RECONSTRUCTING THE COMMON GOOD

Theology and the Social Order

GARY J. DORRIEN

ORBIS BOOKS

Maryknoll, New York 10545

Kim Gifford
1939–1987

Joyce Giles
1926–1987

Jim Campbell
1907–1989

Gene Morris
1914–1989

The memories of their goodness are blessings.

The Catholic Foreign Mission Society of America (Maryknoll) recruits and trains people for overseas missionary service. Through Orbis Books, Maryknoll aims to foster the international dialogue that is essential to mission. The books published, however, reflect the opinions of their authors and are not meant to represent the official position of the society.

Copyright © 1990 by Gary J. Dorrien
Paperback edition published in 1992
Published by Orbis Books, Maryknoll, NY 10545
Manufactured in the United States of America

Library of Congress Cataloging-in-Publication Data

Dorrien, Gary J.
    Reconstructing the common good: theology and the social order /
Gary J. Dorrien.
        p.   cm.
    Includes bibliographical references.
    ISBN 0-88344-659-6 (cloth)   0-88344-797-5 (pbk.)
    1. Socialism, Christian.   I. Title
HX51.D67 1990
335'.7 – dc20
                                                    90-31698
                                                       CIP

Contents

Preface to the Paperback Edition

They are old questions now raised in a dramatically new international context. What would it mean to take liberation theology seriously in a North American context? With what resources could a North American liberationism be constructed? *Reconstructing the Common Good* ventures a response to these often-posed queries. It interprets the history and theory of modern Christian socialism, excluding the Anglican socialist tradition that my previous book examined. It argues that a postmodern liberationism must draw upon existing African-American, feminist, environmentalist, and Latin American movements. And it contends that North American liberationism must do something more, offering a vision of a just social and economic order that can serve as a common project for North America's various progressive movements.

This book was written during the last two years of the Cold War. Several reviewers have questioned whether its impassioned anticommunism didn't bear the marks of its timing. Would I have devoted so much attention to the brutality and failures of Communism if I had written the book a year later? Would I have criticized Latin American liberationists so strenuously for failing "to examine the implications of Communist terror, totalitarian rule, and economic bankruptcy" if I had written the book after the issue became moot?

Other reviewers turned the question around. Did I still believe that the language and politics of democratic socialism could be redeemed in the wake of the West's Cold War victory? Didn't the worldwide triumph of capitalism refute the basic claims of modern Christianity's dominant ethical tradition? Writing in *The Christian Century,* the noted neoconservative ethicist, Robert Benne, argued that the time had come for Christian theologians to turn away from the moral tradition discussed in this book. "I believe that Christian ethicists should rather turn their attention to the possibilities for justice within liberal capitalism," he explained. Though he acknowledged that the decentralized, pluralistic, social democratic politics defended in this book have nothing to do with Communism — and in fact, militantly opposes all forms of state socialism — Benne concluded that the verdict of history has come down against any kind of social democratic politics. He found much company in the sentiment. Socialism is dead, and with its death lies the end of any politics that would seriously attempt to break down existing concentrations of economic power.

v

I believe that this widely proclaimed decree compels respect, but not acceptance. There is no political tradition that has opposed Communist tyranny more assiduously than the social democratic tradition, a tradition that my previous book, *The Democratic Socialist Vision,* examined in some detail. My criticisms of liberation theology in the present book reflect this tradition's longstanding, principled commitment to democratic self-determination as the means by which the common good must be pursued. The strategic and philosophical issues raised by my critique of liberation theology's discussions of socialism have not been rendered moot by the collapse of world Communism, but are relevant to any continuing discussion of liberationist alternatives. Nothing proved so galling to democratic socialists in the past than to be categorized or associated with their Communist opponents. Social democrats have been claiming for sixty years that Communism is suffocating and ultimately unsustainable. Nothing is so galling to them today than to be told that the collapse of the system against which they struggled marks their own demise. The need for greater social and economic equality has not vanished with the passing of the Soviet bloc. The ravages of imperialism, oppression, structural dependency, environmental destruction, and world poverty have not diminished with the triumph of liberal capitalism. Liberationist movements and theologies have emerged in the past generation to struggle against these social evils—which were generated under the very social order that we are now told to accept as the most desirable system attainable.

Modern Christian theology has rarely taken this counsel. From Karl Barth to William Temple to the first-world theologians discussed in this book, modern theology's major figures have vigorously criticized liberal capitalism and condemned the long record of political, military, economic, and cultural imperialism that liberal democratic rhetoric has often rationalized. In the past generation, third-world liberationists have added their voices to this tradition, claiming that any liberationist project must break from the legacy of liberal democracy as they have experienced it. I assume that any liberationist praxis must stand in solidarity with this sentiment. The question is whether the fundamental liberationist critique of liberal democracy can be sustained in a world that has witnessed the objective failures of the primary alternatives to liberalism.

The loudly celebrated triumph of capitalism and the hunger for market freedom that we are witnessing throughout much of the world press the question very hard upon liberationists. This book argues that an affirmative answer can be given to the question if one views liberal democracy as an unfinished project in need of a democratic transformation. The common project for contemporary progressive movements is to expand modernity's democratic revolution by democratizing social and economic power. The effort to democratize power must take place not only at the point of production (as in Marxism) or in the electoral arena (as in liberalism), but also in what Manning Marable calls "the living place"—the postindustrial community where people struggle to attain sufficient health care, child care, housing, a clean environment, public transportation, and community. If it is axiomatic that progressive politics today requires a feminist, racial, ecological, and anti-imperialist consciousness that earlier progressive movements often lacked, it is becoming equally evident that liberation theology also needs to appropriate communitarian critiques of liberal democracy and state socialism.

The language of socialism has become severely problematic for this project, and not only because it was perverted long ago by totalitarians. Democratic socialism has its own legacy of overcentralized collectivism. For most Americans, the term "socialism" therefore conjures up authoritarian images that have nothing to do with freedom, community, or even equality. *Reconstructing the Common Good* employs the language of democratic socialism because this is the language of the tradition it discusses. While I am doubtful that the "S-word" and its associated vocabulary are redeemable at the end of the twentieth century, I will argue that the spirit and principles of decentralized, pluralistic, democratic socialism—by whatever name—are constitutive of any worthy progressive politics for the future. Democratic socialism needs a grammar that is not besmirched by the history of Communism or the statist errors of social democracy's past. The purpose of the present work is not to propose such a grammar, but to assess the relevance of Christianity's socialist tradition for the next generation of liberationist theologies.

One clarification of the book's economic argument is in order. Benne and others have identified the present work's conception of economic democracy with the "market socialist" model developed in the 1930s by the Polish economist, Oskar Lange. As my final chapter observes, there are significant similarities between certain aspects of Lange's model and economic democracy. Lange tried to show that market mechanisms and incentives could be integrated into socialist theory. He argued that a large state sector could coexist with, and benefit from, the pricing and market discipline of a private sector of small enterprises. In his proposal, state planners would simulate and be instructed by the private sector's pricing system. The problem with this scheme, however, as my final chapter notes, is that it retained a highly centralized and collectivist conception of the role of the state. Though he granted a larger role for the market than traditional state socialism, Lange still had centralized planners trying to replicate the enormously complex pricing decisions of markets—a task exceeding the competence or knowledge of any conceivable planning board. Though a considerable degree of state planning is inevitable in any advanced industrial or postindustrial society, the purpose of economic democracy is not to expand the role of state intervention, but to democratize the base of economic power, principally by expanding the cooperative sector.

Like other theorists of state socialism, Lange tried to construct a model that was different in kind, rather than "merely" different in degree, from liberal capitalism. This is the crucial mistake that progressive movements overinfluenced by Marxism must give up. It is this Marxist hangover that has recently caused certain Leftists—notably Robert Heilbroner—to feel deflated by the implosion of the Soviet bloc. For those who drew assurance from the existence of an alternative kind of world system—however debased—the spectacle of the Soviet Union seeking admission to the International Monetary Fund has proved disheartening. The collapse of Communism confronts them with the absurdity of Marx's prescriptions for abolishing the market. One might as well strive to abolish human nature. Economic democracy does not replace the market system with state planning or trade upon utopian expectations of a transformed humanity. It does not necessitate a break from liberal democracy to a non-market system, but requires a further extension of liberal democracy's democratizing logic into the economic system.

If it is true that communitarian social democracy represents a difference in degree rather than a difference in kind from liberal capitalism, the difference is crucial nonetheless. The debate that remains is the debate that social democrats always wanted, focusing on the differences between liberal and social democracy. When we limit democracy to the electoral sphere, we foresake social, economic, environmental, cultural, and political gains toward the common good that only a democratization of power can achieve. This contention—the thesis of Christian socialism from Rauschenbusch to Tillich to Moltmann to Ruether—is no less compelling or relevant in the wake of Communism's overdue collapse. If it is true that liberation theologies of the future need to break free from the Marxist and socialist statism, collectivism, and utopianism with which they have often been tainted in the past, this does not mean that the Christian-Marxist dialogue of the past three decades has produced nothing worth preserving. Marxist socioeconomic criticism has been appropriated by virtually all progressive theologies. Liberationist dialogues with Marxism have prompted many Christians to recover the social meaning of the prophetic biblical faith. It is here, however—in Christianity's own theological tradition—that liberation theology's most vital resources are buried. *Reconstructing the Common Good* explores part of this heritage.

Introduction

This is a study in the history and theory of modern Christian socialism. In my previous book, *The Democratic Socialist Vision*, I argued that contemporary democratic socialism is fundamentally defined by its emphasis on decentralized forms of socialization and democratic control over the process of economic investment. The book focused on the programmatic shift that Western social democratic parties and theorists have made in the past generation toward market-oriented forms of socialization. Though I suggested that the recent reconception of socialism as decentralized economic democracy owes much to the religious (and syndicalist) traditions of democratic socialism, *The Democratic Socialist Vision* dealt with religion only as a subtheme. The present work explores the legacy of modern Christian socialism, defending an argument about the significance of this tradition that was only implied in my earlier book.

To examine religious socialism is to discuss the relationship between two historical forces that are often wishfully declared to be in eclipse. The death of socialism, like the end of religion, has been announced over and again during the past century, yet, as I have argued elsewhere, the human desire for social, political, and economic self-determination has made socialism in some form nearly as durable throughout the world as the phenomenon of religion. If it is true, as Mircea Eliade insisted, that religion is an element in the structure of human consciousness rather than a stage within the history of consciousness, the perdurance of religion in some form can be assumed. In that case, the significant question about religion becomes the question of the form, which, of course, is also the question about socialism.

Because socialism is commonly identified with highly centralized, authoritarian systems of government ownership and control, the very possibility of a decentralized, democratic form of socialism is often defined out of existence. We are thus repeatedly assured that socialism is inherently undemocratic or that the recent Scandinavian experiments in market socialism are not "really socialist." I will argue, however, that strategies for worker-and-community-controlled forms of socialization fulfill the traditional goal of socialism, which is to establish democratic authority over the process of economic investment in the context of political freedom. And I will further contend that the ongoing theological tradition of Christian socialism offers a moral and socioeconomic vision of democratic empowerment that is

1

instructive for the various contemporary reformist, populist, and liberationist movements.

Today, postmodern theorists and others often assert that liberal notions about democratic or human rights are only meaningful within the discourse traditions of liberal societies. As I will explain in chapter 7, I believe that the more extreme forms of this position need to be resisted, since they lead to a moral relativism that undermines the struggle for social justice. When I was a student, I was frequently told by friends and leaders in the antiwar movement that my questions about democracy, freedom, and Communism were meaningless within the context of the Vietnamese conflict. It was claimed that the Vietnamese and Cambodian revolutionary movements were developing indigenous forms of socialism that did not exist within the range of possibilities discussed in the West. Repeating the mistakes of earlier generations of revolutionary tourists, numerous activists returned from their pilgrimages to North Vietnam with glowing assurances about the virtues of Vietnamese Communism and the irrelevance of democratic rights in a Vietnamese context.[1]

Many of those who made or embraced such claims in the 1960s later found their political categories in shambles when Vietnam was turned into a dictatorial prison and the unspeakable horrors of the Cambodian revolution were revealed to the outside world. In reaction, thousands of activists retreated to private concerns and abandoned politics altogether, deflated by their new awareness of the complexity, hypocrisy, and tragedy of political life. Others abandoned only their idealism, and became neoconservatives. Irving Howe has noted that a disproportionate number of the neoconservative converts came from the wing of the antiwar movement that had specialized in attacks upon trade unions and political reformism. When they moved to the Right, they retained their long-held contempt for liberalism.[2]

By contrast, throughout the same period such social democrats as Howe, Michael Harrington, and Michael Walzer regarded the struggle for social justice as primarily the effort to attain *and extend* the goals of political liberalism. During the war, they vigorously opposed American intervention in Vietnam, while insisting that revolutionary movements promoting Communism were no more worthy of support in the third world than Communist parties elsewhere.[3] To them, the only emancipatory form of socialist praxis was one that upheld the values of freedom and democracy as both means and end. When the Socialist International sent its Committee to Defend the Nicaraguan Revolution to Managua in 1981, the socialists repeatedly pressed the Sandinista leadership to maintain a mixed economy, political pluralism, nonalignment, and democratic rights. Harrington recalled that this formula was repeated so often that he wondered if they couldn't save time and energy by giving it a number. The plea itself was utterly serious, however, for, as Harrington explained, once one begins to make compromises on democratic rights, "even for the noblest of reasons or out of respect for the most imperious of historical necessities, one is on the slippery slope that leads to the defense of 'progressive' torture and repression."[4] This book is written in the same conviction.

In his useful study of the three fundamental historical forms of democracy, the eminent political theorist C. B. Macpherson contended that those who presuppose a liberal conception of democracy are obligated to acknowledge their commitment to liberal democracy.[5] The present work is liberal democratic inasmuch as it is rooted in the liberal tradition and assumes the necessity of individual rights to freedom of speech, association, preference, and the like. The present work advances what is often today called a "postliberal" conception of democracy, however, insofar as it extends the boundaries of classical liberal theory. Following Macpherson and Robert Dahl, I will view liberal democracy as a tradition torn between two conflicting visions of what a good society should be.[6] In the classical liberal vision, the right to property is considered superior to the right to democratic self-government, and the equalizing role of government is reduced to a minimum. In the second vision, which was first expressed in the later writings of John Stuart Mill, the right to democratic self-government is considered superior to the right to property, and the role of government is shaped to maximize *actual* equality of opportunity. While it is incumbent upon liberal theorists to reconcile the differences between these conflicting visions so far as possible, the fundamental differences between them are ultimately irreconcilable. Thus, when I argue that democratic socialism is logically and historically continuous with liberal democracy, my references to liberalism will assume the second sense of the term.[7]

The implications of the second understanding of liberalism are sufficiently different from classical liberalism that some theorists have recently insisted upon calling this position "postliberalism." Unlike Samuel Bowles and Herbert Gintis, I will not invest much importance in the question whether the position advanced in this book should be called postliberalism or an extension of liberalism.[8] I do share, however, their basic commitment to a conception of democracy that continues to expand personal rights "and thus to render the exercise of both property rights and state power democratically accountable." Like Bowles and Gintis, I will advance a conception of democracy that affirms all the traditional democratic rights of representative democracy and individual liberty and that "proposes novel forms of social power independent of the state; namely, democratically accountable, chartered freedoms in community and work." Bowles and Gintis rightly observe that the rights to democratic control of investment and production are not only desirable in principle, but also increasingly necessary as means to sustain democratic control of governments.[9]

For the sake of clarity, I will define socialism in a way that largely excludes cultural factors. Following the usage of the Frankfurt Declaration (1951) of the Socialist International, I will define socialism as a system featuring public and cooperative ownership of the major means of production and a mixture of market forces and government planning in making production decisions. The Frankfurt Declaration asserts that authentic socialism can only be achieved by democratic means and that economic power should be decentralized wherever decentralization is compatible with the aims of economic planning.[10] Though it is still commonly assumed that capitalism requires the predominance of market forces and that socialism requires the predominance of government planning, the Socialist International already assumed in 1951 that this distinction was anachronistic in the era of the welfare state. Modern democratic socialism emphasizes decentralization of authority, mixed forms of social ownership, and the necessary role of the market. As I have argued in *The Democratic Socialist Vision*, the fundamental difference between democratic socialism and capitalism focuses upon the question of how the process of economic investment should be organized and controlled.[11] Given that capitalism and socialism are both deeply politicized in the modern world, and given that several of the traditional differences between democratic forms of capitalism and socialism have blurred in recent years, I will seek to avoid various overlapping ambiguities by defining capitalism and socialism primarily according to their differences over the democratization of investment and the question of private versus social ownership of the major means of production.

While I am fully aware that the concept of a "common good" is rejected in various forms of postmodern, Marxist, and neoconservative criticism, I have continued to refer to the idea of a common good because I believe the notion is indispensable to any constructive movement for social justice. To refer to a common good is not to assume that a cross-cultural or universal theory of social need is attainable or even desirable. Neither is it to assume that a developed theory of the common good is ever fully attainable for any particular society. The complexity of the social factors in question, the unlimited amount of information that would need to be assessed, the multiplicity of viable perspectives on the data, and the continuous historical changes within societies themselves preclude the possibility of ever developing a fully satisfactory theory of the common good for any modern society.

To repudiate the notion of a common good on these grounds, however, is to undercut the struggle for attainable gains toward social justice, since it negates the elusive but necessary vision of a just social order that progressive movements need to sustain themselves. To abandon the always provisional and imperfect search for the common social good is inevitably to settle for less than progressive movements should accept. The notion of the common good as a single, all-embracing idea of the good life must be rejected.[12] As Chantal Mouffe has written, the notion of the common good "must be understood to refer exclusively to the shared political ends of a democratic political community, i.e., the principles of freedom and equality for all."[13] The notion of the common good that is needed is therefore both pluralistic and egalitarian, focusing upon a limited range of common political ends. The question of democracy itself, from this perspective, focuses upon the character of relationships that can be constructed on the principles of freedom and equality within political communities. One of the main arguments of this book is that decentralized forms of economic democracy would better serve the common good than the truncated forms of democratic entitlement thus far created under modern capitalism.

I will argue that because all of the theorists examined in this study share two fundamental claims and a preoccupation with the question of modernity, their moral and political arguments can be meaningfully compared in the light of the widely various historical and cultural circumstances that have shaped their work. For all of them, the question of modernity is, first, the question of how to appropriate or to assess the results of modern historical, scientific, and philosophical criticism. Though the differences between modern progressive and liberationist theologies on this question are substantial, all of the figures examined in this study are "modernists" in the sense that they accept the legitimacy of modern critical methodologies.

But the question of modernity concerns more than the critical meaning of religious faith. Most important in the present work, the question of modernity is the question of the praxological meaning of Christian faith in a world shaped by the development of modern corporate capitalism and its accompanying ideologies. I will follow Harvey Cox in defining modernity as the culturally predominant system or worldview that promotes nationalism, technological determinism, bureaucratic rationalism, profit maximization, and the marginalization of religion.[14] In differing ways, all of the figures in this study advance religious arguments for a socialist transformation of modernity. The book will, accordingly, adopt a twofold socioeconomic and theological focus, examining the conception of socialism and the conception of the relationship between the Kingdom of God and historical praxis developed by each theorist.

I am grateful to several colleagues who have read and thoughtfully commented upon my manuscript for this book, including Harry Boyte, Eve Drogin, Robert Ellsberg, William French, Robin Lovin, Mark Rosenman, Kevin Sharpe, Max Stackhouse, Lester Start, Laurin Vance, and Kyle Wallace and to Frank Austin, its copyeditor. I am also indebted to numerous friends in the religious and academic communities of Albany, New York, who inspired, nurtured, challenged, and encouraged me during the six years that I served as a pastor and chaplain in that city. I have dedicated this book to the memory of four of them, but, in a larger sense, this book is also dedicated to all of those in Albany whose goodness and ever-gracious friendship sustained me during the formative period of my vocation.

1

Theology and the Democratic Faith

The notion that the moral claims of Christianity and socialism are complementary has a distinguished pedigree. A generation after the first Christian socialist organizations had been established in Europe, Friedrich Nietzsche argued in *The Antichrist* that socialism is repugnant because of its rootage in the moral principles of Christian theology. "The poison of the doctrine of equal rights for all," he observed, "—it was Christianity that spread it most fundamentally." But in recent times, he explained, the Christian sympathy for "all the failures and all the weak" had become politicized in the socialist movement, which was based on the Christian notion of equal rights for even "the whole scum and refuse of humanity."[1]

Nietzsche thus regarded the kinship between Christianity and socialism as self-evident. A century later, however, despite the existence of a rich theological tradition of socialism, from the pre-Marxist cooperativism of Anglican socialism to the contemporary neo-Marxist theologies of liberation, the argument is repeatedly advanced that socialism is incompatible with an authentic Christian faith. This argument often takes a quite personal form. While generally ignoring the fact that democratic socialists no longer advocate nationalization, such neoconservative writers as Richard John Neuhaus, Edward Norman, and Paul Johnson have repeatedly attacked Christian socialism as a collectivist substitute for authentic religion, arguing that modern theologians have only turned to socialism as a compensation for their loss of religious faith.[2] This contention has been pushed to its extreme limit by Johnson, who has identified William Temple as the prototype of the modern theologian because Temple, according to Johnson, was the first to substitute politics for spirituality.[3]

The problem with this insistently repeated accusation, as I will demonstrate throughout this book, is that it misrepresents an extraordinary tradition of men and women on the basis of a narrowly presumptuous assumption of what it means to be religious. For example, though he was indeed a deeply politicized figure who stood within the historic Anglican tradition of decentralized socialism, Temple was also one of the most profound and devout spiritual writers of this century. Like most of the figures I will discuss in the following chapters, he turned to socialism not to compensate for the loss of his faith, but to live out the moral implications of his abiding religious commitment.

The irony in the position taken by Norman and Johnson is that while they criticize modern theologies for enshrining the values of liberalism, their own dichotomy between the religious and public realms is itself a product of modernity. The point is often made that in the name of separating politics from religion, the neoconservatives invariably promote a highly politicized form of religion of their own. The point is telling, but the deeper contradiction in the neoconservative position is that while neoconservatives present themselves as defenders of the importance of religion, their arguments undermine the social role and moral claims of the churches. As Temple observed of this position: "It is assumed that the church exercises little influence and ought to exercise none. It is further assumed that this assumption is self-evident and has always been made by reasonable people. As a matter of fact, it is entirely modern and extremely questionable."[4] The integrity of Christian faith is compromised not by those who attempt to live out its moral commands in the public world, Temple asserted, but by those who reduce its meaning to an otherworldly spirituality. The irony of the conservative *and* liberal defenses of religion, as Harvey Cox has recently shown, is that they have abetted the post-Enlightenment trivialization of religion while claiming to uphold the social importance of religion.

In his pathbreaking work on this subject, *Religion in the Secular City*, Cox argues that the mainline churches ensured their own survival over the past century by accommodating their theologies to the rationalistic, technological, business-oriented spirit of the modern world. Faced with the advances of modern science and technology, as well as the evident need to justify their own already-marginalized existence in the modern world, liberal theologians responded by developing theological systems that were impervious to scientific or public criticism. While this strategy purchased a crucial measure of respectability for the liberal churches, Cox observes, the problem with the strategy was that it left the churches without a social mission. "The churches were left with little to do in this world but to comfort, console, and prepare people for the next one," he writes. "Making money and making war could proceed without the inconvenient restraints of morality sanctioned by religion."[5] The mainline churches were thus reduced to upholding, and sometimes sacralizing, the socioeconomic structures of business civilization as the price for their protected space on the margins of society.

Cox argues that even the Social Gospel movement conformed to these arrangements. Though he concedes that the theologians of the Social Gospel attempted to reassert the moral values of Christianity in the public realm, Cox asserts that even their writings "usually deferred to the power of the classes that had established the right to govern. They rarely complained about societies dominated by small financial or political elites. What they pressed for was not a change in the structure of domination itself but for some modification in how those who ruled would do so."[6]

As a critique of the church's history and strategy of accommodation, including the limitations of the Social Gospel movement, I find this a compelling assessment, but I will argue that this assessment does not apply to the foremost proponent of the Social Gospel. Walter Rauschenbusch developed a powerful religious and socioeconomic argument for socialism that was continuous with modern liberalism while looking beyond it. In this respect, his work exemplified the appropriation of liberal democracy and liberal intellectual criticism that this book will advocate. While it is frequently argued that "postmodern" liberationist theologies must continue to appropriate the critical rigor of theological liberalism, I believe that the liberal notion of democratic entitlement is equally crucial for any North American theology of praxis. To argue for democratic self-determination in the economic realm is to extend the notion posited by modern liberalism that only democratic forms of political authority are legitimate. Thus, I will argue, while democratic socialism is critical of liberal democracy, it is equally important to affirm that democratic socialism represents the fulfillment of the liberal notion of democratic legitimacy.

Philosophical readers will recognize this argument as the theory of liberal democratic "retrieval" formulated by the late political theorist C. B. Macpherson, and variously amended by Amy Gutmann, David Held, Frank Cunningham, and others. In his important work *The Life and Times of Liberal Democracy*, Macpherson observed that "liberalism" (or "liberal democracy") can be fundamentally regarded as the ideological justification for modern capitalism *or* as the notion that society should strive to ensure that all of its members are equally free to fulfill their capabilities. The former conception of liberalism emphasizes the priority of private property and the right to equality of opportunity; the latter notion emphasizes the priority of democratic self-government and the necessity of an approximate equality of condition as a precondition for actual equality of opportunity. Macpherson's conception of democratic socialism as the extension of liberalism, like my own, was based upon the latter conception of liberalism.[7]

An early version of the same approach can be found in the writings of Rauschenbusch, who attacked the socioeconomic structures of modern capitalism while laying claim to the fundamental liberal principle of democratic empowerment. His writings on socialism thus prefigured much of the recent literature on democratic theory. Though he has often been dismissed as an idealist who failed to take the realities of sin with sufficient seriousness, I will argue that Rauschenbusch's career was driven by his profound awareness of what he called "the kingdom of evil." Despite his numerous limitations and mistaken judgments, he represents to me the kind of idealism that is needed today, because he struggled unfailingly to promote and fulfill the ends of attainable justice in a fallen world.

When I was a seminarian, I once heard Jürgen Moltmann exhort a group of North American theologians to develop their own praxological theologies by studying the works of Rauschenbusch. The recommendation moved me to examine a theorist I had previously dismissed, following convention, as a utopian. Two years later, when Gustavo Gutiérrez spent a year as a visiting professor at Union Theological Seminary, he studied the writings of Rauschenbusch for the first time and urged his students to acquaint themselves with Rauschenbusch's work. Moltmann and Gutiérrez both asserted, as I will argue, that the work of Rauschenbusch represented the most instructive precedent for a North American theology of praxis. Like Moltmann and Gutiérrez after him, Rauschenbusch insisted that democratic empowerment was crucial as both means and end, and that the goal could only be fulfilled in either case by expanding the base of economic power. And like nearly all of the figures I will examine in this book, Rauschenbusch advocated socialism without reducing his faith to politics or identifying the inbreaking reign of God with any particular program.

My subsequent chapters will discuss the arguments of the major figures in the Christian socialist theological tradition (excluding Temple) since the time of Rauschenbusch. While it is unfortunately true that some figures in this tradition have at times equated the meaning of their faith with a given political program, one of my principal arguments will be that the major theorists of Christian socialism have avoided this mistake out of their respect for the transcendent mystery that religion ultimately represents. A totally politicized religion debases the transhistorical meaning of faith while producing, as well, a corrupt form of politics. One of the central questions about the future of the Christian socialist tradition is whether it will continue to distinguish between the transcendent absoluteness of the object of faith and its relative approximations within history.

The emergence of liberation theology has raised this question with special force. I have devoted a substantial section of this book to liberation theology, focusing especially upon the critiques of modernity that the liberationist movement has generated.[8] Because the liberationist movement first arose in societies profoundly unlike Western Europe or North America, liberation theology has naturally taken a more critical perspective toward the political culture of the first world than even the most radical forms of first-world theology. As a contribution to spiritual theology, liberationism is the religious self-expression of the victims of third world history; as a critique, liberationism is fundamentally a critique of the economic and cultural effects of Western capitalism. I have resisted the tendency, however, to treat liberation theology as a foreign discourse operating totally outside the assumptions or norms of first-world theology. While I have accepted the basic liberationist claim that liberationism represents a distinctive methodological departure from progressive first-world theology, I do not believe that this departure exempts liberation theology from criticism or severs its connection with the historic tradition of Christian socialism. While it is important to establish that liberation theology adopts a different and more generative starting point than the theologies of first-world liberalism, it is mistaken to assume that this departure should exempt liberation theology from all first-world theological, political, or socioeconomic criticism.

For the same reason, I have not interpreted liberation theology as a totally novel phenomenon within church history. Although I will argue that liberation theology needs to become more conversant with the literature and praxis of economic democracy, and less preoccupied with debates inherited from Marxism, I regard liberationism as an enormously significant movement that has revitalized the larger Christian socialist tradition. As I will argue in two chapters that discuss the three foundational figures in liberation theology, the key challenge that faces the liberationist movement is to retain its insistence on decentralized democratic empowerment in the face of other options that are less worthy but seem more attainable.

Near the end of his useful monograph on the life and thought of Gutiérrez, Robert McAfee Brown has argued that because of the immense differences in social context between the first and third worlds, a North American liberationist theology will need to use sources from the first world rather than the writings of the Latin American liberationists. Brown has periodically asserted that a North American liberationist theology will need to draw upon the works of Rauschenbusch, Moltmann, Paul Tillich, and others, rather than attempt to transplant the ideas of third-world liberationist theologians.[9]

This is exactly the project I have embarked upon, but, like Brown, I also believe that any transformationist North American theology today must be developed in light of third-world liberationist criticism. As I will argue in chapters 5 and 6, liberation theology is valuable not only for its recovery of the prophetic biblical tradition and its power to inspire the disinherited masses of the third world, but also for its exposure of the limitations of first-world theological and political liberalism. Along with the critiques of first-world liberalism that have been developed in feminist and black theologies, third-world liberationist criticism has revealed the need for an emancipatory vision that transcends the limitations of Western progressivism, including the limitations of traditional Christian socialism. My final chapter, therefore, develops an argument for a postmodern religious socialism that retains the essential features of traditional Christian socialism while reconceptualizing its ends in the light of feminist, black, and third-world liberationist criticism.

Fear of socialism is pervasive in the United States, but I believe that this fact confirms the significance of the religious tradition of democratic socialism. For many years, the major policy proposal of the European and North American socialist parties called for nationalization of essential business and financial enterprises. Eugene Debs, for example, simply assumed that socialization meant nationalization, and in the United Kingdom the Fabian theorists argued that every move toward collectivism represented a victory for democratic socialism.[10] This highly centralized image is what most North Americans still have in mind when they reject "socialism," notwithstanding the fact that the democratic socialist parties of Europe and North America no longer advocate economic nationalization. There is an alternative conception of socialism that originated in the guild and religious movements for socialism, which today is predominant throughout the democratic socialist movements of Europe and North America. Contemporary democratic socialism promotes a mixed economy with regional economic planning and decentralized forms of socialization. Though the turn to economic democracy has been a relatively recent phenomenon within the institutional socialist movement, this approach has been a distinguishing feature of Christian socialism, on both moral and programmatic grounds, since the time of F. D. Maurice.[11]

As I have argued in *The Democratic Socialist Vision*, contemporary democratic socialism is linked with the socialism of Eugene Debs and the Fabian theorists in its insistence on democratic control over society, but contemporary socialism begins with the assumption, on moral and socioeconomic grounds, that decentralized forms of socialization are more humane than the alternatives. The discourse of the Left should be an inclusive, democratic language that appeals to common values of fairness, equality, community, freedom, and peace. Because the Left has often been "radical" in the worst sense, promoting violent images of class warfare and upheaval, it has historically cut itself off from the common moral language of North American citizens. The Left has often managed only to project its own deracinated sensibility, despite the fact that the fundamental socialist principle—the principle of democratic accountability—is deeply rooted in North American political culture.[12] To make concrete social gains in the political contexts of the first world, the Left needs to appropriate the religious tradition of socialism represented by Rauschenbusch, Temple, Tillich, and others, which has insisted that the moral and political language of rights must be applied to the economic order. Though democracy is the cherished ideal of North American political life and is loudly proclaimed by all parties, it exists in the United States only in a truncated form. The programmatic goal of modern democratic socialism, therefore, is to fulfill the democratic revolution that started in the United States, by democratizing economic power.

Because this is an idealistic objective, and because the tradition discussed in this book is undeniably idealistic in its socioeconomic claims, it is perhaps advisable to explain why I do not accept the endlessly repeated assurances that democratic socialism contravenes human nature or is programmatically unattainable. Today it is frequently asserted, often with prooftexts from the works of Reinhold Niebuhr, that such movements as liberation theology are doomed to failure on account of human egotism. Because Left-liberal movements ignore the limitations of human nature, the argument goes, overloading the political system with demands it cannot fulfill, these movements actually undermine the existing structures of social justice.

This argument is often presented as a Niebuhrian conclusion, though the patronage is at least arguable. Niebuhr spent his entire adult life (after leaving the Socialist party) in the liberal wing of the Democratic party. It was far from his spirit to claim, as has been done in his name, that the existing bourgeois societies have fulfilled the limits of attainable democracy. Unlike many of his current "followers," Niebuhr criticized the imperialism of his own country and supported nearly every liberal domestic reform of his time.[13]

More important, the Niebuhrian argument about human nature bears implications that have been ignored in the neoconservative literature invoking his name. In his classic essay on democracy, *The Children of Light and the Children of Darkness*, Niebuhr argued that modern political democracy was created by "children of light" who underestimated the destructive power of individual and collective egotism in society. Niebuhr contrasted the moral idealism of the children of light with the moral cynicism of the fascist and Stalinist "children of darkness," arguing finally that what was needed was a "new religious culture" that would unite moral concern with a realistic attitude toward the nature of power. The problem with the traditional arguments for democracy, in his view, was that they reflected the moral innocence of the children of light, conceiving democracy as the form of polity that enlightened people deserve. Rather than conceive democracy primarily as a symbol of human goodness or progress, or as the political structure that people naturally deserve on account of their inherent moral worth, Niebuhr argued that democracy should be defended dialectically, on positive and negative grounds, as the system that most fairly restrained human egotism. As he famously put it, "Man's capacity for justice makes democracy possible; but man's inclination to injustice makes democracy necessary."[14]

Niebuhr did not deny that the human capacity for fairness is often moved by genuine feelings of compassion and solidarity, but to him it was axiomatic that all such feelings are mixed in human nature with more selfish motives. The crucial point, for him, was that democracy is necessary precisely because human beings are inherently selfish. If human nature were more benign, he observed, the question of the distribution of power in society would not be so crucial. The "benevolent ruling class" would be an actual possibility. But because human beings are so easily corrupted by the attainment of power, Niebuhr argued, democracy is necessary as a restraint on greed and the human proclivity to dominate others.

This is also my own position, which I extend beyond the boundaries of (the later) Niebuhr's analysis, into the realm of economic power. For the same reason that political democracy is necessary, as a restraint on the abuse of unequal power, I will argue that the democratization of power in the economic sphere is a worthy and attainable goal.

The textbook objection to this argument is that it politicizes the economic system, removing the existing wall that separates the political and economic systems within modern capitalism. But the empirical problem with this argument is that modern capitalism is already deeply politicized. Reports by Congress Watch and the Congressional Budget Office have estimated that U.S. government subsidies, bailouts, and other forms of corporate welfare exceed $100 billion per year. Moreover, even these studies usually omit most indirect subsidies, such as corporate income from government programs and regulations, which, if added, would push the true figure for annual corporate assistance to at least $140 billion.[15]

The meaningful question about economic planning is therefore not *whether* advanced economies will be politicized in the future, but in what way they will be politicized. Federal economic planning in the United States presently subsidizes the most powerful corporations and business interests in the country, largely on the basis of what has aptly been called the logic of the broker state.[16] Since the giant corporations in the United States have the most means to lobby for assistance, they are also the chief beneficiaries of government loans, grants, import quotas, tax breaks, bailouts, price supports, indirect subsidies, uncollected taxes, and socialization of expenses and losses. This elementary fact has far-reaching implications. Because the broker state primarily responds to demands placed upon it by powerful institutional interests, economic planning in the United States routinely underfunds low-cost housing, full-employment planning, and other social needs that David Stockman memorably termed "weak claims" — that is, the claims of the poor, who have weak lobbying power.[17]

The most worthy alternative to the broker state arrangement is not to pretend that economic planning does not (or should not) exist, but to democratize the process of economic investment. Modern societies are shaped primarily by those who control the terms, amounts, and direction of credit. To require that every large enterprise have public and employee representatives on its board of directors, therefore, would represent a significant step toward democratic self-determination, since the major industrial and financial corporations have a greater impact on our lives than, for example, the state legislatures that we elect. Since economic planning is now inevitable in some form, the question for our time is not whether it should exist at all, but whether it should be democratized to serve the common good. Toward that end, modern democratic socialism advocates a mixture of worker-owned firms, employee stock-ownership plans, national development banks, community-owned corporations, cooperative banks, private ownership of agriculture and small firms, and decentralized economic planning.[18]

To argue that this is an attainable socioeconomic vision is not to harbor illusions about the goodness of human nature. Some of the literature on economic democracy suggests that democratizing the economic order would engender a more cooperative and less alienated sensibility among wage earners than is presently the case under capitalism.[19] This is, without question, a central objective of economic democracy, but the short-term argument for democratic control of the economy does not hinge upon the expectation of a transformation of worker consciousness.[20] Studies of worker-controlled firms have thus far produced mixed results on the question whether worker control immediately increases workers' sense of vocational satisfaction.[21] Significant changes within a political culture do not occur overnight. Like Robert Dahl, I think it is reasonable to expect that over the course of a generation a more democratized economic order would significantly reduce the sense of alienation and atomization currently reported by wage earners in large firms.[22] To argue for democratic control over the economy, however, is not to assume that democratization would transform human nature, but to hold, as Niebuhr argued in a different context, that the human proclivities for justice and injustice make democratic empowerment both possible and necessary.[23]

This argument underscores the importance of historical perspective. On several occasions I heard Michael Harrington remark that none of us will live to see a democratically transformed society in North America. To struggle for democratic socialism, he often told his North American audiences, is to commit yourself to a vision you will never see fulfilled in your own country. I believe that this reminder sets the question of idealism in its proper perspective. To struggle for democratic empowerment is not to presume that economic democracy would work on a large scale if it were imposed next year on a political culture unprepared for it. Democratic socialism cannot be imposed or transplanted at all. It can only take shape over the course of a lifetime, as hard-won social gains and a growing sense of the common good build the groundwork for a new social order.

The vision of a cooperative commonwealth, therefore, if held with any degree of expectation, must be held as a faith. Religious socialism offers this project a valuable moral language and a crucial insistence on the limiting realities of human sinfulness. Beyond these contributions, however, religious socialism also provides a language of faith for social objectives that are attainable but not seen. This book is an exploration of that project.

2

Walter Rauschenbusch and
the Legacy of the Social Gospel

The zeitgeist is often a vengeful spirit. In 1936, young John Bennett observed that each generation of intellectuals typically downgraded their predecessors beyond all fairness, while exaggerating the novelty of their own wisdom. Though he was already associated with the emerging Niebuhrian perspective on social ethics, Bennett acknowledged that in their eagerness to supplant the Social Gospel of the previous generation, the Niebuhrians often criticized this tradition beyond all fairness. By then it had become commonplace to assume, as W. A. Visser't Hooft argued in *The Background of the Social Gospel in America*, that the Social Gospel theologians were pantheistic utopians who had failed to take seriously enough the transcendence of God and the pervasive reality of evil. This assessment (sometimes without the pantheism) was advanced over and again by the Niebuhr brothers and others throughout the 1930s and afterward, providing the point of departure for a new theological consensus.[1]

Bennett himself occasionally contributed to this literature, arguing that because of their attachment to Progressive-era idealism, the Social Gospel theologians had mistakenly presented love as the answer to policy problems and had failed to prepare American churches for the "malignant realities" and terrors of the twentieth century.[2] The decisive fault with the Social Gospel, Bennett asserted, was that it underestimated the degree to which sin is inexorable in all social and personal contexts, and therefore lacked a sense of the tragic dimension in history.[3]

This argument has been so influential over the past sixty years that in many seminaries the Social Gospel tradition has often been taken up only in light of the Niebuhrian criticisms upon it. At the same time, and for the same reasons, the theologies of Friedrich Schleiermacher and Albrecht Ritschl have often been studied only as the background to the neo-orthodox theologies of the twentieth century. It is true, as Bennett and the Niebuhrs urged, that because the Social Gospel movement was rooted in the theological liberalism of Schleiermacher, Ritschl, and Adolf von Harnack it contained the limitations and mistakes of this tradition. Writing in 1933, Bennett was so convinced of the bankruptcy of this tradition that he declared, "the most important fact about contemporary American theology is the disintegration of liberalism." It is also true, as Reinhold Niebuhr insisted, that some proponents of the Social Gospel "did not believe in sin" and therefore reduced Christian theology to a facile social optimism.[4]

But, as Bennett today would concur, it is mistaken to implicate the major figures of the Social Gospel tradition in the latter indictment, or to presume the death of theological liberalism, or to assume that the social goals of the Social Gospel movement have been discredited by the events of this century. The last point is crucial. Even if most of the Niebuhrian criticisms of this movement were justified, it does not necessarily follow that the spirit or goals of the Social Gospel were too utopian to deserve our consideration. I will argue, in fact, that in the life and work of this movement's outstanding figure, Walter Rauschenbusch, we confront the most instructive precedent for the modern liberationist project. In his analysis of political economics and his conceptions of the kingdom of God and the kingdom of evil, Rauschenbusch anticipated most of the elements of modern liberationism and offered a more regenerative theological vision than the alternatives produced by his numerous critics.

It is reported that as a youth, after he had been asked what he wanted to be when he grew up, Walter Rauschenbusch immediately replied, "John the Baptist." The full irony of this wonderful reply only became evident after his ordination, when he began to practice a type of ministry that his parents would not have recognized. His father, August Rauschenbusch, was the sixth in an unbroken line of Lutheran pastors, but after August emigrated to the United States as a missionary he was drawn to the stricter biblicism of the German Baptist faith. In 1850, the former Lutheran pastor was rebaptized by immersion in the Mississippi River—an act of religious conviction that alienated him from his family and most of his previous friends. Four years later, he married one of his young confirmands, and in 1858—three years before Walter's birth—August was called from the Missouri frontier to a teaching position in the German Department at Rochester Theological Seminary, where he specialized in Anabaptist history. He taught for more than thirty years at the same seminary where his son later attained fame as an author and professor.

August Rauschenbusch was overbearing and depressive, as well as profoundly disaffected from his wife, Caroline. His letters to his sister Maria contained bitter complaints about his wife's supposed mistreatment of their three children and her alleged lack of Christian faith, culminating in August's admission that at times he desperately prayed for his wife's death.[5]

The strife between his parents deeply wounded young Walter, and evidently influenced the development of his lifelong tendency to offer himself as a mediator between contending parties. Though he largely blamed his father for the conflict between his parents, and was occasionally forced to defend his mother from August's verbal abuse, Walter loved his father and admired him for his religious and intellectual seriousness. He was also grateful that his parents encouraged his early interests in literature, history, and languages.

These interests were cultivated in his preadolescence during four years of study in Germany, accompanied by his mother. At eighteen he returned to Germany to study at the Evangelical Gymnasium of Gutersloh in Westphalia and at the University of Berlin, where he strengthened his mastery of six languages. Rauschenbusch later claimed that he experienced religion only as a moral duty until the age of seventeen, when he resolved the adolescent identity crisis in which he was mired by accepting the faith in which he had been raised. He recalled of this experience: "I said to myself, 'I want to become a man; I want to be respected; and if I go on like this I cannot have the respect of men.' This was my way of saying 'I am out in a far country and I want to get home to my country and I do not want to tend hogs any longer,' and so, I came to my Father, and I began to pray for help and got it; and I got my own religious experience."[6]

In later life, Rauschenbusch found the egocentrism in this experience rather unsettling, but it was typical of his honesty and his genuine sense of grace that he continued to recount the story as it had actually occurred and unfailingly expressed his gratitude for it. "Such as it was, it was of everlasting value to me," he recalled. "It turned me permanently and I thank God with all my heart for it. It was a tender, mysterious experience. It influenced my soul down to its depths. Yet, there was a great deal in it that was not really true."[7]

When he returned from the University of Berlin, Rauschenbusch enrolled in the undergraduate program at the University of Rochester and simultaneously began his training for the ministry at Rochester Theological Seminary. The formative experience of his seminary career occurred during his first summer pastorate, in a small German church in Louisville, Kentucky, where he tended a "small but neglected flock" that was torn apart by internal feuds. According to his fond recollection, Rauschenbusch made continuous rounds of house calls in Louisville, mediated long-standing disputes, admonished the purveyors of gossip, "and tried everywhere to awaken in their hearts the love of Christ as the only sure cure for their love of self and sin." The experience confirmed his desire to be a "captain" in what he called "the onward marching army of our people."[8] That was the Social Gospel in preconscious form.

The following summer, after he returned to Louisville for a second field assignment, Rauschenbusch remarked to his parents in a letter that he was only then beginning to believe in the gospel of Christ—though only in the liberalized form that he found credible. As he explained elsewhere, he was determined to "do hard work for God" and to live literally by the teachings and spirit of Jesus, but his religious devotion did not curb his interests in scientific or historical criticism.

Three months after his graduation from Rochester Seminary, Rauschenbusch was considered by the Baptist Mission Union as a candidate for the presidency of Telugu Theological Seminary in India, but his name was dropped from consideration after his former Old Testament professor disclosed that Rauschenbusch had come to embrace liberal views on the authority of the Old Testament. When he was subsequently urged by the Mission Union to apply for an alternative foreign mission, Rauschenbusch, already concerned about a hearing defect that later became deafness, courteously declined.[9] By then, he was determined to carry out the pastoral assignment he had recently begun at the Second German Church (Baptist), on the border of Hell's Kitchen in New York City.

The origins of the Social Gospel are usually traced to the early ministry and writings of Washington Gladden in the late 1870s, but Rauschenbusch's move to New York in 1886 must be counted among the founding events of this tradition.[10] He arrived with the singular pastoral purpose of converting individual souls to Christ and nurturing them in the sanctifying Spirit, lacking any notion of the church's mission as a social calling. Rauschenbusch began to rethink the church's mission almost immediately, however, upon his arrival in New York. He was revolted by the squalid living conditions of his immigrant congregation and deeply shaken by the extent of malnutrition, disease, and illiteracy among the tenement children. He later recalled that his "awakening" to the social mission of the church occurred during his initial months in New York, when he tried to apply his individualistic maxims to an urban situation, "and discovered that they didn't fit."[11] In the face of the widespread and often brutal degradation that he encountered in New York, it became apparent to Rauschenbusch that the church, if it intended to follow Christ, must commit itself to caring for the poor and neglected. Upon failing to find a meaningful or even sympathetic response to this conviction within the church, Rauschenbusch looked for outside alternatives, and found himself working in Henry George's 1886 mayoral campaign. The campaign was based on the programmatic thesis of George's massive work, *Progress and Poverty*, which argued that the state should impose a "single tax" on the unearned increment in the value of land.[12] George's novel form of populism was crushed at the polls, but his campaign and ideas had a profound effect upon Rauschenbusch, who later credited this "apostle of a great truth" for awakening his mind to the social question.[13]

Rauschenbusch's own deepest concern, however, was the social mission of the church. In the early years of his pastorate, he was frequently advised by fellow pastors to drop his preoccupation with "social work" and confine himself to "church work." Rauschenbusch continually struggled to understand, in reaction, why the churches had reduced the prophetic commands of Scripture to the conventions of middle-class individualism. He observed that in the theologies and typical preaching of the churches, the Christian faith was often presented as though the prophetic literature and the teachings of Jesus did not exist. As he began to comprehend that the faith of the churches was a shrunken imitation of the prophetic biblical faith, he underwent what he described as a "second conversion to Christ" that deepened his earlier resolve to live entirely by the teachings and spirit of Christ.

Rauschenbusch was keenly aware, however, that this second conversion had pushed him into theologically uncharted territory, far beyond the religious boundaries he had inherited. It was an experience of creative dislocation. He eventually decided that the churches of his time subscribed to domesticated, shriveled theologies because they sought, above all, to avoid conflict. Though he was slow to resolve the theological problem that his breakthrough in consciousness raised for him, Rauschenbusch threw himself into numerous "social-work" activities, began to study political economics, and formed friendships with two like-minded Baptist pastors.

These friendships were crucial. While Rauschenbusch began to educate himself about politics and economics, studying especially the writings of Henry George, the English socialist Richard Heath, and the American socialist John Spargo, he began lifelong friendships with Leighton Williams and Nathaniel Schmidt. Williams was the son of a wealthy, clerical New York City family and a graduate of Columbia University, Union Theological Seminary, and Columbia Law School. Like Rauschenbusch, he was serving his first pastorate and working in George's mayoral campaign when he and Rauschenbusch first met. Shortly afterward they met the scholarly Schmidt, pastor of the nearby Swedish Baptist Church, who later became professor of Semitic studies at Cornell University. Within weeks of their first meeting, these young, idealistic, intellectual pastors formed what they called "a new Society of Jesus" in which they vowed to uphold "the ethical and spiritual principles of Jesus . . . without subscription to any creed."[14]

They met each week throughout 1887 for Scripture study and discussion, and met again each Sunday afternoon for communion services that Rauschenbusch recalled, years later, for the "tranquil spirit of reverence, contemplation, and sense of Christ's real presence" that their fellowship engendered. Despite Schmidt's move to Colgate Theological Seminary the following year, their deep sense of mutual commitment and affection was sustained for nearly thirty years. When Rauschenbusch published his epochal *Christianity and the Social Crisis*, twenty years after their friendships had begun, Williams wrote that the book presented an accurate summary of the group's social convictions, and complained only that it did not adequately reflect the spiritual basis of their faith.[15] It was undoubtedly in response to this criticism, in part, that three years later Rauschenbusch published a collection of his spiritual meditations and petitions, titled *For God and the People: Prayers of the Social Awakening*.[16]

Perhaps the most revealing example of Rauschenbusch's personal style and perspective during his pastorate was an article that he published in the daily press in 1887. "Beneath the Glitter" contained the distinctive mixture of compassion and outrage that launched the Social Gospel movement.

Fine sight, you think? Yes, the stores are bright, people well-dressed mostly; they all look busy and happy, as they push by . . . "The world is not so bad a world as some would like to make it." That's your verdict, is it, from what you see? You'll go and pooh-pooh this talk about want and degradation and the iron law, and all that. Well, go ahead, you'll only be one of a crowd. . . .

There, do you see that big clothing house on the corner there? Brilliantly lighted; show windows gorgeous; all hum and happiness. But somewhere in that big house there's a little bullet-headed tailor doubled up over the coat he is to alter, and as surely as I know that my hand is pressing your arm, I know too that he is choking down the sobs and trying to keep the water out of his eyes. Why? Because his little girl is going to die tonight and he can't be there. Consumption, pulmonary. Been wasting away for months, can't sleep except her head is on his breast. And then he can't sleep when her panting is in his ears. He has just been draining his life to sustain hers, and yet Minnie is all the world to him. She's the only drop of sweetness in his cup; all the rest is gall. Hard work; nothing to look forward to; wife grown bitter and snarling; and tonight the girl dies. How do I know? Just been there. Her forehead is getting clammy and her whole body rocks with the effort to breathe. She's whispering, "Tell my papa to come," but he'll not be there before one o'clock tonight. Saturday night, you know; very busy; sorry, but can't spare him. O yes, you can say that: ought to go home, permission or none; but that means throwing up a job that he has been hanging to by his fingernails. It will be six months before he gets another. And so he has to sew away and let his little girl die three blocks off. When he gets home he can sob over her corpse; what more does he want? Exceptional case, you think. Not a bit of it. It's the drop on the crest of the wave. . . .

Do you see that old woman with the basket just turned into the street? Yes, the little one with the shawl over her head. Well, that is one of the meekest souls in this city. She and her husband live in two little rooms in a rear house. They pay about the lowest rent I have found in this neighborhood, $6 a month. He earns from $1.50 to $3.00 per week, so you can figure how much they live on. Lazy? No, sir! They have just toiled and toiled all their lives. She has kept house and borne children and washed and scrubbed and saved. Why aren't they better off, you ask? That's what I want you to tell me. Here are these two old people standing at the close of a life of work and frugality, and watching old age and helplessness creeping down on them. And what have they got to face it with? A bit of bare furniture; one son who drank and has drifted out of their sight; another son, a

barber, who just scrapes together enough to feed and clothe his family
while they live and to pay off their funeral expenses after they die; a
few graves across the river; a hope in heaven, and $70 in the savings
bank. . . .

Do you see that girl in front of . . . got to go, eh? Bored you, didn't
I? Yes, guess I am something of a crank on these things. Wish you'd
trot around with me for a week; you wouldn't think so highly of things
as they are.[17]

Drawing upon his pastoral experiences, Rauschenbusch filled the pages
of a new Christian Socialist monthly called *For the Right* with cranky articles
like the above specimen, as well as with more refined pieces on religious
topics. The journal was launched by Williams and Rauschenbusch during
the same year (1889) that the Episcopal socialist W. D. P. Bliss founded
the Society of Christian Socialists and its periodical, *The Dawn. For the
Right* never found a clear focus or large readership, and a number of its
articles were unintentionally patronizing in tone, but the journal was distinguished by its sincere effort to communicate with uneducated readers.

For the nearly two years that *For the Right* stayed in print, Rauschenbusch struggled to find a theological system that would express his own
religious experience and worldview. To the extent that he redefined his
theological position, it was largely a product of intuitive revision. Rauschenbusch recognized that he had outgrown the vaguely liberal pietism he had
adopted during his seminary years. The problem was that, having been
raised to dread the tradition of German theological liberalism, it was difficult for him to imagine that he now belonged to it. This apprehension was
complicated by the fact that even the more progressive German theologians,
such as Harnack, were either cautious or silent on sociopolitical subjects.
Rauschenbusch stewed over the question until 1891, when he took a leave
from his parish to study social movements in England and resume his theological studies in Germany.

The latter experience was formative for him. Through the course of the
year, Rauschenbusch relinquished his inherited fear of German liberalism
and recognized that his own religious sensibility was most satisfactorily
expressed in the theological tradition of Schleiermacher, Ritschl, Harnack,
and Herrmann. As his subsequent writings reveal, Rauschenbusch incorporated the anthropocentrism, evolutionary monism, and moral idealism of
this tradition into his own theological stance. This stance was most decisively shaped, however, in a moment of insight that occurred near the end
of his study leave in Germany, when Rauschenbusch found the unifying
theological principle he had been seeking. As he later recalled:

And then the idea of the Kingdom of God offered itself as the real
solution for that problem. Here was something so big that absolutely
nothing that interested me was excluded from it. Was it a matter of

personal religion? Why, the Kingdom of God begins with that. The powers of the Kingdom of God well up in the individual soul; that is where they are born and that is where the starting point must necessarily be. Was it a matter of world-wide missions? Why, that is the Kingdom of God, isn't it—carrying it out to the boundaries of the earth. Was it a matter of getting justice for the working man? Is not justice a part of the Kingdom of God? Does not the Kingdom of God consist of this: that God's will shall be done on earth even as it is now in heaven? And so, wherever I touched life, there was the Kingdom of God. That was the brilliancy, the splendor of that conception—it touches everything with religion; it carries God into everything that you do, and there is nothing else that does it in the same way.[18]

This insight led Rauschenbusch to conclude that the problem with the churches was that they no longer dared to imagine the meaning of the petition "Thy Kingdom come." Rauschenbusch had heard "Kingdom" language all of his life, but as the actual implications of the idea first washed over him he wrote that the effect was like a revelation, as if the peak of a mountain had suddenly broken through the clouds. "It responded to all the old and all the new elements of my religious life," he wrote. "The saving of the lost, the teaching of the young, the pastoral care of the poor and frail, the quickening of starved intellects, the study of the Bible, church union, political reform, the reorganization of the industrial system, international peace—it was all covered by the one aim of the Reign of God on earth. That idea is necessarily as big as humanity, for it means the divine transformation of all human life."[19] The Kingdom of God, as he later put it, should not be viewed as an appendage or an epilogue to Christian doctrine; it should be conceived, rather, as "the first and most essential dogma of the Christian faith." Rauschenbusch characterized the kingdom as "the lost social ideal of Christendom" and insisted that the ideal could only be recovered by taking seriously the example and teachings of Jesus.[20] "Here was the idea and purpose that had dominated the mind of the Master himself," he elsewhere explained. "All his teachings center about it. His life was given to it. His death was suffered for it. When a man has once seen that in the gospels, he can never unsee it again."[21]

The most creative period of his ministry occurred after Rauschenbusch returned to the United States in 1892, regenerated by his experiences abroad. In addition to their traditional pastoral tasks, he and Williams resumed several neighborhood projects and launched others that included a deaconess home, an association for working women, an institute for working men, the Amity Theological School, and other ventures that were substantially financed by Williams's mother. At the Baptist Congress of 1892, they presented their emerging theological position for consideration, which emphasized the centrality of the kingdom and the authenticating authority of the Spirit. Rauschenbusch and Williams argued that because the concepts of the kingdom and the Spirit were biblical and all-inclusive, yet also immune from historical criticism, they could provide the basis for a theological renewal within the church. A similar position was advanced by John Whittier, who told the Congress that the Quaker doctrine of the inner light could be "the stronghold of Christianity against the critical and agnostic spirit of our age." Rauschenbusch and Williams immediately associated themselves with this argument, while cautioning that the idea of the kingdom was needed to prevent the reduction of Christian experience to mystical inwardness.[22]

When this position proved to be too revisionist for most of the delegates, Rauschenbusch and Williams organized a progressive caucus within the Congress that became, the following year, the formally constituted "Brotherhood of the Kingdom." The group was led by Rauschenbusch, Williams, Schmidt, and the subsequently eminent theologians William Newton Clarke and Josiah Strong. Though most of its original members were Baptist pastors, the Brotherhood was open to all Baptist communicants, male and female, and was eventually opened to members of other denominations. The spirit of the group was expressed in its constitutional preamble, which declared that the Spirit of God was moving the church toward a truer understanding of the nature of the Kingdom of God. "Obeying the thought of our Master," it declared, "and trusting in the power and Guidance of the Spirit, we form ourselves into a Brotherhood of the Kingdom, in order to re-establish this idea in the thought of the church, and to assist in its practical realization in the life of the world." Members of the Brotherhood vowed to "exemplify obedience to the ethics of Jesus" and to "propagate the thoughts of Jesus" through their preaching and writing.

This association became Rauschenbusch's intellectual and spiritual home. Much of Rauschenbusch's time in Germany had been spent working on a lengthy manuscript that, upon his return, was reviewed and amended by Williams and Schmidt. Though the book was not published in Rauschenbusch's lifetime, he developed the basic ideas it contained in a series of separate papers written for journals and for Brotherhood meetings.[23] During the same formative period of his ministry, Rauschenbusch's spiritual life was fed by the annual Brotherhood retreats at Williams's farm in Marlborough, New York. Despite occasional rifts between Rauschenbusch and Williams, the Brotherhood held together for twenty years, functioning as a spiritual fellowship and as a kind of Fabian Society for the emerging Social Gospel movement.

Like the Fabians, the Brotherhood writers were skilled pamphleteers. Perhaps the most noteworthy of these efforts was a rather strident piece of theological historiography in which Rauschenbusch offered a typology of the historic misrepresentations of the kingdom. "A Conquering Idea" was written against the backdrop of a growing dispensationalist movement. The essay opened with the observation that the kingdom had been misrepresented most often through its identification with heaven, or the heavenly afterlife. In this common misrepresentation, Rauschenbusch argued, the kingdom becomes our anticipated destination beyond this life, and not a reality within our present or future life on earth.

A closely related distortion of the biblical doctrine was the replacement of the idea of the kingdom by the idea of individual salvation. Rauschenbusch asserted that in the biblical conception, such as in the eschatological pronouncements of Jesus, the kingdom is always a collective ideal that absorbs the human race "as a great unity." But to Americans, he ruefully observed, the organic biblical conceptions of the kingdom or original sin or the church as the body of Christ seemed incomprehensible. They floated upon the "millpond of modern theology," he wrote, "like the bowsprit of a sunken ocean vessel." Modern Christians therefore routinely reduced the collectivist ideas of Scripture to the question of individual salvation, Rauschenbusch explained, "because they understand nothing but individualism."

He identified ecclesiastical triumphalism as the third historic misconception of the kingdom. By Rauschenbusch's reading, the defects of Roman Catholicism were rooted in this fundamental distortion, in which the biblical idea of the kingdom was swallowed up in the idea of the church. Rauschenbusch acknowledged that Catholicism was a product of the early church's disillusionment after the kingdom promised by Jesus had failed to arrive. The idea of the church as the fulfillment of Christ's mission could be traced, he noted, to the early Church Fathers, who theorized that the kingdom had come into the world with (and in) the emergence of the church. Though he was often severely critical of Roman Catholic authoritarianism, Rauschenbusch conceded that the ecclesiological interpretation of the kingdom was a shrewd and partly truthful solution to the problem of the delayed Parousia. Like the otherworldly and the individualistic interpretations, he argued, the ecclesiological interpretation of the kingdom was based on a truism of the faith. "Heaven is a truth; individual salvation is a truth; the church as the body of Christ is a tremendous truth." But none of these ideas, he wrote, "neither singly nor combined, make up the full idea of the Kingdom of God."

The problem with the churches was that the full idea of the kingdom was unknown within them. Rauschenbusch argued that the substitution of heaven for the Kingdom of God on earth had made certain churches socially negligent or irrelevant and thereby "substituted asceticism for a revolutionary movement." The same churches often completed this distortion by reducing the organic, biblical idea of the kingdom to the individual's search for eternal salvation. By fostering this shriveled concept of the kingdom, he observed, the churches promoted an ethos of egocentric self-absorption, characterized by "religious selfishness" and a lack of interest or concern for others unlike themselves.

On the other hand, the theocratic substitution of the church for the kingdom negated the eschatological identity of the church and left most of the people in the world "unsanctified even in theory." Rauschenbusch was sensitive to the suggestion that his argument was historically implausible, since it implied that the biblical doctrine of the kingdom had been lost for nearly nineteen centuries. He pointedly recalled, however, that the Pauline doctrine of justification by faith had been lost until it was rediscovered by the sixteenth century Reformers. Rauschenbusch submitted that just as Luther and his generation had been called to recover the meaning of Pauline theology, so were modern Christians called to reclaim the message and significance of the synoptic Christ. "And perhaps that ideal of Christ is large enough," he wrote, "to include in one tremendous synthesis all the terms that are crowding into the life of this second age of renaissance."[24]

The latter phrase reflected Rauschenbusch's faith that despite the dramatic growth of millenarian and other sects in his time, the kingdom was "moving to victory" in the various movements for peace, economic justice, and freedom. Moreover, Rauschenbusch resisted the typical Progressive tendency to write off the booming millenarian movement as a know-nothing backlash. His researches into millenarian beliefs led him to argue, in "A Conquering Idea," that the millenarians had taken hold of one end of the biblical theology of the kingdom. "They have it in a bizarre form," he observed, "but they have it." The relentless millenarian focus on the fulfillment of history *in this world*, at the end of time, brought a biblical sense of urgency and eschatological expectation into this movement that was missing in the mainstream churches. Rauschenbusch argued that the millenarian movement owed its considerable energy to its grasp of this end of the biblical faith.

He continued that the socialists held the other end. Though they did not pray "Thy Kingdom come," Rauschenbusch asserted that it was the socialists, far more than the churches, who struggled to fulfill the biblical vision of a just social order. The socialist movement represented the kingdom of God "with God left out." Despite their antireligious posture, the socialists had become the keepers of the biblical dream that society could be organized for the sake of all its people. Insofar as it took up the struggle for social transformation that the churches had abandoned, Rauschenbusch therefore asserted, the socialist movement had become more Christian than the churches.

To Rauschenbusch, the project of the Brotherhood was to recover the organic vision of the kingdom that had been broken into otherworldly, individualistic, ecclesiastical, millenarian, and socialist fragments. While the kingdom *is* in heaven, he affirmed, it must also come to earth; while it begins in the depths of human hearts, it is not meant to stay there; while the church is "the channel through which ethical impulses pour into humanity from God," it is not identical with the kingdom; while the perfection of the kingdom may be transhistorical, the kingdom is also a present reality. Rauschenbusch insisted that the kingdom must never be reduced to any of its constitutive elements, because the kingdom is precisely "the sum of all divine and righteous forces on earth."[25] The sin of the churches and of the socialist movement was to settle for less than the Kingdom of God. "One of the special tasks of our Brotherhood," Rauschenbusch therefore wrote in 1895, "is to wed Christianity and the Social movement, infusing the power of religion with social efforts, and helping religion to find its ethical outcome in the transformation of social conditions."[26]

Rauschenbusch married Pauline Rother, a Milwaukee schoolteacher, in 1893, and raised five children with her in a marriage that was far more loving and secure than the marriage of his parents. His career as a pastor ended eleven years after his arrival in New York and nine years after a bout with Russian grippe left him almost totally deaf. He coped with his deafness bravely, carrying on his pastoral tasks as well as he could, but the handicap unavoidably limited his effectiveness as a pastor and activist, and Rauschenbusch unfortunately never learned to find humor in the awkward situations it occasionally caused. Though he was never known to whine about the loss of his hearing, and his wife unfailingly helped him cope with it, his inability ever to make light of it suggests that his impairment was a constant source of heartache to him. For the remainder of his adult life, Rauschenbusch endured a constant, surflike noise in his ears. In his letters, he sometimes referred to his condition as his "physical loneliness."

After he realized that his hearing would never return, Rauschenbusch turned with even greater concentration toward the written word, and also began to look for an academic position. The latter came in 1897, when he accepted an appointment to teach New Testament, English, and other subjects in the German department at Rochester Theological Seminary. Five years later, he was appointed professor of church history at his former seminary.

Dores Sharpe has recalled that Rauschenbusch always taught for a verdict. His lectures were apparently as vivid, dynamic, and polemical as his writings. Shortly after his return to Rochester, Rauschenbusch also offered his services to the small churches in the area that could not afford to pay for outside speakers. For nearly twenty years, he gave numerous sermons and lectures in these churches without remuneration.

Despite his love for the lecture circuit, however, and his sense of obligation to the small churches, Rauschenbusch was always foremost a writer. In addition to the hundreds of articles he wrote for a variety of newspapers and journals, he wrote the unfinished *Revolutionary Christianity* and also published several German-language books, including hymn translations and a life of Jesus.[27] At the same time he also wrote a series of essays that summarized the religious and social beliefs held in common by the members of the Brotherhood of the Kingdom. These essays were periodically presented to the Brotherhood and revised in light of group discussion and criticism. In the summer of 1905, Rauschenbusch began to work on a book that would contain his revised Brotherhood essays as well as several chapters of new material based on his current reading. *Christianity and the Social*

Crisis was published in 1907, shortly before Rauschenbusch left for his sabbatical in Germany. He feared that the book would be attacked by reviewers and perhaps even cause his dismissal from the seminary, but when he returned to the United States the following year Rauschenbusch found that he had tapped the zeitgeist.

Christianity and the Social Crisis went through six printings in its first two years and made Rauschenbusch famous. Though he had worried that his espousal of socialism would cost him his teaching position, Rauschenbusch's arguments did not reveal, or hide behind, any sense of ambivalence. The book announced at the outset that "the essential purpose of Christianity is to transform human society into the Kingdom of God by regenerating all human relations and reconstituting them in accordance with the will of God."[28] *Christianity and the Social Crisis* offered a biblical and historical argument in defense of this thesis, and closed with a programmatic analysis of the church's social mission in the modern world.

The biblical argument was based mainly on Rauschenbusch's interpretation of the prophetic literature ("the beating heart of the Old Testament") and the synoptic gospels. Rauschenbusch argued that most religions promoted the worship of power, by conceptualizing religion as a way to reconcile human beings, through ritual, with the powers of nature or force or wealth. But the prophetic biblical tradition eschewed the worship of power, condemned the evils of injustice and oppression, and insisted that "ethical conduct is the supreme and sufficient religious act." It was this prophetic stream of faith and hope that Jesus embodied, Rauschenbusch claimed, except that in Jesus even the nationalistic features of prophetism were discarded.

Like the readings of modern structuralist critics, Rauschenbusch read the parables of Jesus as polemical in intent.[29] In his interpretation, however, the synoptic parables of the sower, the tares, the net, the mustard seed, and leaven were meant to replace a catastrophic (or apocalyptic) idea of the kingdom with a more realistic, developmental concept. That is, by his reading, the parables were protests against the worldview of late Jewish apocalypticism, rather than products of it. Following the Harnack-Herrmann theory of Christian origins, Rauschenbusch assumed that the apocalyptical sections of the synoptic gospels, such as Mark 13, were retrojections of the later church's own apocalyptic mentality into the kerygmatic narratives. He explained, "It is thus exceedingly probable that the Church spilled a little of the lurid colors of its own apocalypticism over the loftier conceptions of its Master."[30]

This typically liberal deprecation of apocalypticism reflected Rauschenbusch's rootage in the nineteenth century tradition of German literary criticism, which claimed to have identified the Jesus of history within the layers of later church theology. Rauschenbusch worked out of this tradition for the rest of his life, repeating its assertions as unchallenged fact and dismissing out of hand the devastating criticisms it received in the post-

Harnack era of Scripture scholarship. While it is evident from contemporary form and redaction criticism that nineteenth-century criticism made unwarranted claims about the origins of apocalyptic and the historicity of the didactic New Testament texts, the same conclusions were already presented in Rauschenbusch's time in Albert Schweitzer's brilliant treatise *The Quest of the Historical Jesus*. With powerful irony, Schweitzer demonstrated in 1906 that the so-called critical theologians of the past century had merely projected the values of nineteenth century liberalism onto the figure of Jesus.[31] Several years later, when Schweitzer's argument became the cornerstone of a new theological consensus on the origins of Christianity, Rauschenbusch's failure to appropriate the argument made his own theology seem outmoded.

If it is clear that Rauschenbusch's theological position was undermined by his failure to keep up with the Scriptural scholarship of his time, however, it is also noteworthy that his writings contained one important (though indirect) response to the kind of argument advanced by Schweitzer. While Rauschenbusch continued to cling to his liberalized image of the historical Jesus, his principal argument was that the teachings of the prophetic tradition and the early church concerning greed, injustice, oppression, humility, and compassion were unarguably certain. These teachings were summarized, he argued, in the ethics of Jesus, as refracted by the New Testament. What Rauschenbusch feared was that the Schweitzerian emphasis on the eschatological mentality of the historical Jesus would obscure (once again) the importance of the New Testament's moral commands. Though Rauschenbusch mistakenly tried to exempt Jesus from this judgment, he acknowledged that all of the biblical writers made assumptions about the world that were now outmoded. The worldview of the New Testament writers was clouded, he observed, by the expectation of an immanent Parousia and the more immediate reality of Roman oppression. Rauschenbusch noted that the most prominent example of this fact was Paul, whose writings were profoundly shaped by historical and cultural factors that modern North Americans do not share. Yet within modern North American churches, he complained, "it still passes as a clinching argument for Christian indifference to social questions that Paul never started a good government campaign."[32] In this way, he asserted, the churches clung to the letter of the New Testament while smothering its spirit.

The contrary has often been asserted against him, but Rauschenbusch did not overlook the wide disjunction between the biblical and modern worlds. Rather, he drew attention to this disjunction, in order to emphasize the transcending importance of the moral command to build the kingdom. Though his exegetical arguments were undermined by his personal desire to trace this command back to the Jesus of history, his theological reconstruction was otherwise as credible as the alternatives, and more socially regenerative than any of them. Rauschenbusch rightly feared that the

Schweitzerian reconstruction (despite Schweitzer's personal mysticism) would produce yet another form of theological otherworldliness. On personal, spiritual grounds, Rauschenbusch acutely understood the attractions of otherworldly religion, but as a Christian socialist he abhorred the historical legacy of otherworldliness, which had turned Paul "into a personified code of law" and sacralized brutally oppressive governments. *Christianity and the Social Crisis* therefore ended with a straightforward argument for socialism.

One of the most common criticisms of Rauschenbusch's socialism has charged that it was based entirely on moral grounds. This reading has sometimes been supported by citing Rauschenbusch's address to the Rochester Labor Lyceum in 1901, where he derided the doctrine that socialism was simply the assertion of organized proletarian interests. "I tell you that if you could get that view to prevail," he said, "if you can establish it that it is purely a matter of selfishness, and that the sense of justice, the ideal of brotherhood, the longing for a truer and nobler life count for nothing, you have cut the heart out of the social movement. You have turned one of the sublimest movements the world has ever seen into the squealing of a drove of pigs where the rear pigs are trying to push away the front pigs and get their noses into the trough too."[33]

That is vintage Rauschenbusch. Because he always held the moral vision of a common good above the value of any group interest, including the interests of the proletariat, it is often claimed that Rauschenbusch's socialism was entirely idealistic. It is certainly true, as his speech to the Rochester unionists affirmed, that the moral vision was always paramount for Rauschenbusch. It is also true that in direct opposition to Marxism, his political orientation was reformist, and he repeatedly appealed to what he variously called the religious sentiment, spirit, or temperament. Yet despite the assurances of his Marxist and academic critics, it is not true that Rauschenbusch ignored the class struggle or based his socialism entirely on moral ideals. In the concluding chapter of *Christianity and the Social Crisis*, which asserted that socialism is "the logical outcome of the labor movement," Rauschenbusch emphatically argued that moral idealism of any kind was useless unless it was connected to the collective proletarian struggle for justice. He decried the "vain" attempts of idealists to reform the reigning social system "against the solid granite of human selfishness." In the face of the brutal realities of the class struggle, he argued, moral idealism *by itself* was socially bankrupt. "The possessing classes are strong by mere possession long-continued," he explained. "The law is on their side, for they have made it. They control the machinery of government and can use force under the form of law."[34] Contrary to the prevailing image of him as a romantic idealist, Rauschenbusch insistently defended socialism before hostile church and civic audiences because he keenly understood the realities of the class struggle. When he argued that the churches should be in the proletarian movement, he made the argument on moral grounds, but his basic moral assertion was that the class system should be abolished.

Nothing made Rauschenbusch angrier than to see the churches of Christ toadying up to the powerful. Because of his own family background in German Lutheranism, as well as his personal identification with the Anabaptist tradition, Rauschenbusch was haunted by the history of the German class struggle during the Reformation era. His writings frequently returned to the subject. For him, the peasant rebellion of 1525 was a continuing tragedy that illustrated the meaning of the class struggle and shaped his perspective on it. With evident feeling, Rauschenbusch recounted the process by which Martin Luther aligned his church with the German princes and barons, and thus eventually sacralized their war against the peasants. In that war, Rauschenbusch bitterly recalled, the German state "slaughtered probably a hundred thousand, devastated entire districts, broke the backbone of the German peasantry, and retarded the emancipation of a great and worthy class by centuries."[35] Though the peasant rebellion and the simultaneous Anabaptist movement were both "essentially noble and just," he wrote, "both were quenched in streams of blood and have had to wait till our own day for their resurrection in new form."[36]

Rauschenbusch concluded that the moral truth of the Anabaptist martyrs was a glorious, but socially wasted, virtue. Moral virtue should serve the ends of justice. But the achievement of justice depends on the organized determination of an exploited class, he wrote, "which makes that truth its own and fights for it." The struggle for social justice requires nothing less than the truth of its cause and the collective solidarity of the oppressed. "If there is no such army to fight its cause," Rauschenbusch therefore declared, "the truth will drive individuals to a comparatively fruitless martyrdom and will continue to hover over humanity as a disembodied ideal."[37] The sign of moral seriousness was that one was led by it into acts of solidarity with the oppressed class. Just as the Protestant and democratic principles of religious and political liberty had been fulfilled when the movements representing these causes forged alliances with the emerging middle class, he argued, "so the new Christian principle of brotherly association must ally itself with the working class if both are to conquer."[38] Rauschenbusch ended *Christianity and the Social Crisis* with an appeal to the churches to become the "soul" within the body of the proletarian struggle for socialism. For him, the function of the soul was to be a chastening as well as an inspiriting force within that corporate struggle.[39]

If Rauschenbusch was more realistic about the class struggle and the limitations of moral idealism than his critics have often claimed, however, it is nonetheless true that, at least until the outbreak of World War I, he shared the belief in Progress that was characteristic of nineteenth-century liberal idealism. Throughout the 1890s, for example, he observed with astonishment that the millenarians actually refused to believe that the world was getting better. To him it was obvious that the advances in science, the growth of education, the proliferation of new inventions and medicines, the maturation of democracy, and the expansion of the churches marked "an improvement in the net quantity of God-fearing righteousness on earth."[40] Rauschenbusch conceded to the millenarians that the evils of the modern world were "appalling in amount," but he was greatly impressed, as the millenarians were not, with modern scientific, technological, and political efforts to reduce the amount of evil in the world.

Rauschenbusch's most developed theological expression of this sentiment was offered in his second major work, *Christianizing the Social Order*, which appeared in November, 1912 — the same month that Eugene Debs won twelve million votes in the U.S. presidential election. It was the high tide of American socialism. The influence of the burgeoning Social Gospel movement had been revealed earlier the same year by the promulgation of the "Social Creed" by the Federal Council of Churches. The Federal Council was a national association of thirty-three denominations, founded in 1908, that drew its Social Creed almost verbatim from the Methodist Social Creed of 1908. These creeds called for a "living wage" in every industry, abolition of child labor, the elimination of poverty, and a more equitable distribution of wealth.[41] The proclamation of such a creed by Protestant churches, or even the existence of a Federal Council of Churches, would have been inconceivable a generation earlier, but in 1912 the newly instituted Federal Council was stacked with such Social Gospel stalwarts as Gladden, Strong, Rauschenbusch, Shailer Matthews, Harry F. Ward, Charles Stelzle, Frank Mason North, and Graham Taylor. It functioned as a kind of laboratory for Social Gospel ideas that infiltrated the churches and seminaries, largely through the clergy.

The publication of *Christianizing the Social Order* was itself a sign of the success of the prewar Social Gospel movement, since the book was essentially a collection of the Earl Lectures that Rauschenbusch delivered at Pacific Theological Seminary in 1910 and the Merrick Lectures he gave the following year at Ohio Wesleyan University. It opened with a restatement of Rauschenbusch's interpretation of church history, emphasizing that Christ's own theology of the kingdom had been gradually replaced by an otherworldly, hellenized theology ostensibly *about* Christ. As the prophetic texts of the Old and New Testaments were systematically "etherealized" by allegorical interpretation and the larger process of hellenization, Rauschenbusch argued, the core idea of the New Testament was altogether distorted. "The eclipse of the Kingdom idea was an eclipse of Jesus," he wrote. "We had listened too much to voices talking about him, and not enough to his own voice. Now his own thoughts in their lifelike simplicity and open-air fragrance have become a fresh religious possession, and when we listen to Jesus, we cannot help thinking about the Kingdom of God." Just as the Reformers of the sixteenth century had modernized theology by returning to the language and vision of Paul, Rauschenbusch asserted, the Social Gospel was modernizing theology by returning to Christ "and to his faith in the possibility and certainty of the reign of God on earth."[42]

As his title implied, *Christianizing the Social Order* marked a new stage in Rauschenbusch's faith that the world was getting better. He drew encouragement from the theory of evolution, which "has prepared us for understanding the idea of a Reign of God toward which all creation is moving." Although evolution was still disputed by biblical and ecclesiastical conservatives, Rauschenbusch observed that the progressive currents in the churches had embraced evolution as a valuable new paradigm for theology. "Translate the evolutionary theories into religious faith," he announced, "and you have the doctrine of the Kingdom of God."[43] That was religious progressivism in a nutshell, which *Christianizing the Social Order* explicated in nearly five hundred pages.

By "Christianizing" society, Rauschenbusch explained, he did not mean putting the name of Christ into the American constitution, or attempting to create any form of state religion. Rather, to Christianize the social order meant to bring it "into harmony with the ethical convictions which we identify with Christ." Rauschenbusch expressly acknowledged that the ethical values of Christ were not peculiar to the Christian tradition. The whole point, in fact, was that the Christian moral values of sacrificial love, freedom, compassion, fairness, humility, and equality were actually the values of all people of good will, whether religious or not. The point was to bring society into conformity with the moral values of "our collective conscience." Rauschenbusch conceded that his aim was to moralize the social order, but he argued that the substitution of this term for Christianize "would be both vague and powerless" to most women and men. It is appropriate to retain explicitly Christian language, he contended, not only because this language is more concrete and compelling, but also because the worthiest moral values of the West are traceable to the teachings, life, and spirit of Christ. The moral principles by which we should judge the social order are rooted in Judaism and Christianity, Rauschenbusch argued, but he denied that any kind of sectarian implication should be drawn from this fact, for "Christianizing means humanizing in the highest sense."[44] Throughout his later writings, Rauschenbusch used "democratize," "moralize," and "Christianize" as interchangeable terms.

The overall, inordinately optimistic thesis of *Christianizing the Social Order* was that although an unchristianized economic system threatened to destroy the social progress of the past century, most of the U.S. social order was nonetheless already Christianized. Rauschenbusch pointed to the democratization of modern sex roles, education, the churches, and the political system as evidence that the authoritarianism of the past had been Christianized in the past two centuries. In all areas except one, he asserted, it was widely assumed in modern American and European societies that only *democratic* social structures and *democratic* forms of political authority were legitimate. The churches had been Christianized, for example, often unwillingly, as a result of their loss of temporal power and unearned wealth. As a descendant of the Anabaptist tradition, Rauschenbusch recalled with pride that the "radical and pure types" of Christianity had provided the most suitable environments for the democratic revolution, but his overriding point was that most of the churches had since become part of the same social transformation. For Rauschenbusch, the democratization of the churches was an important sign of a better world in the making.[45]

The holdout was the economic system, the "unregenerate section of our social order." Though Rauschenbusch allowed that most businessmen as *individuals* were as moral as anyone else, he regarded the capitalist system as "a form of legalized graft" that engendered "a spirit of hardness and cruelty" that threatened, in turn, the recent social gains in U. S. civic and political life. While other sectors of the country's social life were increasingly characterized by a commitment to the public good, he wrote, the subordination of U.S. economic life to the law of profit undermined the stability of all social gains and degraded the other social sectors and professions that it touched. The perdurance of the logic of capital, he wrote, "means a surrender of the human point of view, a relaxing of the sense of duty, and a willingness to betray the public—if it pays."[46] To a Christianized mind, "the ugliest fact is the vindictiveness with which the private interests fight righteousness."[47]

Rauschenbusch argued that the fundamental social problem was not so much the profit system as it was the autocratic power "unrestrained by democratic checks" that capitalism gave to owners and managers. Insofar as it represents a fair return on one's useful labor and service, he wrote, profit has a sound moral basis. Rauschenbusch conceded that even the wage system could be morally justified where free land is available, or a certain kind of labor is scarce, or an employer is especially generous. But wherever labor markets are crowded, he observed, the entrenched power of the capitalist class becomes more predatory as it effectively "taxes" the working class through lower wages. Rauschenbusch listed numerous other ways by which unearned profits could be gained, but the focus of his critique was the moral evil of underpaid labor, which he characterized as "a tribute levied by power."

The reason that the labor question had intensified in the past century, he argued, aside from the rising sense of democratic entitlement, was that control of the instruments of production under capitalism had increasingly shifted to a small class of owners and managers, who made unearned profits off the exploited labors of the weak.[48] Rauschenbusch asserted that whenever profit exceeds a just return or is disassociated from direct work, "it is traceable to some kind of monopoly privilege and power—either the power to withhold part of the earnings of the workers by the control of the means of production, or the ability to throw part of the expenses of business on the community, or the power to overcharge the public."[49] The unearned profits gained by these means, he wrote, amounted to legalized graft.

As its title implied, *Christianizing the Social Order* was more idealistic than *Christianity and the Social Crisis*. The emphasis on the class struggle in Rauschenbusch's earlier writings was played down in his later work, but *Christianizing the Social Order* nonetheless contained Rauschenbusch's most developed argument for socialism. To Rauschenbusch, the fundamental problem with capitalism was that it negated the property rights of the working class. Though a modern American worker has democratic entitlements in the political sphere, he noted, in the economic sphere the same worker "has only himself," lacking any rights over property. The property with which he works is too expensive for him to own, yet most industrial property, Rauschenbusch observed, was financed by the savings of working people, through their banks and insurance companies. "But therewith the money passes out of the control of the owners," he wrote. "What a man deposits today may be used next week to pay Pinkertons who will do things he abominates."[50]

The essential question, therefore, was whether the process of investment could be democratized. The objective of economic democracy, he explained, was not to eliminate property rights, but to expand property rights under new forms. Rauschenbusch recalled that when the legislative process in Great Britain was owned by the landlords, the property interests of that class were quite naturally written into law. The sign of a realized democracy, he argued accordingly, would be the attainment of property laws that served the interests of the working class, for "political democracy without economic democracy is an uncashed promissory note . . . a form without substance."[51]

Rauschenbusch's conception of socialism strangely retained one vestige of Marxist utopianism. He repeatedly asserted that under socialism, because the power to charge monopoly prices would be abolished, prices would be based *entirely* on service rendered.[52] This holdover from the utopian socialist literature was out of place in Rauschenbusch's writings, since he otherwise opposed centralized collectivism and accepted the necessity of the market for a democratic society. Rauschenbusch exaggerated the extent to which economic democracy could ever replace economic competition, in part because of his weakness for utopian rhetoric, but his programmatic focus on the ultimate importance of investment was the overriding factor in his work.

Though he lived in an age when socialists typically produced "blueprints for a new humanity," Rauschenbusch understood that *democratic* socialism would require a situationally defined mixture of cooperative and public ownership of essential industries and private ownership of small enterprises. Rauschenbusch favored cooperative ownership whenever possible, but he recognized that the mix of ownership modes would always be a matter of contextual judgment in a democracy. While he accepted the Marxist theories of surplus value and the class struggle, he rejected the materialistic determinism of the existing socialist movement as well as the movement's rationale for centralized authority. He was thus a precursor of modern democratic socialism. In recent years, the theorists of liberal socialism have drawn attention to the socialist implications of John Stuart Mill's egalitarianism, arguing that Mill's position logically led to a form of socialism that is continuous with the liberal democratic tradition. An early form of the same argument was implicitly advanced by Rauschenbusch, who claimed as his position the vision of decentralized socialism offered in Mill's *Principles of Political Economy*, where Mill envisioned workers "collectively owning the capital with which they carry on their operations, and working under managers elected and removable by themselves."[53]

It is true, as John Cort has noted, that Rauschenbusch sometimes failed to distinguish among direct workers' ownership, mixed forms of cooperative ownership, and public ownership of production.[54] The issue is important in the present context because it brings out the difference between the narrow and the wider conceptions of economic democracy. Today, those who organize cooperative firms in the United States must do so without special government assistance and often without adequate financing or advice from banks. Most cooperatives operate on the traditional principle that those who own a company's capital have a right to control the company. On this principle, workers must be the primary investors in a firm in order to control it, which often means that the firm will be undercapitalized as the price of workers' control. The narrow form of economic democracy thus continues to measure human value in terms of exchange value. The kind of liberal socialism of which Rauschenbusch was a precursor, however, represents a strategy not only to empower workers, but also to empower those who do not earn wages: homemakers, the disabled, welfare families, retirees, the unemployed. Modern liberal socialism, as exemplified by the Meidner Plan for Economic Democracy, promotes the mixed model of cooperative ownership that Rauschenbusch suggestively advocated. With far greater specificity than is typical in contemporary liberationist theologies, he developed a detailed argument that all land-based natural monopolies (such as mines, oil and gas wells, water power, and harbor facilities) should be socialized and that the unearned rental values of private land should be recovered through taxation. He considered the private ownership of land and the buildings upon it to be socially justified, provided that the unearned rental values of land were returned to the community that created them.[55]

Though he tried to be optimistic on this score, Rauschenbusch worried that the political culture of the United States was too individualistic to accept economic democracy, and he lamented that North Americans only seemed to achieve a sense of common purpose when they engaged in war. Like William James, he argued that Americans have traditionally glorified their wars, not because they love violence, but because they enjoy the sense of social solidarity that war alone has historically generated. The moral alternative to war, by Rauschenbusch's reading, was socialism. He argued that a major cause of the lack of public spirit in American life was the comparative lack of public property. The only constructive way to promote a sense of common purpose in America, he therefore concluded, was to work for as much of the socialist program as was attainable. If a public spirit in America was to be developed on the basis of a common good rather than on militarism, he asserted, a transformation of the individualistic American consciousness would be required.[56]

Despite the fact that it contained over four hundred pages of political economics, Rauschenbusch insisted that *Christianizing the Social Order* was "a religious book from beginning to end," because the kingdom of God "means the progressive transformation of all human affairs by the thought and spirit of Christ."[57] In this sense, he regarded his arguments for socialism to be as religious as his commentaries on Scripture or his devotional writings. Rauschenbusch was also deeply devout in the traditional, individual sense, however, and because he was anxious to communicate his faith to a mass audience, he published a collection of his spiritual meditations in 1910. *For God and the People: Prayers of the Social Awakening* revealed the inner, religious source of Rauschenbusch's outward compassion and energy. It contained petitionary prayers for a wide variety of occasions, grouped according to subject and the time of day. Rauschenbusch's evening prayers, and his prayers for the unemployed and the destitute, were especially moving. "O Thou who art the light of my soul," he wrote at the end, "I thank Thee for the incomparable joy of listening to Thy voice within, and I know that no word of Thine shall return void, however brokenly uttered."[58] For many readers, the publication of this volume dispelled the common misconception that the Social Gospel had substituted politics for faith.

For God and the People was followed in 1912 by another statement of Rauschenbusch's personal faith, *Unto Me*, which he addressed to social workers.[59] This small book attempted to conjoin the personal and social meanings of faith—a project that Rauschenbusch carried out most successfully in his subsequent work, *The Social Principles of Jesus*, published in 1916. *The Social Principles of Jesus* was a popularized synthesis of Rauschenbusch's theological views, written in the form of a handbook on the teachings of Jesus. The book was written for the YMCA under the direction of the Sunday School Council of Evangelical Denominations, and as a study book for church classes it eventually became Rauschenbusch's most widely distributed work. He explained at the outset that the book was offered to dispel the "haze" with which the churches had "enveloped" the social teachings of Christ.[60] In a catechetical format, Rauschenbusch discussed the synoptic teachings on poverty, property, compassion, violence, and the like, presenting Jesus as an advocate for social justice and the kingdom. The kingdom of Christ, he concluded, "overlaps and interpenetrates all existing organizations, raising them to a higher level when they are good, resisting them when they are evil, quietly revolutionizing the old social order and changing it into the new." The kingdom sometimes suffers terrible reversals, he noted, as in the catastrophe of the current war, but Rauschenbusch insisted that the kingdom is nevertheless always coming, even on "the wrecks of defeat." The kingdom is only revealed in our experience in fragments, he wrote, "but such fragmentary realizations of it as we have, alone make life worth living."[61]

That was the tone of his final work, as well. *A Theology for the Social Gospel* was published in 1917. By the time that he wrote this comparatively dispirited work, Rauschenbusch's idealism was deeply shaken, but he argued nonetheless that the Social Gospel would outlast the war. In his opening pages, Rauschenbusch conceded that the war now "dwarfed and submerged all other issues," including those traditionally raised by the Social Gospel, but he observed that the war *itself* had become the most pernicious social problem of all, which revealed the need for an enlargement of the Social Gospel vision. What was needed was a moral and economic concept that translated the earlier class analysis of the Social Gospel into international terms. The war had been caused, he asserted, by "the same lust for easy and unearned gain" that the Social Gospel had always opposed. "The social problem and the war problem are fundamentally one problem, and the Social Gospel faces both." Against those who had given up on the Social Gospel on the grounds that the war had destroyed the progressive political culture that the movement needed to survive, Rauschenbusch insisted that the Social Gospel movement was filled with repressed energy that would eventually regenerate the larger progressive movement, once the war was over.[62]

Rauschenbusch himself struggled to believe this assessment. *A Theology for the Social Gospel* offered a systematic theology for the existing and future Social Gospel movement. The author's struggle to maintain his faith in the future of this movement was apparently reflected, however, in the book's prose style, which lacked the compelling energy of Rauschenbusch's other major works. In *Christianizing the Social Order*, for example, Rauschenbusch offered a neo-Hegelian interpretation of history as "the sacred workshop of God" in which women and men "realize God" by cooperating with the work of the Spirit. He asserted that all history is the "unfolding of the purpose of the immanent God who is working in the race toward the commonwealth of spiritual liberty and righteousness."[63] This highly suggestive conception of the relationship between divine reality and history was the kind of idea that Rauschenbusch meant to develop further in *A Theology for the Social Gospel*, but, with one exception, the book fell short of his intention. *A Theology for the Social Gospel* presented a series of restatements of Rauschenbusch's previous theological ideas, often without the imagination or idealist dialectics of his previous writings. The result was the same theology with less spirit.

The exception was Rauschenbusch's discussion of sin, which took up six consecutive chapters. The emphasis on sin and the subdued tone of the book were undoubtedly attributable to the war, but Rauschenbusch observed that his perspective was rooted in the writings of his theological mentors, Schleiermacher and Ritschl. Following the interpretation first offered by Ritschl, Rauschenbusch argued that the solidaristic conception of sin, and not the theory of subjective religion, had been Schleiermacher's most important contribution to theology. Just as Schleiermacher and Ritschl had emphasized the centrality of the religious consciousness of solidarity, and therefore posited the existence of a hereditary racial unity of sin, Rauschenbusch asserted that the Social Gospel must also affirm the social reality of original sin and the supernatural power of evil.[64]

Building upon the organic historicism of Schleiermacher and Ritschl, Rauschenbusch argued that classical metaphysical theologies had been correct to insist upon the solidaristic transmission of evil, but, in Rauschenbusch's estimation, these theologies unfortunately overloaded the idea with a theory that "tried to involve us in the guilt of Adam as well as in his debasement of nature and his punishment of death." This theory "logically fixed on us all a uniform corruption," he noted. But if the human will is unavoidably, uniformly corrupt, Rauschenbusch asked, what is the point of morality or education? He argued that the problem was not with the idea of a unity of sin, but with the exaggeration of this idea into a doctrine of essential depravity. By exaggerating the biological transmission of evil in the human race, the classical theologies had overlooked the various and equally destructive means by which evil was transmitted through social tradition. This defect in the traditional theologies had engendered reactionary social consequences, Rauschenbusch argued, because it undercut the theological basis for moral efforts to resist the spread of evil. He observed that most of the vices and crimes of adults, such as drug addiction, social cruelty, perversity, racism, and ethnic feuds, were transmitted from one generation to the next through socialization, not through heredity. "When negroes are hunted from a Northern city like beasts, or when a Southern city degrades the whole nation by turning the savage inhumanity of a mob into a public festivity," he argued, "we are continuing to sin because our fathers created the conditions of sin by the African slave trade and by the unearned wealth they gathered from slave labour for generations."[65] The social reality of the kingdom of evil was a profound truth overlooked in certain liberal theologies and trivialized in traditional notions about the work of the devil. That we are implicated in the historical evils of our ancestors was, for him, a social fact that only the Social Gospel seriously addressed.

It is ironic that Rauschenbusch has so often been accused of ignoring the reality of sin, when he was actually acutely conscious of personal and social evil. His "idealism" was simply his enduring conviction that the manifold social evils of bigotry, militarism, and indifference, as well as the structures of evil created by a parasitic ruling class, could be socially redeemed through moral effort and democratization. Though he respected, to a point, the classical metaphysical explanations of the origins of evil, he sought to correct the reductionism implicit within these theories by emphasizing the universality of sin as a *historical* fact. Without this emphasis on the sociohistorical transmission of sin, he rightly argued, the value of every strategy to overcome social evil was undermined.[66]

Rauschenbusch ended *A Theology for the Social Gospel* on a wilfully optimistic note, claiming that "the era of prophetic and democratic Christianity has just begun."[67] His letters of the same period, however, reveal that he continually struggled to believe this assertion. Though he was never a strict pacifist, Rauschenbusch repeatedly condemned the waging of aggressive or imperialist wars, and he frequently expressed his abhorrence of war as the ultimate enemy of social progress.

The outbreak of World War I wounded him for personal reasons, as well. While his loyalty to the United States never wavered through the course of the war, Rauschenbusch's perspective was deeply affected by the fact that he was nearly as at home in Germany as in the United States. His expression of this perspective angered many Americans. Shortly after the war began, Rauschenbusch argued in an article titled "Be Fair to Germany" that Germany was no more militaristic than its neighbors, and that the United States should remain neutral in the war. This widely criticized article was followed the next year by Rauschenbusch's declaration of opposition to American military sales to England, and later followed by his opposition to American military preparedness.

It was often noted by his critics that Rauschenbusch never condemned the German invasion of Belgium with more than a passing phrase, or a characterization of it as a "blunder." This was a serious failing, for which he was vehemently attacked by newspaper editors and preachers. His affection for Germany, his hatred of war, and his overriding desire for reconciliation during a period of intense anti-German feeling in America often led Rauschenbusch to seem defensive toward Germany. It was for reasons that had nothing to do with lack of patriotism, however, that he was led to oppose U. S. participation of any kind in the war. As the country's involvement in the war grew deeper, and the charges of disloyalty rang in his ears, he gradually withdrew from the public debate. His family later recounted that Rauschenbusch was unrelievedly preoccupied with the war in his last two years of life, but because he was badly burned by the charges of lack of patriotism he wrote very little about it. "I am glad I shall not live forever," he wrote sadly to Algernon Crapsey. "I am afraid of those who want to drag our country in to satisfy their partisan hate, or because they think universal peace will result from the victory of the allies."

While he never embraced absolute pacifism, Rauschenbusch's abhorrence of the war moved him to join the pacifist Fellowship of Reconciliation in 1917. That year, he delivered a speech at a special meeting of the F.O.R. that reflected his shift in temperament and style. Like his book of the same year, *A Theology for the Social Gospel*, Rauschenbusch's speech to the F.O.R. was pacific in tone and occasionally simplistic in argument, presenting a Christian case for near-pacifism that lacked the vigorous, dialectical style of his earlier writings. Though he unfailingly insisted that the

Social Gospel movement would regenerate Progressivism after the war had ended, he perceived that the movement was paralyzed from without, and rapidly disintegrating.

Rauschenbusch became seriously ill early in 1918, the victim, by his own account, of his many years of overwork and his deep depression since the outbreak of war. "Since 1914 the world is full of hate," he wrote in March, "and I cannot expect to be happy again in my lifetime."[68] Two months later, he wrote to Lemuel Call Barnes of the American Baptist Home Mission Society that although his life had been physically very lonely (a reference to his deafness), and often beset by attacks from conservatives, he had been upheld by the Spirit of Christ, which "has been to me the inexhaustible source of fresh impulse, life and courage. . . . My life would seem an empty shell if my personal religion were left out of it."[69]

He died of brain cancer on July 25, 1918, during the last weeks of the war. A few weeks before his death, Rauschenbusch expressed his experience of the ever-gracious being of God in a poem, "The Little Gate to God." Part of it ran:

In the castle of my soul
Is a little postern gate,
Whereat, when I enter,
I am in the presence of God.
In a moment, in the turning of a thought,
I am where God is.
This is a fact.

This world of ours has length and breadth,
A superficial and horizontal world.
When I am with God
I look deep down and high up.
And all is changed.

The world of men is made of jangling noises.
With God it is a great silence.
But that silence is a melody
Sweet as the contentment of love,
Thrilling as a touch of flame.

In this world my days are few
And full of trouble.
I strive and have not;
I seek and find not;
I ask and learn not.
Its joys are so fleeting,

Its pains are so enduring,
I am in doubt if life be worth living.

When I enter into God,
All life has a meaning.
Without asking I know;
My desires are even now fulfilled,
My fever is gone
In the great quiet of God.
My troubles are but pebbles on the road,
My joys are like the everlasting hills.
So it is when I step through the gate of prayer
From time into eternity.[70]

It has often been said that Rauschenbusch died with a broken heart, but his friend and biographer, Dores Robinson Sharpe, has put the matter in perspective. Sharpe concedes that Rauschenbusch experienced profound sorrow and depression in the closing years of his life, but the judgment that Rauschenbusch was broken by the war, Sharpe argues, underestimates his moral courage, and his faith. For Rauschenbusch, the reality of the kingdom, "the energy of God realizing itself in human life," was a powerful force "in all tenses," as he put it, throughout his adult life.[71]

As a church historian, he was well aware that the idea of the kingdom had been distorted or buried for most of the church's lifetime. He was equally conscious of the parallels between the world war and the religious wars of the sixteenth century. Rauschenbusch greatly feared that the war of his time would damage the progressive movement as seriously as the wars of the sixteenth century distorted the early Protestant movements, but it was a matter of faith to him that the kingdom would be fulfilled in any case.

Though he had numerous faults, some of which are painfully glaring today, I believe that his supposed chief fault—his idealism—was actually his most exemplary feature for the modern church. As Martin Luther King, Jr., once observed, Rauschenbusch undoubtedly overestimated human nature and overidentified the kingdom with the movements for democratization. In these respects, he was the child of nineteenth-century progressivism. Yet King identified Rauschenbusch as one of the foremost influences on his life and thought, primarily because Rauschenbusch offered him an energizing, religious vision of a better world.[72] In Rauschenbusch's life and work, as in King's, the vision was sustained in a way that did not fall into utopianism, self-righteousness, or radical militancy. He was not "radical" in any sense except the *democratic* sense, and he regarded democracy and utopianism as mutually exclusive. The only certainty that one can offer about a democratic future, Rauschenbusch characteristically remarked, is that things will not happen in the way that one expects.[73]

I have argued that, with occasional lapses, Rauschenbusch was not a utopian, and that his idealism was actually his most exemplary trait. Rauschenbusch had failings of another kind, however, that are noteworthy in light of the standard criticisms against him. Far from being the utopian or radical leftist often portrayed in the literature about him, Rauschenbusch sometimes fell short of the most important progressive movements of his time, largely because of his rootage in the church. He repeatedly remarked, with regret, that it was not the church that had led him into the social movement in the first place. What he occasionally failed to see afterward was that his devotion to the church sometimes restricted or distorted his conception of social progress. For example, though his writings contained favorable references to Susan B. Anthony and other feminist reformers, Rauschenbusch's religiously based assumptions about familial roles made him ambivalent toward the suffrage movement. In this matter, as in his support for Prohibition, he reflected the social conservatism of the churches, which extended to the Social Gospel movement.[74]

This conservatism also extended to race. Though the Social Gospel theologians were critical of the ravages of slavery and racial hatred, most of them accepted the recent Supreme Court rulings on "separate but equal" segregation, just as they unreflectively presupposed the superiority of the Anglo-Saxon racial line. Rauschenbusch rarely discussed race at all, but his occasional asides revealed similarly ambivalent feelings on the subject. Throughout the Baptist Congress debates over immigration in the 1880s and early 1890s, he argued vigorously for an open immigration policy and criticized all racially based arguments for closed immigration. Yet in one of his fund-raising appeals for the German department at Rochester Seminary, Rauschenbusch asked in 1895, "Are the whites of this continent so sure of their possession against the blacks of the South and the seething yellow flocks beyond the Pacific that they need no reinforcement of men of their own blood while yet it is time?" And in his Rochester commencement day address of 1902, he counterposed the needs of the Anglo-Saxons and the "princely stock," the Teutons, with the demands of the "alien strains" arriving from other parts of the world.

Max Stackhouse has observed that by "Teutonic," Rauschenbusch generally referred to a "tun"-oriented cultural tradition that was more democratic than, for example, the Latin tradition. The point is well taken. Rauschenbusch's purpose was to protect democracy. He feared that democratic gains in the United States could be lost if immigrants from authoritarian countries came to the United States in disproportionate numbers. His arguments were based not so much upon racial fear as upon his concern about the fragility of democratic political cultures. Yet his references to the "princely Teutonic stock," the "yellow hordes," and the like contained unmistakably racist connotations. His overall intention was always to promote democratic ends and assert that the United States accepted all races as equal. But as Paul Minus has observed, Rauschenbusch was also preoccupied with the task of making the most effective argument for acceptance of German immigrants. Under the pressure of that concern, he implied that some immigrants were more equal than others. He thus undermined his own argument for democracy, using language that must be considered racially offensive.[75]

Rauschenbusch's worldview was also emphatically pre-ecumenical in regard to Catholicism. To him, the tragedy of church history was that the Catholic Church had hellenized the prophetic, kingdom-oriented teaching of Christ, turning Christianity into a form of ecclesiastical neopaganism.[76] The Episcopalian socialist and friend of Rauschenbusch, Vida Scudder, once exhorted him to tone down his attacks on Catholicism, but Rauschenbusch considered the problem of Catholic authoritarianism to be a matter of crucial political and theological principle. Though it is fair to say, as Robert D. Cross has written, that Rauschenbusch's interpretation of church history reads today "as virtually a parody of the extreme Protestant critique on Catholicism," it is also fair to recall that official Catholic teaching in Rauschenbusch's time was theologically precritical and violently anti-ecumenical.[77] Rauschenbusch's animus against Catholicism was based on his perception that the Catholic Church was a socially and theologically reactionary force that had thwarted liberalism and offered itself as a substitute for the kingdom. The fact that these arguments had a progressive ring at the turn of the century is a measure of the changes that have occurred within Roman Catholicism and liberal Protestantism since that time.

In his recent assessment of the Social Gospel tradition, the eminent church historian Martin Marty has emphasized the racial and feminist failings of Rauschenbusch, as well as the limitations of his moralism. Marty contends that Rauschenbusch only came close to socialism in his support of Henry George's single-tax program and further claims that Rauschenbusch rejected a class analysis in favor of a moralistic appeal to the power of love. Asserting that Rauschenbusch and the other Social Gospel reformers were chiefly characterized by their "programmatic timidity and gentility," Marty concludes that the irony of the Social Gospel tradition is that it was ever considered radical.[78]

I recognize and appreciate that this reading is offered as an ironic interpretation of the character and legacy of the Social Gospel. For the most part, despite their often soaring rhetoric, the Social Gospelers were indeed far more timid and accommodating than they presumed. Marty's emphasis on the irony of this fact marks an important corrective to much that has been written about the Social Gospel tradition. It is certainly true, as Marty asserts, that Rauschenbusch and most of his Social Gospel colleagues were not temperamentally "radical" or militant in any way. Rauschenbusch was in the movement, not because he was alienated, or afflicted with the *ressentiment* defined by Nietzsche and Scheler, but because he was faithful to his understanding of the moral imperatives of Christian faith. He detested violence and authoritarianism of all kinds and emphatically rejected the notion that a democratic transformation of the social order could ever be constructed on the ruins of a class war. His discomfort with the radical, often antireligious sensibility of the U.S. Socialist party prevented him from ever joining it.

It is mistaken to assert, however, that Rauschenbusch was not a socialist, or that he ignored the class struggle. Though he clearly preferred to argue for socialism on moral grounds, he also insisted with equal clarity that "we must not blink the fact that idealists alone have never carried through any great social change. . . . For a definite historical victory a great truth must depend on the class which makes that truth its own and fights for it."[79] Throughout his career, Rauschenbusch made withering attacks on the "parasitic" and "predatory" ruling classes, whose self-interest, he wrote, "makes them impervious to moral truth if it calls in question the sources from which they draw their income." Even in his most pacific work, *A Theology for the Social Gospel*, he powerfully criticized those "upper class minds" who have been able throughout history "to live parasitic lives without any fellow-feeling for the peasants or tenants whom they were draining to pay for their leisure."[80] In *Christianizing the Social Order*, he mounted a sustained attack on monopoly profits and the private control of the investment process, and identified himself with the decentralized form of socialism advocated by John Stuart Mill.[81]

Rauschenbusch favored decentralized forms of socialization over nationalization, not because he was "timid," but because he understood that in most cases decentralized cooperative ownership represented the most democratic and economically efficient alternative to the capitalist system. With all of his failings and limitations, he prefigured the modern liberationist and democratic-socialist movements in ways that are instructive. Long before the problems with highly centralized, nationalized economies were documented, Rauschenbusch perceived that a mix of decentralized public and cooperative enterprises would better serve the common good. He advocated the abolition of class rule, which he attributed to the power to charge a monopoly price, by asserting the necessity of democratic rights over property.[82] Rauschenbusch's programmatic vision was thus the vision of modern liberal socialism, emphasizing the values of economic democracy rather than the totalizing rhetoric about "rationalizing all of society" found in the Marxist literature of his time. Marty observes that Rauschenbusch accepted the legitimacy (and even necessity) of private property, but the acceptance of private property on some variable scale has been a feature of democratic socialism since the time of Mill, Ferdinand Lasalle, and Eduard Bernstein.

Moreover, the fact that Rauschenbusch only worked in one partisan Left campaign should not be taken to indicate his lack of political seriousness. Rauschenbusch envisioned a socialist movement in which the churches would someday play a humanizing role, but his own efforts were poured into the churches themselves, which were far from socialism. That is, he preferred to work for a social transformation within the churches, rather than to offer a token religious presence to the existing socialist movement.

That was part of his idealism. Rauschenbusch wanted the churches to be part of the larger progressive movement, but he keenly understood that most of the churches were far from making such a commitment. He devoted himself to raising the level of social consciousness within the churches, however, because he believed that the churches had an invaluable role to play in the public realm.

In an era when the mainstream churches have largely lost their public voices in the United States, and even the word "liberal" has become an epithet, I believe this aspect of Rauschenbusch's legacy is most significant. By continually accommodating themselves to a dominant political culture that emphasizes the rights of property over the rights of democratic self-government, the mainstream churches have undercut their claim to a social mission within that culture. By contrast, though he valued inclusiveness and modernity as much as anyone, and even accepted the desire for respectability that motivated church leaders, Rauschenbusch believed that the churches should struggle to become a collectively regenerative force within society. Because the word "gospel" was sacred to him, he only embraced the term "Social Gospel" in the last two years of his life, but he believed throughout his adult life that the church should advance the liberal, democratic, religious values of the Social Gospel with a missionary spirit.

In his various writings, he propagated this faith with terms (such as "Christianization") that would be inappropriate today, and his optimistic temperament led him to overestimate the degree to which U.S. society had already become democratized. The corrective to the latter fault, however, was present in Rauschenbusch's own work. As he repeatedly insisted, somewhat inconsistently with his optimistic assessment of the U.S. social order, the lack of democracy in the country's economic life undermined the existence of U. S. political and civil democracy. In one crucial respect, this is what made Rauschenbusch more realistic than the chorus of "realistic" critics who followed him. The most discerning of these critics acknowledged Rauschenbusch's emphasis on sin, but then claimed that this emphasis contradicted his social idealism. In their view, though Rauschenbusch was clearly aware of the pervasiveness of sin, his social views were not sufficiently chastened by this awareness.[83] Because human beings are naturally selfish, the argument goes, "realists" must accept a trade-off between political and economic democracy, rejecting the latter in order to consolidate democratic political gains.[84]

It was exactly this notion, however—that freedom and equality are contradictory—that Rauschenbusch insistently rejected. To him, the reality of sin did not discredit economic democracy any more than it damaged the case for political democracy. He believed, rather, that the omnipresence of evil made the democratization of power necessary. That is, in order to check the amount of evil that any powerful group can cause, Rauschenbusch argued that economic democracy is as necessary as political democracy. Without a gradual democratization of economic power, he warned, the existence of political freedom would be jeopardized. Rauschenbusch understood that there are problems with economic democracy, just as there are problems with political democracy, but he argued that the evils of undemocratic authority always outweighed in the long run the problems associated with self-determination.

While it is true that much of Rauschenbusch's language, his biblical exegesis, his cultural conservatism, and his optimism are dated, I believe that the core of his work is as relevant as ever. His religious and political arguments for socialism have been appropriated by the theorists of contemporary liberation theology. His decentralized, cooperative vision of socialism prefigured the program of the modern democratic socialist movement.

Above all, he understood that all movements for social progress need an energizing vision of a better world. He spent his life calling the churches to go beyond their strategies of accommodation, to embrace a biblical vision of social and economic transformation. In every age, he once remarked, those who struggle for greater social gains are patronized by the sad smiles of the wise. "Let them smile," he said. "I would rather join in the Exodus and lay my bones to bleach on the way to the Promised Land than to make bricks for Pharaoh forever, even if I could become an overseer over other slaves and get big spoonfuls from the garlicked fleshpots of Egypt."[85] He explained over and again that he advocated democracy, not utopia. "We shall never have a perfect life," he wrote, "Yet we must seek it with faith. ... At best there is always but an approximation to a perfect social order. The Kingdom of God is always but coming. But every approximation to it is worthwhile."[86]

That is the living spirit of the Social Gospel.

3

Paul Tillich and the Theology
of Religious Socialism

In the later years of his life, when he was widely recognized as one of the outstanding theologians of his generation, Paul Tillich occasionally surprised his students by remarking that he still considered himself a socialist. To most of his North American students, Tillich was not a political figure at all, but the author of the massive *Systematic Theology* and other works that synthesized modern theology, philosophy, art, and psychology. Though his students were sometimes vaguely aware that Tillich had been the major theorist of "religious socialism" in pre-Nazi Germany, his reputation in the United States was based upon three decades of theological work that seemed to address every related discipline *except* political economy. Tillich once told James Luther Adams that of all his books he was most proud of *The Socialist Decision*, but during his lifetime this often-quoted remark was incomprehensible to most of Tillich's North American audience.

With the emergence of liberationism as a major theological movement, however, a renewal of interest in Tillich's socialist writings has taken place. Numerous theologians have observed in recent years that the themes of modern liberation theology were prefigured in Tillich's socialist works, and some have further argued that these writings are valuable sources for the liberationist project of the future. I believe they are right. The search for a humane socialism, in critical dialogue with Marxism, is a theological project that Tillich advanced. Some of the most important questions in liberation theology were suggestively, and at times powerfully, developed in Tillich's socialist works.

With the recent renewal of interest in these writings, however, has often come a rather curious reluctance to criticize Tillich's judgments or to critically assess the value of his theorizing for the contemporary situation. I will argue that Tillich suffered an unfortunate failure of nerve and conviction in his postwar intellectual career, but I will also argue that his prewar writings defined a vision of socialism that is still instructive today.

Tillich was the son of a Lutheran pastor and school superintendent who epitomized his social type, the late nineteenth-century Prussian state servant. To be a functionary of the Prussian state, as Tillich later observed, was to accept the worldview expressed in Kant's *Critique of Practical Reason*, in which one submits to "the primacy of the idea of duty above everything else, the valuation of law and order as the highest norm, the tendency to centralize the power of the state, a subjection to military and civil authorities, and a conscious subordination of the individual to the organic whole."[1] In 1914, when Tillich went to the Western front as a chaplain in the kaiser's army, he was already a doctor of philosophy, an ordained Prussian Evangelical minister, and a husband, but the overriding loyalty in his life, as in his father's, was to king and fatherland. He later recalled that although he had been too philosophically sophisticated to believe in the "nice God" of popular superstition, he was otherwise, at the age of twenty-eight, a sheltered academic who entered the war as ignorant of politics as anyone, and as eager to serve Germany.[2]

When Tillich emerged from the front four years later, having survived two nervous breakdowns, the sight of mass graves, the grotesque disfigurement and death of friends, the seemingly endless nightmare of cold weather, bayonet charges, and explosions, and his own desperate sense of futility, he entered the military base at Spandau as a traumatized, but deeply radicalized, figure. He later recalled that it was only during the war that he first began to comprehend the existence of the class struggle, as well as the fact that the church was widely regarded as the "unquestioned ally of the ruling groups."[3] The war was the occasion of his first direct contact with the proletariat. Though he had originally supported the German war effort with enthusiasm, over time he became increasingly disgusted that the churches on both sides were promoting and sacralizing the war in the name of Christ. In the trenches, it seemed to him that the world was ending. When a friend sent him a picture of herself sitting on a lawn, clothed in a white dress, Tillich wrote to her saying it was inconceivable to him that something like that still existed.[4]

The intellectual cleric who had entered the war to fulfill his moral obligation, and who had then experienced revulsion toward the slaughter around him, found his only moments of wartime uplift through his reading of Nietzsche's *Thus Spoke Zarathustra*. Nietzsche's ecstatic affirmation of life and his searing assault on moral and civic conventionality proved intoxicating to the repressed chaplain. For a brief period during 1916, while he sat in the French forest reading Nietzsche, Tillich experienced a respite from his emotional torment and began to imagine the possibility of a postwar life. The only kind of theology that could be written after the war, he thought at the time, would have to address the "abyss in human existence" that the war had revealed.[5] He later recalled that he had entered the forest a dreaming innocent, and emerged from it a wild man.

Tillich left the front in August 1918, less than two months after receiving the Iron Cross (First Class), and spent the remaining four months of the war at the Spandau military base in Berlin, where he witnessed the final disintegration of the kaiser's government. The war killed nearly two million Germans, wounded another four million, and ran the national debt to $44 billion. Although Tillich did not witness the final collapse of the German army, he observed the strikes and uprisings in the streets of Berlin that led, in November, to the abolition of the German monarchy and the inauguration of a republic. By then, Tillich was beginning to feel emotionally prepared to resume his life in a new world, and for the first time he felt drawn to politics.

The following month he made his first public political statement. While preparing to leave the army, Tillich accepted a junior faculty post at the University of Berlin and was also appointed by the new provincial government (which called itself an "Evangelical" rather than "Royal" consistory) to a post as a city pastor. Tillich accepted the position, while criticizing the church's insistence on retaining its privileges as a state church within the new government. Shortly afterward, when the provisional government floated a proposal to separate the church from the state, Tillich signed a statement published by the New Church Alliance that supported the principle of ecclesial disestablishment. This statement was repudiated, in turn, by Lutheran hierarchs and officials, who viewed disestablishment as a threat to their influence and authority, and who eventually forced the new German republic to retain the state church.

The New Church Alliance argued that the postwar German church should reject the militarism and nationalism of the past and discard every remaining vestige of ecclesiastical imperialism. Somewhat to his own surprise, these had become Tillich's own positions, which deepened his sense of alienation from the existing church. Though he did not remain active in the New Church Alliance, Tillich independently took the same road that the Alliance later took as an organization—into the newly organized religious socialist movement.

Tillich's attraction to politics was sparked by the November revolution; yet, despite the fact that he had only recently rejected the monarchicalism of his father and his church, from the beginning of his conversion to socialism he regarded the Social Democratic party (SPD) as a badly compromised and incoherent organization. Thus, instead of joining the SPD after the war, Tillich immediately identified with the Independent Social Democrats, the socialist party to the left of the Social Democratic party. Tillich never formally joined the Independents, but he voted for their candidates, spoke at one of their rallies in 1919, and formed friendships with party members. The SPD had somewhat reluctantly assumed power in the aftermath of the November revolution, and had subsequently formed a coalition government with the Catholic Center and Liberal Democrat parties after the national elections in January. Tillich acknowledged that the SPD was bound by "historic necessity" to play a mediating role in the Weimar Republic, but he argued at the time that the SPD could only represent the socialist vision, and serve the common good of Germany, by moving left. In his judgment, the party was ideologically bankrupt and seemed totally preoccupied with petty electoral tactics. For the rest of his life, Tillich argued that his commitment to the militant socialism of the Independents had been strategically correct, especially in light of the fact that the SPD coalition governments had used the army against the Communists and Independents. The SPD had failed, he would say, in part because it had failed to be socialist.

Still dressed in his army grays and Iron Cross, Tillich taught his first postwar course, "Christianity and the Social Problems of the Present," at the University of Berlin in 1919. The subject matter reflected his own urgent desire to explore the religious and social implications of the various political movements, parties, and ideologies of the postwar world. For the historical sections of his lectures, he drew heavily upon Ernst Troeltsch's *Social Teachings of the Christian Churches*. At the time, Troeltsch himself was a leader in the Democratic party, a moderately conservative party to the right of the SPD, but Tillich avidly promoted his work and rightly claimed that it would become a classic text. Tillich was intensely interested in the crosscurrents of social, political, religious, artistic, scientific, and philosophical reconstruction in Europe, and often interrogated his students about what was being taught in other classes.

From a later vantage point, perhaps the most striking feature of Tillich's early postwar work is that it contained nearly all of the distinctive marks of his mature theology. Only three months after his release from the army, for example, Tillich presented a lecture to the Kant Society in Berlin, "On the Idea of a Theology of Culture," in which he expressed the fundamental thesis of his subsequent lifework—that religion is the substance of culture, and culture the form of religion. Though he later toned down its political substance, Tillich's theology of culture was originally conceived as a project within the tradition of religious socialism.

"Religious socialism" was founded in Germany at the turn of the twentieth century by Christoph Blumhardt, Hermann Kutter, and Leonhard Ragaz; in 1920, Tillich joined the small group in Berlin that identified with this tradition. The group was led by two pastors, Gunther Dehn and Karl Mennicke, and included among its approximately twelve members the economists Eduard Heimann and Adolf Lowe, who became lifelong friends of Tillich's. As Heimann later recalled, the Berlin group was a small collection of "naïve, optimistic, esoteric, eccentric academicians" who gathered to discuss the practical and theoretical problems of postwar reconstruction.[6] They were politically unaffiliated socialists who sought to revive the prophetic spirit in the churches and synagogues—half of them were Jewish—while refraining from any identification of socialism with the kingdom of God, or even with any political party. Their central identifying idea was eventually provided by Tillich, in his reinterpretation of the New Testament concept of the *kairos*.

Kairos in Greek is literally the "right time" (distinguished from the "formal time" of *chronos*), but in Tillich's appropriation of the term the *right* time implied a redemptive transformation of consciousness. The *kairos*, for Tillich, was the moment in time when the eternal, which is ethically normative, breaks into the ambiguous relativity of existence and thus creates something new within history. In the manner of his philosophical mentors, Hegel and Schelling, Tillich theorized that the crucial turning points in world history have all reflected the universal *kairos*, in which "the eternal has broken into the temporal," and he further argued that the current period of European history was such a (potential) turning point. In its *ultimate* sense, he asserted, the *kairos* is the center of history, because it is the interpretive key to the whole of history and all its parts.[7] In its *special* sense as a decisive force in the present situation, Tillich wrote that the *kairos* is "the coming of a new theonomy on the soil of a secularised and emptied autonomous culture."[8] The problem with traditional socialism was that socialism was the product of the same deracinated, secular culture that it purportedly opposed. Tillich argued that a genuinely emancipatory socialism would have to transcend both medieval heteronomy and bourgeois autonomy, while offering a transformative vision that was not cut off from the past or from the realm of the transcendent. The concept of the *kairos* as the fullness of time functioned as a boundary concept, for Tillich, between religion and socialism. Religious socialism represented more than a new economic system. "It is a comprehensive understanding of existence," he later wrote, "the form of the theonomy demanded and expected by our present *kairos*."[9]

Tillich believed in the early 1920's that Germany was uniquely prepared for religious socialism, precisely because Germany had been humiliated in defeat. The bankruptcy of bourgeois civilization should be most apparent, he thought, to those who had been ravaged by the war. By the end of the war, Tillich had adopted a socialist perspective on the causes of the war, arguing that it was largely a struggle between imperialist powers for the right to control markets outside Europe. Though the war had destroyed the international socialist movement, Tillich argued that a truer form of socialism could be inaugurated in the German ruins of the war, if only Germans would accept the true reasons for their debasement. He took comfort in the traditional Christian doctrine that brokenness is the precondition for transformation. Tillich and his friends in the "*kairos* circle," as the Berlin group became known, therefore used their various editorial and platform opportunities to advocate a "theonomous" vision of socialism outside the circles of party politics. They argued that the current period of German desolation was actually a precious historical moment that contained kairotic possibilities. Tillich's doctrine of the *kairos* was undoubtedly a generalization of his personal experience following the war, which explains his tendency in later life to exaggerate the political impact of the *kairos* group. In his *Systematic Theology*, Tillich acknowledged that awareness of a *kairos* in history "'is a matter of vision," and therefore subject to errors in interpretation or application.[10] But he was unarguably right to attribute momentous importance to the postwar conflicts in Europe. When the tide later began to turn toward fascism, he should have been one of the first to comprehend what had happened, though, unfortunately, he was not.

The Social Democrats were ousted from power in the national election of 1920, largely because the election followed closely upon the adoption of the Weimar Constitution (in August 1919) and the explosion of German outrage against the terms of the Treaty of Versailles. Though the Social Democrats had only reluctantly accepted the conditions of the Versailles treaty, which included redrawn borders and a crushing burden of economic reparations, they were widely regarded by Germans as traitors for signing the treaty. The Weimar Republic itself was commonly viewed by Germans as an alien, foreign-imposed *Unrechtstadt*, a bastard state. This contempt was symbolized in several German universities by the reestablishment of formal ceremonies that celebrated the founding of the Reich on January 19, 1871.[11] At the same time, the Independent, Nationalist, and Communist parties all opposed the Weimar Constitution outright, having been excluded from the governing coalitions of the postwar period. These parties and others fought their battles in the streets. After three years of strikes, sporadic rioting, factional street fights, and widespread looting and disorder, an abortive putsch was led in 1923 by the young Adolf Hitler.

The same year, Tillich published his foundational essay, "Basic Principles of Religious Socialism," which he offered as a summary of the convictions of the *kairos* circle. He began with a distinction between the "sacramental" and "rational" orientations. The sacramental worldview is defined by an epiphanic consciousness, whether in the primitive or pantheistic consecrations of matter as divine, or in the identification of certain objects or concepts as holy. Sacramentalism presupposes an organic, communitarian consciousness in which history is viewed as myth. Everything in life is understood and valued in relationship to the sacred symbols of faith. In a sacramental context, individual life is dominated by sacred relationships to some mixture of the family, soil, tribe, cult, class, nation, or political system. Tillich argued that the source of sacramental power is its foundation in sacred myth, which confers meaning upon the perceived relationships between past and present, humankind and nature, and individual and community.

The rational orientation, by contrast, is based not upon an epiphanic consecration of nature, but upon form and law (*Recht*). Tillich acknowledged that form and law also exist in the sacramental consciousness, but he argued that in sacramentalism form and law are directed toward the holy (*das Heilige*) rather than toward the right (*das Richtige*). In the rational orientation (as, for example, in Kantian philosophy) even the holy is judged according to critical standards of right. Historical criticism, demythologization, and all other forms of "enlightened" criticism are products of the rationalist consciousness, which is methodologically relentless in its demystification of the world. Tillich was sympathetic toward rationalism to the extent that the spirit of modern scientific inquiry and democratic values could be identified with the rationalist consciousness, but he criticized rationalism on socioreligious grounds, arguing that rationalism had produced the sterile, deracinated culture of the bourgeoisie. The fundamental defect in the rationalist consciousness was that it absolutized autonomy.

Tillich posited religious socialism, dialectically, as a third orientation that united the sacramental and rationalist worldviews, but which also transcended them. Religious socialism is essentially a *prophetic* orientation, he wrote, that unites the mythological and critical interpretations of history as it transcends the split between heteronomous and autonomous authority. "It has the holy, but only as it permeates law and form; it is free from sacramental indifference, but it does not succumb to rational purgation."[12] Religious socialism is thus a necessary corrective to existing socialism, because religious socialism is inherently prophetic. Tillich argued that the prophetic character of the socialist movement had been compromised in recent years by electoral opportunism and theoretical obfuscation, and he insisted that everything depended upon whether the movement could subordinate these co-opting elements to a higher, prophetic vision.

The defining feature of Tillich's theological vision was the *kairos*, the fulfilled moment of time in which the present and future meet, "and from whose concrete tensions the new creation proceeds in which sacred import is realized in necessary form."[13] Thus, in the consciousness of the *kairos*, the sacramental and rationalist orientations are united in a new form, which Tillich called *theonomy*, "the unity of sacred form and sacred import in a concrete historical situation." As the ultimate content of the kairotic consciousness, theonomy is a condition in which "the spiritual and social forms are filled with the import of the Unconditional as the foundation, meaning, and reality of all forms." Theonomy transcends the mythological consciousness of sacramentalism and the deracinated emptiness of rationalism. While there are various forms of theonomy, Tillich asserted that in an ideal theonomy, religion and culture would not merely coexist, since true religion is the substance of culture, just as culture is actualized religion. "Every coordination of the Unconditional and the conditioned makes the Unconditioned conditioned and the conditioned Unconditioned," he explained. The vision of theonomy is concretely fulfilled whenever "form and import" are actualized as a unity.

Tillich's theological vision was not, however, simply a politicized version of cultural neoprotestantism. Though Tillich is rightly viewed as a cultural theologian in the tradition of Schleiermacher and Troeltsch, he was too deeply scarred by the war to regard culture in Schleiermacherian terms.

Prewar European theological liberalism had typically reconciled religion and the modern world by reinterpreting the gospel to fit the values of the modern world.[14] The operative assumption was that by virtue of its educational, scientific, and economic advances, the culture of bourgeois civilization was the bearer of moral and intellectual norms by which religion should be judged. This assumption was repeatedly displayed in the "biographies" of Jesus written in the nineteenth century (most of which portrayed Jesus as a sympathetic bourgeois), but even the more sophisticated theologians of the nineteenth century, such as Harnack and Herrmann, tended to reduce Christianity to a religious rationale for "progress" and other liberal values. The massive illusions that riddled the "life-of-Jesus" books were dissected by Albert Schweitzer in *The Quest of the Historical Jesus*, published in 1906.[15] The biographers of Jesus could be compared to a man who stared down a well, Schweitzer concluded, seeing only his own dim reflection. Unlike Rauschenbusch, Tillich seriously appropriated Schweitzer's arguments. For Tillich, what remained of the comfortable neoprotestant faith died in the French forest. Cultural neoprotestantism was inadequate, in his estimation, primarily because it underestimated the depth and pervasiveness of evil in the world.

Tillich's theology was therefore marked by an insistent emphasis on the reality of a nihilating, demonic force within nature. Since every culture in the world conflates divine and demonic elements, he argued, theology must maintain a dual relationship to culture. Religion must contain within itself a "yes" and a "no" to culture. Tillich allowed that when confronted with distorted or destructive social forces, it can be, at times, appropriate for Christians to retreat into the faithful confines of a sacred community. He identified the early church, medieval mysticism, and traditional Lutheranism as examples of such a culturally rejectionist retreat from the world.

But a church that permanently withdraws into a religious ghetto, he countered, becomes demonic itself, because it forsakes its vocation in the world. For Tillich, it was axiomatic that the church has social obligations and that *all* forms of religion, including the most sectarian, are inevitably shaped in some manner by prevailing cultural norms and values. Therefore, the cultural Protestantism of nineteenth-century liberalism and the cultural isolationism of traditional Lutheranism were equally mistaken, the former because it underestimated the force of evil in the world, the latter because it tried to escape from the evil in the world.

The church is meant to redeem evil *in* the world through the power of the Spirit. Tillich argued that culture religions of all kinds are deformed through their lack of a prophetic spirit. "The only proper attitude toward culture and also toward socialism," he asserted, "is that characterized by the double demand of *reservatum* and *obligatum religiosum*."[16] The *reservatum religiosum* rejects the identification of religion with culture, or of religion with any particular form of politics, but the *obligatum religiosum* insists upon the obligation of the church to be an agent of transformation within the world. By stripping religion of its prophetic substance, culture religions not only trivialize religion, Tillich contended; they also "rob culture of its import" by dissipating the substance of culture, which is religion.

Even by German intellectual standards, Tillich's thought operated at a high level of abstraction, yet he repeatedly insisted that religious socialism could only be adequately defined through the concrete struggle for it. The fundamental struggle, in his assessment, was not against secularism (which is an element within religion), but against the demonic. Tillich defined the demonic as "the contradiction of unconditioned form, an eruption of the irrational ground of any realization of form that is individual and creative."[17] Like the multivarious manifestations of divine reality, the demonic is always revealed through some concrete form, though never exhausted in it. The basic difference between the divine and the demonic, Tillich explained, is that divine energy is positive, and the demonic negative, toward unconditioned form. Religious ecstasy, for example, can be either divine or demonic; both divine and demonic energy have an ecstatic element. The crucial difference between them is that the ecstatic element in the divine is creative and life-giving, whereas demonic ecstasy is destructive. The demonic is the nihilating force within life that pulls toward nothingness, the reversal of creation. In the biblical myth of creation, God created everything out of nothing. Demonic forces try to return everything to nothing. In his lectures, Tillich sometimes startled his students by speaking quite seriously of Satan. Though he always acknowledged his uncertainty as to whether evil was personal, he considered the mysterious reality of the demonic, in some ontological form, to be self-evident. In his early, theological formulation, the struggle for religious socialism was a fight against the persisting demonic aspects of sacramentalism and rationalism.

Tillich's conception of religious socialism was postmodern in the sense that he appropriated modern liberalism while insisting on the need to go beyond it. He argued that in the struggle against the demonic elements of mythic sacramentalism, for example, religious socialism must adopt rational, liberal, and democratic elements.[18] Yet, at the same time, Tillich insisted that religious socialism must oppose the sterile materialism of the bourgeoisie, which the socialist parties had unfortunately adopted. Despite his highly abstract language and his tendency to offer verbal solutions to practical problems, Tillich resisted the latter tendency in himself by refusing to conceive socialism in either moralistic or purely theoretical terms. He based his argument for socialism on the class struggle and on the prophetic demand for justice, arguing that religious socialism is not a perfectionistic ideal but an attainable vision that includes sacramental and rationalist elements. Religious socialism begins, he asserted, as a struggle against the numerous forms of injustice, dehumanization, inequality, and authoritarianism that sacramental systems have rationalized throughout human history. Tillich therefore asserted that whenever religious socialists are faced with a choice between liberal democracy and theocratic sacramentalism, they must always support or make alliances with the former. The road to religious socialism runs through liberalism.[19]

The problem with liberal modernization, Tillich argued, is that it strips nature of its sacramental power and thus turns nature into an economic instrument. As Marx observed, the result is spiritual death through the commodification of all social existence. "The more a thing becomes a commodity," Tillich explained, "the less it exists in an eros-relation to the possessor and the less intrinsic power it possesses. In this inner emptiness, however, the thing becomes the object of the subjective eros and of the subjective will to power."[20] Under capitalism, the naturally human desires for pleasure and domination become directed toward a subverted, totally commodified social system; thus the brake on these desires, which a sacramental relationship to nature had provided, no longer exists. Whatever the subjective will to power (or desire for dominance) takes away from nature, Tillich observed, it simultaneously loses for itself, "and it thus becomes a thing in the oppressive process of a limitless industrial economy."[21]

Tillich held that the class struggle was not a universal social phenomenon, but rather "an expression of the demonic character of capitalist economy," yet he emphatically argued that the class struggle could not be resolved simply by socializing the economy.[22] He assumed that socialism must be more than a program of economic socialization, and he faulted the existing socialist parties for advocating a secular state socialism that was merely an economic "counterconcept" to modern capitalism. For Tillich, authentic socialism required a transformation of consciousness, replacing the subjective will to power with a universal religious eros. If the goal of socialism is not theonomy, he argued, a victorious socialist movement will only rationalize more collectivized forms of hubris, power worship, and dehumanization. Socialism must reject all forms of authoritarianism. It must affirm the democratic constitutional state "as a universal form," Tillich asserted, but it must also seek to fill this form with "the sacred import of a creative theonomy." Socialism is, in part, the struggle for democratically legitimate forms of social authority and the realization of formal equality "to the breaking point."[23]

Tillich did not suppose that social gains in the direction of religious socialism should be left undefended. He remarked that while people often romantically assume that pacifism has something to do with religious socialism, pacifism in fact nullifies socialism, because it fails to protect the social gains that define socialism. To serve justice is to advocate whatever is necessary to attain or maintain justice. To renounce the coercive power of the state, Tillich therefore argued, was to nullify the struggle for justice, since only the power of the state can successfully restrain the reactionary or destructive desires of human beings in a fallen world.

Although Tillich conceived socialism as the fulfillment of democracy, he also renounced all romantic notions about the supposed goodness or purity of the proletariat. He argued that one of the most formidable barriers to a revitalized socialist movement was the moral and intellectual backwardness of the working class, which willingly consumed "the *kitsch* in art and science, in morals and jurisprudence."[24] Tillich bemoaned the "demonic force of inferior value" that he found widespread in German culture, and he argued that the socialist movement needed to address the social and moral ravages of capitalism as seriously as it attacked the economic problems. Here, as in his theory of the sacramental origins and power of racism, Tillich offered a line of criticism that anticipated themes later developed and perverted by the theorists of German fascism.

"Basic Principles of Religious Socialism" closed with a reiteration of Tillich's assertion that religious socialism must not be identified with any particular party. He cautioned that the existing socialist parties were riddled with their own seemingly intractable "demonries" and argued that religious socialists must also keep their eyes open for "theonomous elements" in other parties and movements.[25] The strategic goal of religious socialism was not to become a religious faction in a larger party. Tillich seemed to realize that the socialism of the Independent party was a political dead end, and he renounced the pacifists and populists for their utopian illusions, yet his own position was utopian in one sense. He wanted religious socialism to generate a transformation of the German political and economic systems, but without being involved *in* politics. By the time he gave up that remaining vestige of utopianism, it was very late in the day for German democracy.

Tillich married Hannah Gottschow, his second wife, in 1924, and at the same time accepted an associate professorship of theology at the University of Marburg where he succeeded the ailing Rudolf Otto. Despite the presence of Otto, Rudolf Bultmann, and Martin Heidegger at Marburg, Tillich immediately found the university depressing for its provincialism. Following the dissolution of his first marriage, he had lived a rather bohemian existence in Berlin, where he habitually toured the cafes and became sexually involved with numerous women. Tillich was promiscuous for most of the rest of his life, a fact that has been bitterly chronicled by his wife, Hannah (who was also far from monogamous), and analyzed more sympathetically by his friend, the psychoanalyst Rollo May.[26] The nature of Tillich's relationships with women, sexual and otherwise, is a complicated subject, but for present purposes it is only relevant that Tillich's erotic awakening after the war also drove him to develop intense interests in expressionist painting, psychoanalysis, music, literature, and politics. "I have come to know the Boheme," he wrote early in 1924, but that spring, shortly after his second marriage, Tillich made the career move to Marburg, a quaint university town on the river Lahn, sixty miles north of Frankfurt. Hannah Tillich has recalled that in Marburg "everything seemed coarse and unbearable" to both of them, including the food, the muddled Hessian accent, the claustrophobic encircling hills, and the socially and sexually repressive atmosphere.[27]

Besides missing the cosmopolitan atmosphere of Berlin, Tillich also came to miss his University of Berlin students, who had accepted his theological liberalism and appreciated his political and cultural interests. At Marburg, the majority of students were Barthians who regarded Tillich's theology as warmed-over nineteenth-century culture-protestantism. Tillich finally attracted approximately thirty students at Marburg and became friends with Otto, but when a full professorship at the Institute of Technology in Dresden was offered to him the following year he took the post with grateful relief.

His first commercial success, *The Religious Situation*, was published as he prepared to move to Dresden. *The Religious Situation* traded heavily upon Max Weber's concept of the "spirit of capitalism," which Tillich identified, like Weber, as the self-assertive, competitive ethos of the modern industrial world.[28] Like Weber, he asserted that capitalism despiritualized the natural world in order to commodify everything within it. In its unrelenting drive to provide the maximum number of consumers with the maximum number of commodities, Tillich argued, the capitalist system "seeks to arouse and to satisfy ever increasing demands without raising the question as to the meaning of the process which claims the service of all the spiritual and physical human abilities."[29] This critique echoed Weber's indictment of the same "specialists without spirit and hedonists without heart," but Tillich's response to the problem went far beyond Weber's nonreligious liberalism. Tillich fastened upon the spiritually destructive logic of capitalism, arguing that in this system of rationalized selfishness "there is no trace of self-transcendence, of the hallowing of existence. The forms of the life-process have become completely independent of the source of life and its meaning."[30] As an alternative to the deracinated spirit of capitalism, Tillich advocated a form of praxis that he termed "faithful realism" (*glaubiger realismus*).[31]

This was a dialectical concept. Faith, in Tillich's language, is a perspective that transcends any particular experience or datum, but realism is a perspective that focuses on particular experiences and data. Faith is inherently transcendental, but realism rejects transcendence. Tillich argued that a realistic assessment of history and nature is necessary, but insufficient, because realism cannot reveal the larger or deeper meaning of anything. He pointed to the cold emptiness of positivist and pragmatist philosophies as evidence that realism needs the insights of faith. Those who fail to hold the dialectic of realism and faith in balance, he observed, inevitably lapse into some form of faithless realism or unrealistic idealism.

Tillich identified faithful realism most specifically with religious socialism, but his larger argument in *The Religious Situation* was that a "faithfully realist" revolt against modern civilization was already taking place in modern art, philosophy, and science. He contended that in their various ways the expressionist and post-expressionist movements in painting, the Nietz-schean and Bergsonian philosophies of life, the Freudian discovery of the unconscious, and the Einsteinian revolution in physics were all character-ized by a fundamental openness to the Unconditioned (Tillich's God-term), or at least to the transcendent. The most significant currents in modern intellectual life, by his reading, were in revolt against the denatured secu-larism of the bourgeoisie. Tillich argued that this openness to the unlimited in modern intellectual life created a new, and potentially kairotic, situation for religion. His assessment of the churches, however, was less hopeful. Following Troeltsch, Tillich argued that the churches were generally unpre-pared for the modern world, especially in the social sphere. While the liberal elements in the churches had long surrendered to modernity, reduc-ing religion to the cultural values of bourgeois civilization, Tillich observed that even the most reactionary, antimodern elements in the churches were working out new compromises with the capitalist order. Though these ele-ments remained essentially precritical in their theologies, in the social sphere they were beginning to rationalize an accommodation with the exist-ing system. By increasingly accepting the modern relegation of religion to the sphere of private experience, for example, the churches cooperated in their own social marginalization. Tillich observed that this strategy pur-chased a new institutional respectability for the Catholic and mainstream Protestant denominations, but at the price of trivializing or distorting the social meaning of Christian faith.

The political economics of Tillich's socialism was only vaguely suggested in *The Religious Situation*, but the final chapter contained a striking descrip-tion of the *religious* content of religious socialism. Tillich noted that under capitalism the "religious symbols of eternity" had been pushed to the mar-gins of society. The goal of religious socialism, by contrast, is theonomy, "the free devotion of finite forms to the eternal."[32] Tillich argued that the kind of *religion* that was needed to sustain religious socialism would be a union of the mystical and the prophetic spirits. Religious socialism needed to combine the religious substance of mysticism, exemplified by Rudolf Otto's *The Idea of the Holy*, with the prophetic tradition of Jewish and Christian criticism.[33] Tillich specifically mentioned the "neo-reformed" the-ology of Karl Barth as the outstanding modern example of prophetic crit-icism. He acknowledged that Barth's soaring affirmation of divine transcendence and his rejection of all anthropocentrism in theology offered a modern religious vision of formidable power and penetration. Tillich expressed his fear, however, that the prophetic aspect of Barth's theological project would fade as the "prophetic disturbances of our days" dissolved into normalcy. That is, Tillich feared that Barth's prophetic edge was only sustained by the widespread sense of political crisis in Europe. If the political situation were to become more stabilized, he thought, Barth's theological project could easily become merely a sophisticated form of otherworldliness.

Tillich's own approach was to unite the most meaningful elements of the church's mystical and prophetic traditions. He insisted in a later essay that neither of these traditions is religiously or socially meaningful if it fails to illuminate one's present, concrete situation. "Revelation is revelation to me in my concrete situation, in my historical reality," he wrote in 1928. He concluded that the most serious crisis for the church lay in its failure to unite "contemporaneity and self-transcending power" in its witness to the world.[34]

In 1929, at the age of forty-three, Tillich was named professor of philosophy and sociology at the University of Frankfurt, a position he held for the four most satisfying years of his German career. This was his first full professorship at an accredited German university, and Tillich exulted in his professional success, his new circle of colleagues and friends, and the beauty of Frankfurt's geographical surroundings. He immediately attracted a large number of students and acquired a reputation as a generous, unpretentious, and sympathetic teacher who enjoyed intellectual and personal interaction with his students. Tillich was open to a fault, treating even his Nazi students with respect. His first doctoral student, Theodor Adorno, affectionately nicknamed him "Pacidius" for his pacific temperament. Tillich rarely took disagreements personally, and nearly always, with genuine interest, solicited the views of others, even when they were strongly critical of his own. He listened intently, and possessed the pedagogical skill and personal graciousness to find wisdom in every student's question. Though he was tormented throughout his career with doubts about the validity of his thought—especially during his years at Frankfurt, when he was the only theologian on the faculty—Tillich's intellectual self-doubts rarely led to defensiveness or anger of any kind. He was extraordinarily open toward students, colleagues, and friends, in part because he always expected to learn from them and to develop his ideas through them.

Shortly after his arrival at Frankfurt, Tillich helped to engineer a faculty position for Max Horkheimer, who then became director of the *Institut für Sozialforschung*. Later famed as the "Frankfurt School," Horkheimer's institute was an independently endowed, humanistic-Marxist association that included, among others, Leo Lowenthal, Friedrich Pollock, Adolph Löwe, Karl Mannheim, Kurt Riezler, Karl Mennicke, Adorno, and Tillich. Like Tillich, the Frankfurt "critical theorists" were more inclined toward theory than practical political engagement, and, theoretically, most of them were socialists positioned between the compromised revisionism of the SPD and the totalitarian collectivism of the Communist party. Tillich found a home in this company of Hegelianized Marxists. His growing fame and his friendships with Löwe, Adorno, and others made his tenure at Frankfurt the happiest period of his life.

But there was a drawback. Despite his occasional religious anxieties, Tillich's life at Frankfurt was otherwise so personally satisfying to him that he failed to recognize what was occurring in the world outside his rarefied circle. Though he was disgusted by the Nazi movement, and though he wrote lengthy articles about political theory and ideology, his absorption in the Frankfurt academic and social life often caused him to appear oblivious to the actual German political crisis of the moment. For all of his interest in politics and his insistence on the importance of concreteness in theology, Tillich's disconnection from the outside community caused him to underestimate the growing strength of the Nazi movement. He wrote highly sophisticated essays on the class struggle and on the political failings of the churches without seeming to notice that his own writings failed the test of concreteness.[35] His own theorizing was not tested by experience.

During the first three years of his term at Frankfurt, Tillich's main concession to the actual political situation in his country occurred in 1929, when he held his nose and joined the Social Democratic party. The dramatic gains of the Nazi movement had made just enough of an impact upon Tillich's consciousness to move him to join a revisionist party that he disdained. This example of political realism distinguished Tillich from most of his friends, but Tillich's aversion to the actual tasks of party and union organizing caused him to keep his distance from SPD politics. He was even further removed from the activities of the churches. Tillich's efforts on behalf of religious socialism were thus largely confined to occasional public lectures and to his academic lectures and essays on the theory of socialism. Most of Tillich's essays on socialism during his Frankfurt period were published in the journal *Neue Blätter für den Sozialismus* ("New Leaves for Socialism"), but his most significant essay of the period was published as a pamphlet in 1931 under the title "The Protestant Principle and the Proletarian Situation."

Tillich acknowledged at the outset of this essay that the Protestant and proletarian movements appeared to have nothing in common. He admitted that the mainline Protestant churches had been wedded since their inception to the bourgeoisie, whether in the feudal-patriarchal form of the bourgeoisie (as in central Europe) or in the liberal-capitalist form (as in western Europe). Far from advocating the transformation of the social order on religious or moral grounds, Tillich observed, Protestantism had typically reduced the mission of the church to the religious needs of the self, while sacralizing the capitalist order as an order of divine providence. Thus, from a historical as well as from an ideological standpoint, the opposition between Protestantism and proletarianism seemed to be irreconcilable.

Tillich acknowledged that without a transformation of its own "inherent character" Protestantism did seem irreconcilable with the proletarian movement. But he argued that this assessment of the problem misconstrued the true "inherent character" of Protestantism, which should never be identified with any of its historical forms. Tillich asserted that the defining feature of Protestantism is not any given doctrine or ecclesiastical form, but the Protestant principle, the principle of resistance against all forms of human pretension, authoritarianism, and idolatry. As he expressed it, what "makes Protestantism Protestant" is that Protestantism contains within itself a critical, dynamic principle that transcends all of its historical configurations. The inherent character of Protestantism is not revealed in any particular confessional or social form, he argued, but in the life of faith, in which historically relative texts, doctrines, and sacraments are valued as relative means to grace. Tillich insisted time and again that to place one's faith in anything less than the Unconditional is idolatry. If one believes in God on the basis of Scripture or tradition or logical arguments, then what one believes in is Scripture or tradition or logical arguments, and not God.

True faith, Tillich argued, is the state of mind "in which we are grasped by the power of something unconditional which manifests itself to us as the ground and judge of our existence." [36] The being of God is not an object beside or above other objects. Rather, the power that grasps us in the state of faith is "a quality of all beings and objects," the quality that points beyond the finite existence of all beings and objects to the "infinite, inexhaustible, and unapproachable depth of their being and meaning." If the Unconditional were less than Being itself — that is, if God were a being — then reality would be greater than God. The only faithful (that is, nonidolatrous) conception of divine reality, Tillich therefore argued, is one that refrains from defining the mode or nature of the divine mystery, and which especially avoids the conception of God as one object among others. Since all human language is the product of multifariously limited human experience, it is axiomatic that human language can never define the nature of divine reality, which transcends the limits of space and time. This axiom is the core of the Protestant principle, which Tillich characterized as a "guardian" against all attempts to overdefine the unconditioned mystery.

For Tillich, this principle had social implications. Though the Protestant churches had effectively sacralized capitalism as an "order" of the divine will, he argued, the deepest impulse within Protestantism opposes this legacy. Tillich asserted that the Protestant churches could only begin to fulfill their social mission, and take root in the lower and working classes, if they first submitted to the judgment of the Protestant principle. "The inadequacy of Protestantism in the face of the proletarian situation," he insisted, "is the result of the contradiction between the Protestant principle and Protestantism as it actually is."[37]

He argued that a transfigured, prophetic Protestantism could forge an alliance with the proletarian movement, based on the common presuppositions that the human situation is perverted and that history is driven by class conflict and greed. Tillich pointed to the deep strain of Augustinian realism about the human condition that existed in Protestant theology and argued that, unlike the Catholic and humanistic traditions, classical Protestantism had preserved Augustinianism in a way that spoke to the condition of the proletariat. Catholicism claims to repair the fissure in being between human beings and God through the graces of its sacramental system, while humanism denies that human beings are depraved in the first place. Against these contrasting attempts to conceal the truth about the human situation, Tillich observed, Protestantism has long insisted that human nature and all of its products are distorted by sin. Unlike the various strategies of concealment, which tend to reduce sin to the fateful experience of finitude, classical Protestantism has held that human evil is ultimately traceable to the perversion of human nature as revealed in hubris and concupiscence. Tillich thus asserted that, like the proletarian movement, authentic Protestantism recognizes that all personal and social existence is permeated with evil.

Like the proletarian movement, however, the Protestant churches have often trivialized their own doctrine of evil by promoting unworthy doctrines of redemption. Orthodox and liberal programs vary within Protestantism, Tillich noted, yet all of them share the same fundamental strategy, which is to domesticate the mystery of divine reality and thereby make God more accessible. Orthodox Protestants bridge the gap by reducing God to a set of doctrines, while liberal Protestants typically reduce God to human scale by making God accessible through morals or education. Tillich elsewhere acknowledged that proletarian movements similarly trivialized the significance of evil through their utopianism, which pretends that human evil will not outlast the next revolution. In any case, he argued, the overriding fact is that all of these strategies are ideologies in the Marxist sense of the term, examples of false consciousness. To fight against these ideologies, and to avoid falling into any of them, Tillich argued that a prophetic Protestantism must persistently expose the false consciousness that pervades them. "It must show how the man-made God of Catholicism was in the interest of the feudal order, of which the medieval church was a part; how the ideology of Lutheranism was in the interest of the patriarchal order, with which Lutheran orthodoxy was associated; how the idealistic religion of humanistic Protestantism is in the interest of a victorious bourgeoisie."[38] Because the class struggle is a fact, he asserted, all theologies serve given class interests, including those that are held to surpass such concerns.

Tillich derided the "hopeless mechanism" and materialism of the socialist parties and argued that a religious presence in the proletarian movement could rid the movement of its vacuous atheism. He cautioned that before the churches could ever be prepared to play such a role in the proletarian movement, however, they needed to renounce their functionally reactionary dichotomy between the sacred and the secular and acknowledge that "everything is secular and every secular thing is potentially religious."[39] From a religious socialist standpoint, the "holy" is not one value beside others, but the presence of the Unconditioned in all values and in the whole of being. Tillich's theological socialism thus began with a principled rejection of the various dualisms inherited from the Catholic, Lutheran, Calvinist, and Anabaptist traditions.

Tillich admitted that the modern churches seemed innately predisposed to deny their actual role in the existing social order. Since they typically refused to acknowledge that they fulfilled any political function, they routinely rejected a socialist reading of their social mission as "politicized" and therefore profane. Tillich charged, however, that this was a massive illusion. The churches like to pretend that they are "neutral" on the momentous sociopolitical issues of the time, he observed, but they can only maintain that pretense as long as they are cut off from the poor and working classes. He noted that the churches had cultivated the self-deception that they were neutral on farm issues, for example, while every farm laborer knew that the claim was preposterous; the established churches always took the side of the landowners. The alienation of the proletarian classes from these churches, he implied, was therefore not a mystery. "The Church's attempt to frame an apologetic message without considering the class struggle was doomed to complete failure at the outset," Tillich later recalled. "Only religious socialism could carry the apologetic message to the proletarian masses."[40] But as he ruefully noted, the churches preferred to maintain the fiction that they were above the class struggle. Though a remnant of the German church later resisted the nazification of religion by embracing the antihumanistic supernaturalism of Barth, Tillich observed that even this group ignored the class struggle.

The central paradox of Tillich's own life during this period, however, was that despite his astute political consciousness, his militant and elaborately defined socialism, his revulsion toward the Nazi movement, and his numerous friendships with Jews—his friends called him "Paulus among the Jews"—he also indulged in massive political self-deceptions, refusing to recognize the seriousness of the Nazi movement. As late as 1932, Tillich continued to dismiss the notion that the Nazis were capable of gaining power in Germany. At Frankfurt, he was so intensely engaged in his small world of seminars, lectures, and elegant parties that he refused to believe it could all disappear. Though he wrote highly sophisticated essays on the theory and politics of socialism, his friends also noted a childlike optimism in him that prevented him from recognizing the strength of the Nazi movement.[41] In 1932, he continued to deliver eloquent speeches on socialist theory that failed to mention even the existence of National Socialism. Though it was not true (as his friend Gunther Dehn thought) that Tillich was actually oblivious to the Nazi threat during this period, Tillich willfully struggled to convince himself that the Nazis were too uncouth and reactionary to take power in Germany.

While his friends in the SPD urged him to become more active in party politics, and while Adorno urged him to attack the Nazis more directly in his writings, Tillich continued to take the high road until the summer of 1932. In July of that year he witnessed a savage attack upon Jewish and Leftist students at Frankfurt by Nazi students and storm troopers. Tillich dragged the injured students to safety and then made an enraged public speech—in his capacity as Dean of the Philosophical Faculty—that defended the rights of the victims and demanded the expulsion of the Nazi students.

The sight of the storm troopers in Frankfurt stunned Tillich into a more direct form of resistance, but at the very moment when he was most disposed to work with the Social Democrats, the latter suffered a collective failure of nerve by deciding not to resist the illegal seizure of power by Franz von Papen, the reactionary German chancellor. The proletarians in the SPD left the party in disgust. Many of them joined the Communists, who were fighting the Nazis in the streets. The Weimar Republic was disintegrating. Later that summer, as he vacationed in the mountains of Sils Maria, Switzerland, and recalled the sight of the storm troopers. Tillich's finally awakened sense of impending catastrophe moved him to write *The Socialist Decision*.

He began with a dialectical analysis of modern socialism. Tillich argued that three separate interpretations of socialism were contending for control of the democratic socialist movement and that they were grounded in three different generations in recent socialist experience. The older generation, represented by the leadership of the European socialist parties, mechanically subscribed to the concepts of the state-socialist tradition, which was the product of nineteenth-century positivism and its accompanying myth of progress. Tillich passed over the differences between the social-democratic and anarcho-syndicalist branches of classic democratic socialism and argued that in *all* of its forms this tradition had engendered a determinist, scientistic worldview that was still, in 1932, the defining feature of the organized socialist movement. Classical socialism posited the existence of economic laws in history that would be fulfilled by the inevitable triumph of the international proletariat. Tillich observed that this worldview was not credible to a younger generation of socialists, however, who confronted the spectacle of totalitarianism in the Soviet Union, as well as the permutations of capitalism beyond the social system that Marx had analyzed. In reaction to the stultifying and increasingly antiquated dogmatism of classical socialism, these younger socialists, such as Hendrik de Man, rejected the classical Marxian concepts of the class struggle, the dictatorship of the proletariat, and the labor theory of value. They attempted to reconceive socialism in voluntaristic terms, emphasizing moral criticism of capitalism and the morally regenerative possibilities of a decision for socialism.

In his typical way, after identifying the deterministic and voluntaristic traditions in modern socialism, Tillich offered his position as a synthesis of the others. His position, he explained at the outset, "holds fast to Marxism and defends it against the activism of the younger generation," while also rejecting the fossilized version of Marxism that the socialist parties propagated.[42] Earlier that year, two of his fellow contributors to the *Neue Blätter für den Sozialismus* had discovered and published Marx's previously unknown early writings under the title *Economic and Philosophic Manuscripts of 1844*.[43] This discovery of Marx's early writings gave powerful support to Horkheimer and his Frankfurt School colleagues, who had argued for a humanistic reading of Marx. Tillich shared their excitement, but in *The Socialist Decision* he cautioned that socialist theorizing must deal with the "real" Marx, who was a *unity* of the younger humanist and older materialist. "Only if the one is interpreted by the other is a true understanding of Marx possible," he wrote.[44] Unlike the ethical socialists of his time, Tillich began with the Marxist assumption that the class struggle is fundamental to socialism.

Tillich wrote *The Socialist Decision* in the rather desperate hope that a new Left coalition could still be forged in Germany among the proletarian, religious, and social democratic elements. During the same period, a coalition of peasants, church groups, and social democrats in Sweden forged an alliance that inaugurated the Scandinavian-style welfare state.[45] Tillich envisioned a similar realignment in Germany in the face of the political gains made by the Nazis, who were attracting the lower and middle classes for reasons that Tillich acutely understood. *The Socialist Decision* contained an insightful explanation of the emotional power of Nazi mythology, which Tillich later admitted he had written, in part, to overcome the "mythical-romantic element" in himself.[46] Any serious alternative to fascism, he thought, must take the subjective need for a collective vision as seriously as the Nazis did.

Tillich regarded socialism as a form of proletarian self-expression that gave the proletariat a meaning within and beyond the "conditioned" world. Because of its inherent capacity to create and confer meaning, he argued, socialism has a religious character, even when it opposes organized religion. The immediate problem was that this was also true of the Nazi movement, which Tillich interpreted as a perverted form of religion. The Nazi movement derived its deep emotional power from its foundation in religious myth and its capacity to generate a meaningful collective vision upon this foundation. Tillich recognized, in the summer of 1932, that the Nazis had already outstripped the churches and the socialist parties in this critical area, but he argued that despite the evident failures of the European religious and socialist movements, a correctly constituted Left coalition could still impede the rush toward fascism and thus prevent "a self-annihilating struggle of the European peoples."[47]

The Socialist Decision analyzed the mythical and historical roots of capitalism, fascism, Communism, and socialism, distinguishing between two main types of political orientation. Tillich asserted that orientations of the first type are grounded in myths of origin, while those of the second type are grounded in prophetic criticism of these myths.[48] Within these terms, he interpreted the Nazi movement as a form of religio-political romanticism founded upon mythic appeals to soil, blood, and social solidarity. Tillich postulated that there are two basic forms of political romanticism, which he identified with the imperial German state and the Nazi movement. The first form was the classic conservative type, which had been superseded by the rise of the bourgeoisie but which still existed among the landowning aristocracy, certain elements of the peasantry and the churches, and the older generation of military officers. Conservative romanticism typically defended an organic, monarchical model of social order in which the function of the church was to sacralize the founding myths of origin and the social structures built in their name. Tillich noted that the organic type is conservative in the literal sense of the term, seeking to preserve the given myths of origin in their traditional religious form. Conservative political romanticism was (and is) therefore economically and culturally premodern.

The second form of political romanticism, the revolutionary type, featured a more paradoxical relationship to the myths of origin and to modernity. Tillich theorized that revolutionary romanticism, typified by the Nazi movement, tried to restore its own posited myths of origin by overthrowing the existing social order, including the structures of bourgeois democracy. It was therefore "revolutionary" in the ordinary sense of the term. In the case of the Nazi movement, the mythic appeals to soil, blood, and national solidarity were vividly evident, but Tillich observed that all romantic movements of the revolutionary type are founded on a paradox. Unlike the conservative form, which emphasizes the values of preservation and stability and a sense of continuity with the traditions of the past, the revolutionary form is deracinated, emphasizing newness and upheaval, despite its appeals to myths of the past. Thus, instead of interpreting the myths of origin in terms of an organic traditionalism, the theorists of fascism were forced to substitute vitalistic philosophical theories in order to rationalize their appeals to the bonds of soil, nation, and race. Fascist ideologues therefore appropriated (and often distorted) the philosophical writings of Nietzsche, Sorel, Pareto, and Spengler. Tillich observed that by dressing up their ideology in modern philosophical garb, however, the fascist intellectuals were cutting themselves off from the original meanings of their own myths. Tillich read this contradiction as a sign of fascist hypocrisy and as a sign of its potential for violence.[49]

The Socialist Decision concluded that only a different kind of religio-political movement could prevent the stampede toward fascism and possible world war. The kind of movement that was needed would accept modernity while going beyond it. What was needed, Tillich implied, was religious socialism — a postmodern praxis that embraced the liberal, democratic, and critical elements of the bourgeois revolution, but which rejected its irreligious, "autonomous" elements. Like the various fascist movements in Europe, religious socialism was critical of modernity, and affirmed, in some form, the sacramental values of the myths of origin. But Tillich insisted that true socialism is the antithesis of National Socialism, because socialism includes the prophetic ethos of Protestantism as well as the humanistic values of the Enlightenment and of nineteenth-century liberalism.[50] Socialism, for Tillich, was the only worthy vision of the future for the Western world, because only socialism holds together and fulfills the positive, accumulated values of the Western tradition.

The practical problem with this argument was that religious socialism had few adherents. Classical democratic socialism was characterized by a liberal disdain for religion, relegating religion to the realm of barely tolerated private judgment. The German socialist tradition originated during the post-Hegelian era of nineteenth-century German history, when a resurgent state church sacralized a peculiar kind of reactionary state that Tillich characterized as "bourgeois feudal." In this situation, the infant socialist movement naturally allied itself with those bourgeois parties that opposed the state church. Tillich noted that the socialist movement had been characterized ever since by a negative attitude toward religion. This attitude was reinforced by the illusion that the presumably scientific dogmas of socialism could suffice as a substitute for religion. The historical result, Tillich observed, was that the socialist parties had continued to denigrate religion long after the bourgeois parties made their peace with the churches. Thus, the only remaining institutional vessel of bourgeois anticlericalism was the socialist movement.

Tillich acknowledged that if religion were equated with the social record or the theological doctrines of the churches, antireligious sentiments were largely justified. But he rejected this definition, arguing that religion "means living out of the roots of human being."[51] Religion should not be conceived as a separate sphere of human existence alongside other spheres, but as "the power supporting and determining all spheres."[52] Tillich argued that from a religious-socialist perspective this was the only acceptable concept of religion, since all of the alternatives were sectarian. He implied that although the socialist enmity toward the churches had been justified in the past, what socialism needed in the postmodern era was a more reflective appreciation of religion. Tillich asserted that the socialist movement should engage the churches, not in order to use them for purely political purposes—the way the Nazis did—but in order to bring out their true nature. In this way, the socialist movement could free the churches from their "ecclesiastical torpidity" and help them rediscover their own prophetic ethic of justice. "Socialism has to strengthen the prophetic as opposed to the priestly element in the churches," he wrote, adding elsewhere that the prophetic spirit of the Old Testament was the "eternal adversary" of fascist mythology and dogma.[53] *The Socialist Decision* closed with an appeal for a prophetic witness from the churches, declaring that only a spirit of prophetic expectation could triumph "over the death now threatening Western civilization through the resurgence of the myth of origin."[54]

To "decide" for socialism and to wait in expectation for its realization, Tillich argued, was not to indulge the Marxist fantasy that the outcome of history was predetermined, or to pretend that the crises of modern civilization could be resolved through economic collectivism. He favored a commanding-heights strategy of selective socialization in which the major means of production—such as the banks, heavy industry, major manufacturing concerns, and landed estates—were nationalized, but in which market freedom for other enterprises was otherwise guaranteed. He argued that nationalization of major concerns and the construction of a state-planning apparatus were necessary in order to rationalize the process of investment and make the investment process serve the common good. Tillich insisted, however, that it was equally imperative to avoid the "bureaucratization of the whole economy," and thus argued that market freedom was essential in order to regulate the correlations of supply and demand.[55] Tillich was evidently not familiar with the guild-socialist literature, and like most socialists of his time he assumed that socialists required a program of nationalization. Despite this assumption, however, he understood that only a totalitarian form of socialism could abolish the market system altogether. Though he stringently criticized other aspects of social-democratic revisionism, Tillich's programmatic conception of socialism was in the mainstream of the social democratic tradition.

He finished *The Socialist Decision* in November 1932, and awaited its publication with keen anticipation, hoping that the book might contribute in some way to the formation of the coalition that he envisioned. The previous month, Tillich had attended one of Hitler's rallies, which he found terrifying as well as disgusting. His wife later recalled that he saw the demon in Hitler's eyes. The experience moved Tillich to complete *The Socialist Decision*, but at the end of January 1933, while the book was still in production, Hitler was appointed chancellor over a coalition government. The following month the burning of the Reichstag building gave Hitler a patriotic pretext to attack the Communists. The March elections gave him a solid majority, and on March 21, Hitler was granted dictatorial powers by an enabling act of parliament.

He moved swiftly. Before even the boycotts of Jewish businesses or the abolition of trade unions, the Third Reich issued a decree that prohibited the publication or distribution of certain books, including *The Socialist Decision*. The book had been printed too late to leave the warehouse, and on April 13 Tillich was among the first group of professors to be suspended as an enemy of the state. His imaginary coalition of proletarians and middle-class Protestants had chosen fascism. On May 10, Tillich witnessed a Nazi rally in Frankfurt at which hundreds of books, including his own, were condemned and thrown into a bonfire. He later recalled, "Time had run backward for two hundred years."[56]

From that point on, the story of Tillich's life becomes more familiar to North American readers, and much less relevant to an interpretation of modern Christian socialism. When a Columbia University committee met to discuss the plight of the suspended German professors, the president of Union Theological Seminary, Henry Sloane Coffin, volunteered to provide a position for Tillich for one year. The invitation was eventually sent to Tillich by Reinhold Niebuhr, and, though Tillich was initially reluctant to accept it, by the end of the summer he realized that the Nazi government was too deeply entrenched for him to sustain any hopes of regaining his position. Horkheimer and Adorno pleaded with him to leave Germany to save his life. Finally, near the end of October, at the age of forty-seven, he departed for New York, fearful that the United States was provincial and that he would be homesick and dissatisfied there. Instead, he eventually found a new home and enormous success, though in a context in which he found it necessary to downplay his socialism.

Tillich's shift away from socialist theorizing and activism occurred gradually over his first decade in the United States. Though he immediately joined the Fellowship of Socialist Christians (which Niebuhr had founded in 1931) upon his arrival in the United States, Tillich eventually came to regard the country as an unsuitable cultural and socioeconomic environment for socialism. Unlike Niebuhr, who abandoned socialism in the late 1930s, Tillich regarded himself as a socialist for the rest of his life. When the subject was raised, he did not shrink from trying to explain to North Americans that socialism was not what they assumed. As a Marxist, however, Tillich believed that without a class-conscious or politicized proletariat there was no point in attempting to develop a theological or even a political argument for socialism in the United States. The only form of religious socialism that could be sustained in such a context, he argued, was the kind of ethically idealistic or utopian socialism that he had always opposed. Tillich therefore turned to other cultural and theological interests, including the completion of his *Systematic Theology*. He never entirely overcame his feeling that there was something unseemly about advocating socialism in the United States, the colossal bastion of capitalism that had, after all, rescued him from Nazi Germany. When his friend James Luther Adams began to assemble and translate Tillich's early writings for American editions in the late 1940s, Tillich insisted upon deleting his essays on the class struggle, claiming that their republication "would ruin me in this country."

In his autobiographical essay of 1952, Tillich explained that he had backed away from his earlier commitment to socialism, "with resignation and some bitterness," because of the apparent impregnability of the cold war. He had earlier envisioned a theonomous third way between capitalism and Communism, but in the bipolar postwar world, he remarked, the remnants of democratic and religious socialism had been crushed.[57] Third-way strategies seemed utopian in a situation where all other political issues were subordinated to the conflict between capitalism and Communism. Because Tillich expressed this judgment so often and with such vehemence, in 1949 the editors of *The Christian Century* mistakenly titled one of his autobiographical essays "Beyond Religious Socialism." For many years afterward, Tillich repeatedly expressed his displeasure with the title. "If the prophetic message is true," he wrote in 1952, "there is nothing 'beyond religious socialism.' "[58] He insisted for all of his life that the content of the prophetic biblical faith was most completely revealed, in the modern world, in the faith of religious socialism. He only doubted, in the post-war situation, that the socialist faith could be held with any degree of expectation or political seriousness.

Like his friend Herbert Marcuse, then, who wrote that in the cold-war era psychological categories had become political categories, Tillich increasingly adopted the language of depth psychology rather than Marxism to express his sociopolitical ideas.[59] Tillich's continuing commitment to religious socialism can be read between the lines of such a comparatively depoliticized work as *Love, Power, and Justice*, where he defined justice as "the form in which the power of being actualizes itself."[60] In this treatise, written in 1954, Tillich offered a conceptual analysis of the relationship between justice and power, arguing for a synthesis between realism (which reduces justice to power politics) and idealism (which ignores the necessity of compromise and force). His continuing commitment to socialism was even more explicitly revealed, nine years later, in his discussion of the Kingdom of God in the third volume of his *Systematic Theology*, which reaffirmed the vision of theonomous socialism that had marked his earlier career.[61]

Throughout these works and others of his later career, however, Tillich's arguments operated at a level of abstraction that virtually defied any attempt to draw out concrete implications. Over the rambling abstractions of his third volume of systematics, one is often tempted to write the words that the eminent physicist Wolfgang Pauli once scrawled on a colleague's paper: "This isn't right; this isn't even wrong." Most of Tillich's interpreters have accepted his judgment that a more forthright defense of socialism would have proved useless (or worse) in the cold-war United States. Ronald Stone, for example, has argued that Tillich was right to mute his political concerns in a country where religious socialism did not "fit." Yet Stone acknowledges that Tillich only considered the subject in a rather narrow context. He failed to consider the worldwide impact of capitalist investment priorities, or even that millions of people in the third world live in grotesque misery and destitution.[62]

It is often suggested that if Tillich had lived to see the emergence of liberationist theologies, his own Eurocentric vision would have expanded and his commitment to the socialist project would have been restimulated. I think there is good reason to accept this suggestion, *without* accepting Tillich's judgment that the struggle for socialism is or was ever futile in the United States or was negated by the realities of the cold war. If religious socialism is in any way the bearer of the prophetic faith, as Tillich insisted, it seems imperative that this faith should be continually presented to the world, regardless of the consequences. The prophetic tradition is a *faith* because it "hopes in things not yet seen" in history and it hopes with a sense of historical expectation. The factors that Tillich bemoaned in North American political culture — the lack of a radicalized working class and the near-deification of the cold war — have remained the most formidable obstacles to the development of a viable North American socialist movement. The fundamental responsibility of North American socialists, however, regardless of the difficulties, is to keep offering the vision of democratic socialism, which is the vision of a realized democracy. Though it is clear that Tillich agreed with this argument, he shrunk from living it out. As a grateful refugee, and later a citizen of the United States, he was naturally disinclined to criticize the nation that had welcomed him in his time of danger and need. He was not temperamentally suited for conflict and often went to extraordinary lengths to avoid it. And as Wilhelm and Marion Pauck have catalogued in sometimes embarrassing detail, it is also true that Tillich "fell for his public image" in later life and became inordinately impressed by his own importance and influence. The same judgment has been offered by Hannah Tillich, who has vividly described his insatiable need to be idolized.[63] I think it is evident that Tillich's commitment to socialism was undercut during his American career by his desire for recognition and approval, especially for the approval of such powerful acquaintances as Henry Luce. When he delivered the featured address at the fortieth anniversary party of *Time* magazine in 1963, Tillich remarked that social critics in America no longer needed to fear martyrdom, but were forced instead to struggle "against being absorbed by the culture as another cultural good."[64] Tillich was speaking of himself, but his high-society audience proved his point, without comprehending the meaning of his speech or the irony of the occasion, by loudly applauding his presentation. Tillich liked to pretend that the adulation he received from *Time* proved the "astonishing lack of prejudice in the American tradition," but he was surely aware that Henry Luce's magazine would not have honored a serious socialist. By then, despite his assurances, he was not taken as one.

Today the symbiosis between religion and socialism is a central concern of various liberationist theologies. Unlike the era in which Tillich wrote his depoliticized words, today there is an intense theological concern with the issues that engaged Tillich's early interest. Today, Tillich's critical appropriation of Marxism and his theory of religious socialism are elements of the liberationist project. Virtually all liberationists subscribe to Tillich's vision of an alliance between religious and socialist movements in which each side enables the other to fulfill its original purpose. Unlike most liberationists, Tillich was an orthodox Marxist in his conception of the class struggle. He assumed that socialism could only be achieved through the revolutionary praxis of an organized proletariat. The problem with this assumption, however, was that it undercut Tillich's own commitment to socialism when he arrived in a country that lacked an organized proletariat. This assumption would have the same effect upon modern liberationism if it were embraced by liberation theologians, since throughout the third world a proletariat in the Marxist sense only exists in a few cities. As I will argue in chapter 7, modern religious socialism must transcend the limitations of the Marxist and social-democratic traditions and offer a new emancipatory vision that includes movements for racial justice, feminism, ecological preservation, gay and lesbian rights, disarmament and noninterventionism, and decentralized socialization of financial and business enterprises. Tillich supported these movements as separate causes, often ahead of his time, but he never attempted to conceptualize them in a unifying vision. That is the postmodern theological project.

Today, among those engaged in this project, the question of the relationship between history and eternity is vigorously debated. Tillich faced the question at the outset of his theological career, in "Basic Principles of Religious Socialism," when he distinguished between the *obligatum religiosum* and the *reservatum religiosum* — the obligations and limits of religious engagement in political life. Throughout his career he maintained, in accordance with this distinction, that all religious commitments in politics must be bound by the principle of dialectic. Every political movement, no matter how righteous, must recognize the Yes and the No that it represents. Several months after his arrival in America, Tillich was forced to reassert the necessity of the distinction when his old friend Emmanuel Hirsch published a theological defense of fascism, *Die gegenwärtige geistige Lage im Spiegel philosophischer und theologischer Bessinung* ("The Present Cultural Situation in Philosophical and Theological Perspective," never published in English). Tillich's response, "Open Letter to Emanuel Hirsch," was published in the German journal *Theologische Blätter*.

He was not surprised that Hirsch had become a propagandist for the triumphant Nazi movement. Tillich had known Hirsch well enough to expect that development. What shocked him, and prompted his vehement response, was Hirsch's outright equation of the Christian and Nazi faiths and his perversion of Tillich's own ideas in making the argument. Having opposed religious socialism for the past fourteen years, Tillich observed, Hirsch had now presented a theology of fascism that reproduced, in distorted form, virtually every concept of religious socialism. The book was a peculiarly contorted form of plagiarism. Tillich noted that Hirsch had copied not only his concepts of the *kairos*, the boundary, the demonic, and the myths of origin (among others), but also the entire religious-socialist interpretation of European history, including the Tillichian dialectic of heteronomous, autonomous, and theonomous reason. Hirsch presented the Nazi movement as the fulfillment of the religious-socialist vision (without actually mentioning religious socialism, or his dependence on Tillich's writings), but he could only produce this interpretation, Tillich remarked, by perverting the eschatological idea of the *kairos* "into a sacerdotal-sacramental consecration of a current event." Religious socialism, holding to the *reservatum*, categorically rejected the notion that its vision could be fulfilled "in one romanticized event or another." The entire argument of religious socialism, Tillich explained, was "oriented toward this rule."[65]

Having reproduced the religious socialist interpretation of modern history and theology, however, Hirsch twisted it to his own grotesque purposes, equating the German nation with a blood-bond, interpreting the Christian eucharist as a reinforcement of this bond, and celebrating the triumph of fascism as an event nearly equal in religious significance to the death and resurrection of Christ. "You have approximated the year 1933 so closely to the year 33," Tillich commented, "that it has gained for you the meaning of an event in the history of salvation." Tillich recalled that when he joined the socialist movement, he entered as an uncompromising critic and revisionist, ever opposed to all forms of utopianism, which he defined as "the absolutizing of a finite possibility." The whole idea of the *kairos*, he explained, was to appropriate "the significance of the historical moment for the formation of the future, yet without becoming utopians, for at the end of every utopian enthusiasm stands disappointment and doubt." Tillich admonished Hirsch that as a theologian in the Nazi movement, his proper task was to uphold the integrity of his religious tradition against all ideological and utopian enthusiasms. "Your book shows me," he wrote, "that you have neither seen it nor fulfilled it."[66] The fundamental issue, then and today, was the integrity of the *reservatum* and the *obligatum*. Hirsch was still Lutheran enough to grant the individual a *reservatum* in his or her personal relationship to God, but his overriding commitment to fascism led him to disavow the same right for the church. In the new civilization, he assumed, the church would unequivocally serve the state. But with that assertion, Tillich observed, even the personal *reservatum* had been effectively canceled, since it had been rendered "impotent over against the *Weltanschauungen* or myths that sustain the totalitarian state."[67] As Richard Neuhaus has aptly noted, Tillich's concept of socialism was the antithesis of Hirsch's totalitarian crime against the spirit.[68] Writing in 1934, Tillich did not claim to know whether the Nazi government would "succeed" in the ordinary political sense of the term. He admitted that he could not prove that Hirsch was wrong about the Nazi capacity to rebuild the economy or revive the German national spirit. He expressed his certainty, however, that Hirsch had committed a grave theological sin through his utopianism, which Tillich regarded as demonic because it absolutized a relative historical movement.

But for Tillich, the question of theological integrity did not end there. He pushed Hirsch to recognize the demonically blasphemous *and* totalitarian implications of his theology by asking him: "Are you, precisely as a theologian, called to subordinate the sacramental consanguinity of Christianity, which is given with the Lord's Supper, to the natural historical consanguinity?" The Nazis were denying that Jewish Christians possessed the right to equal fellowship within Christian churches because they lacked the blood-bond. As a theologian, Tillich pleaded with Hirsch, how can you possibly repudiate the biblical notion that the spiritual unity of the body of Christ transcends all other bonds of race, family, nation, ideology, or class? And as a theologian, he asked, how can you subordinate the divine fellowship of Word and sacrament to the ideological myths of the Nazi government? That was the totalitarian crime against the spirit.

Near the end of his letter, Tillich explained how religious socialism differed from all forms of political sacralization: "Religious Socialism knew, when accepting the doctrine of the *reservatum religiosum*, that the religious can never be dissolved into the socialist, that the church is something quite apart from the *Kairos*, that is, from the promise and demand that Religious Socialism saw in the broadly visible irruption of the new social and spiritual arrangement of society." Hirsch had taken over most of the concepts of religious socialism, Tillich concluded, but, because he opposed the basic principle of religious socialism, his appropriation of Tillich's theology entirely perverted it. "You took over the *obligatum* but gave up the *reservatum*—the charge that is basically the theme of my whole letter."[69]

I believe that Tillich's theology of religious socialism has much to offer the modern liberationist project. His analysis of the conflict between heteronomy and autonomy, the crises of modernity, and the mythic roots of totalitarianism are relevant in the modern context. His theories of religion, religious language, the demonic, and the Unconditioned are as compelling today as when they were first conceived. His critical appropriation of Marxism, his critique of socialist materialism, and his attempt to revive the prophetic element in religion are elements of virtually all liberationist theologies. Though he unfortunately assumed that "socialization" of major enterprises meant nationalization, his conception of socialism was programmatically in the social-democratic tradition, and his emphasis on the necessity of free markets for most enterprises prefigured the decentralized vision of modern market socialism. His interpretation of the *kairos* as a proleptic eschatological and prophetic reality anticipated the theological vision of Moltmann's theology of hope. Most important, however, Tillich's dialectic of the theological *obligatum* and *reservatum* is instructive for the modern liberationist project. Throughout his career, Tillich rightly insisted that no historical movement or idea contains the "unrefracted yes" of the Unconditioned. As he wrote in his memoirs, "the Kingdom of God will always remain transcendent, but it appears as a judgment on a given form of society and as a norm for a coming one."[70]

4

Jürgen Moltmann and
the Dialectics of Hope

When it became apparent, in the early 1960s, that the systems of Tillich and Rudolf Bultmann were losing their predominance over modern theological discussion, numerous alternatives were offered. Intellectual fads of the 1960s produced a profusion of "theologies" of the death of God and the end of religion, but one project that began during that era has made a far more valuable and enduring contribution to modern theology. The post-Bultmannian redirection of modern theology was signaled in 1964 with the publication of Jürgen Moltmann's *Theology of Hope*. In this epochal work, which appropriated the neo-Marxist ontology of Ernst Bloch, the distinctive marks of contemporary progressive and liberationist theologies were first presented. As José Míguez Bonino has rightly observed, the theologian to whom the modern theology of liberation is most indebted is Jürgen Moltmann.[1] His work therefore marks the starting point for reflection on contemporary religious socialism.

Moltmann's concern with the phenomenon of hope is rooted in his experiences as a prisoner of war. He has explained, "I belong to the generation that experienced for itself the end of World War II, the destruction of a state with all its institutions, the tyranny and shame of one's own country, and a long captivity." Moltmann was drafted into the German army at the age of sixteen and assigned to an anti-aircraft brigade in Hamburg, where on two occasions, he was the only member of his unit to survive mortar fire attacks. He was sent to the front in Holland in 1944, where he surrendered the next year "to the first British soldier I met in the woods."[2]

And so he survived. For the succeeding three years he was confined to prison camps in Belgium, Scotland, and England. He has recalled that in the Belgian camp he saw how other prisoners "collapsed inwardly, how they gave up all hope, sickening for the lack of it, some of them dying." Moltmann was saved from the same fate, by his account, only by a religious

77

conversion that began when an army chaplain gave him a copy of the New Testament and Psalms.

As the son of an "enlightened" Hamburg family, Moltmann was disdainful of religion and predisposed not to read the book at all. But when he finally began to read it, largely out of boredom, he was surprised to find that the words of Scripture fed his imagination and emotional need. "They opened my eyes to the God who is with those 'that are of a broken heart,' " he has recalled. "He was present even behind the barbed wire—no, most of all behind the barbed wire." But whenever he tried to claim or comprehend this experience of the presence of God, the experience eluded him.

> All that was left was an inward drive, a longing which provided the impetus to hope. How often I walked round and round in circles at night in front of the barbed wire fence. My first thoughts were always about the free world outside, from which I was cut off; but I always ended up thinking about a centre to the circle in the middle of the camp—a little hill, with a hut on it which served as a chapel. It seemed to me like a circle surrounding the mystery of God, which was drawing me towards it.[3]

These ineffable experiences and the nurturing support of a Christian community led Moltmann to become interested in theology, which he was allowed to study, during his final year of imprisonment, in an English educational camp run by the YMCA. After reading the first volume of Reinhold Niebuhr's *The Nature and Destiny of Man*, Moltmann wrote to his parents that he was considering a pastoral or theological career. His father, a Freemason, replied by reminding him of his duty "to procreate the family" (apparently unaware that Protestant pastors could be married). "I came out of the camp a theologian," Moltmann recalls, "much to the distress of my father."

He has elsewhere recalled that many of his acquaintances who survived the war and their own imprisonment were "burnt children" who tended afterward to shun the fire. "We were weighed down by the somber burden of a guilt which could never be paid off; and what we felt about life was an inconsolable grief. It is understandable that there were some of us whose motto was 'count me out,' and whose aim was to withdraw into private life for the future." When Moltmann finally returned to Germany in 1948, however, he was determined to struggle for a social transformation of his country, having found during his imprisonment "the power of a hope which wants something new, instead of seeking a return to the old."[4]

He received his doctorate in theology from the University of Göttingen in 1952 and served as pastor of the Evangelical Church of Bremen for the succeeding five years. Moltmann was personally inclined to remain in the pastoral ministry, but at the urging of his teacher Otto Weber he accepted a position as a theology professor in Wuppertal in 1958, and then joined the theological faculty of Bonn University in 1963. The following year he published *Theology of Hope*.[5]

The origins of Moltmann's emphasis on hope were thus rooted in his personal experience, but the special significance of hope as a theological principle only occurred to him in 1960, after reading Ernst Bloch's *Das Prinzip Hoffnung (The Principle of Hope)*. He has recalled, "I remember very well spending a whole vacation in Tessin with his book *Das Prinzip Hoffnung* without noticing the beauty of the Swiss mountains."[6] That encounter is one of the formative events of contemporary theology.

As a historical argument, *Das Prinzip Hoffnung* is most readily understood against the background of Bloch's later work, *Avicenna und die Aristotelische Linke,* which reinterpreted the concept of materialism in Aristotelian, medieval, and Renaissance philosophy. Bloch contended that although Aristotle's arguments were more immanentistic than those of Plato, his metaphysical position was still essentially idealistic. Since Aristotle assumed that the potentiality of matter was passive in its process of actualization, he concluded that the actualization of matter occurred within a prestructured universe of forms. In Aristotelian theory, the movement toward form proceeded through the innate desire to experience God as pure form.

Bloch argued that the key to medieval Aristotelianism was its gradual relinquishment of Aristotle's idealism. Avicenna and Avërroes, for example, discarded the Aristotelian assumption that equated potentiality of matter with passivity. This metaphysical revision, which changed the focus of actualization from the *given* to the *developing*, became more explicit in the pantheism of Giordano Bruno, who identified God with matter as self-actualizing potentiality. Despite his materialistic ontology and his rejection of the pre-existence of forms, however, Bruno retained an element of Aristotelian idealism through his God-language.

According to Bloch, it was this remaining idealistic element within Renaissance materialism that Ludwig Feuerbach effectively criticized and which Marx superseded in his theory of dialectical materialism. Because Marx regarded form, or superstructure, as the self-actualization of matter, Bloch argued, he was able to provide the only viable alternative to idealism. For Marx the possibility of self-actualization was determined by the historical configuration of matter at any given time.[7]

It was at this turn in the argument that *Das Prinzip Hoffnung* advanced a novel thesis. Over against the Aristotelian view, in which form preceded matter, Bloch presented a reinterpretation of Marxism which proposed that matter had *not yet* acquired its essential form. In Bloch's reading, Marxism did not depend upon an anamnesis of the necessary, but upon hope for historical possibilities. Essence belonged not in the "already" (Aristotle's *to ti ēn einai*), but in the "not yet." Bloch supported this reading by claiming that Marx did not reduce the higher forms of culture to economic causes, as in the vulgar Marxism of Karl Kautsky, but rather situated them dialectically within the self-actualization of matter. Although culture is always the product of given historical configurations, Bloch observed, cultural forms often outlive the particular material substrate from which they arose. This phenomenon of "cultural surplus" (*Kultureller Ueberschuss*) Bloch attributed to what he considered the fundamental dynamic of all human endeavor: the principle of hope that transcends material conditions. Bloch argued that the relationship between this principle and the philosophy of dialectical materialism was particularly evident in the Marxist critique of religion.

Bloch's assessment of religion focused on Marx's thesis that religion is both an example of alienation and a protest against it. While the first half of this thesis situates the phenomenon of religion within the materialistic dialectic, the second half reveals the principle of hope. As an outcry of hope within oppressive historical contexts, Bloch argued, the Christian faith has its essence not in the theocratic or Constantinian compromises with the world but in a revolutionary future-orientation. Though Bloch accepted the Feuerbachian argument that religious ideas are actually the projected "wish-beings" of alienated consciousness, he insisted that the fundamental Christian idea was the vision of the kingdom of God. Bloch therefore interpreted the Christian notion of God as the futural realm of *homo absconditus* into which humankind is drawn, through the principle of hope, to project its wish for an achieved essence.[8]

As he studied this intriguing interpretation of religion, Moltmann wondered why modern theology seemed lifeless by comparison. If Bloch could breathe life into dialectical materialism, he thought, why couldn't theologians reinterpret their own tradition with equal imagination? Bloch's further argument about the central importance of hope reawakened the same intuition in Moltmann, and inspired his pathbreaking first book:

> I asked myself: "Why has Christian theology avoided this theme that really ought to be its own theme? What is the place of the primitive Christian spirit of hope within current Christianity?" I then began to work on my *Theology of Hope*. Out of biblical theology, the theology of the apostolate and of the kingdom of God, and the philosophy of hope, came the patterns of a tapestry in which everything fitted together well. I didn't want to be Bloch's heir or to establish any competition. I was thinking of a treatment in Christian and theological traditions parallel to the philosophy of hope.[9]

Theology of Hope was, in part, an attempt to come to terms with the Feuerbachian-Marxist critique of religion. Despite the fact that "dehellenization" had been on the agenda of critical modern theology for the past century, Moltmann noted that the vertical and substance patterns of Greek thought were still so deeply ingrained in Western theologians that virtually all modern theologies remained hellenistic. To Moltmann, the most telling example of this fact was the theology of Rudolf Bultmann. Though Bultmann had revitalized the modern theological discussion of hellenization through his writings on demythologization, Moltmann observed that even these writings presupposed a vertical conception of divine reality.

Moltmann insistently argued, by contrast, that the hellenistic conception of the divine nature is an alienating construct in exactly the sense that Marxists criticized. Rather than hypostatize divine reality above or before the world, *Theology of Hope* contended that the eschatology of Scripture offers a nonalienating, nonhierarchical concept of God that holds the present and the future together. That is, Moltmann argued that Scripture assumes a horizontal conception of divinity in which the past and the future are constantly related as "contradiction in identity." Though Christian theism has repeatedly rationalized and even sacralized worldly monarchies, ecclesiastical hierarchies, and nearly every form of oppression, he observed, the operative images of God on which traditional theism has been based are not derived from Scripture. Moltmann contended that the key to a dehellenized reconceptualization of divine reality could be found in the biblical theme of eschatology. "From first to last," he wrote, "and not merely in the epilogue, Christianity is eschatology, is hope, forward looking and forward moving, and therefore also revolutionizing and transforming the present. The eschatological is not one element *of* Christianity, but it is the medium of Christian faith as such, the key in which everything in it is set, the glow that suffuses everything here in the dawn of an unexpected new day." Understood in this way, he explained, eschatology is no longer one doctrine among others in theology, but the presupposition of all others. "There is therefore only one real problem in Christian theology, which its own object forces upon it and which it in turn forces on mankind and on human thought: the problem of the future."[10]

Unlike the language of classical Christian theism, which presupposes the spatial concepts of hellenistic philosophy, Moltmann argued that biblical language is predominantly temporal. In his essay "Theology as Eschatology," which exposited the chief ideas of *Theology of Hope*, Moltmann explained that the God of the Bible is always "ahead of us in the horizons of the future opened up to us in his promises." One implication of this metaphysical position was that because God comes to the present from the future, God does not directly affect or replicate the historical causes from the past. "God is not the ground of this world and not the ground of existence, but the God of the coming Kingdom which transforms this world and our existence radically." Although one therefore appropriately speaks of the deity of God "only in connection with his coming Kingdom," Moltmann insisted that God is causally active in the present as the power of the future, bringing the present forward. As the power of the future, he asserted, God works *into* the present in the same way that the future is always "in mastery" of the present.

It becomes the power that contradicts the present past (guilt) and the resulting transiency of the present (death), and creates, through conflict with the human condition shaped by past and transiency, the powers that overcome it. If such future is the present mode of God's being, God becomes the ground of the freedom from past and transiency and of the possibilities of the new, and, through both, the ground of the transformation of the world.[11]

It has often been noted that this argument closely resembles the metaphysical logic of process theology, but *Theology of Hope* avoided the purely metaphysical arguments that process theologians employ. As Christopher Morse and Lonnie Kliever have demonstrated, Moltmann's explanation of how the future effects the present was influenced, in part, by the Blochian philosophy of hope and *grounded* on the biblical concept of promise.[12] Moltmann interpreted Scripture itself as the record and witness of God's historically generative promises, from the covenant with Israel, to the universalization of the covenant in Christ, to the fulfillment of history. Unlike the traditional concept of eschatology as a theological epilogue or doctrine of the "last things," Moltmann argued that the eschatological vision of the Bible is ultimately an all-embracing vision of God as the totally liberating power of the future. Through the dialectic of promise and fulfillment, he asserted, the promise of God is historically revealed in the eruption of the future into the present. The future is the self-revelation of God, who is "not in us or above us but always before us." For Moltmann, the divine promise was therefore not a discursive statement, but a creative *act*, the creation of history itself.[13]

True to his Barthian heritage, Moltmann emphasized in *Theology of Hope* that the divine self-disclosure continuously shatters "natural" human knowledge. Though the "overspill" of God's promise is concretely revealed in the world through history, Moltmann argued, the human mind is not empowered to receive divine revelation through natural reason, but only through a faithful encounter with the biblical witness to God's promises. It was this radical, universal, eschatological consciousness of Scripture that Moltmann counterposed, in *Theology of Hope*, to what he considered the fragmented, anthropocentric religion of modern theology, typified by Bultmann's theology.

Bultmann was Moltmann's target not only because of his preeminent stature in modern theology, but also because his individualistic theology symbolized, for Moltmann, the modern church's acquiescence to the trivialization of religion under modernity. Bultmann's theology was based on the notion of the invasion of the eternal into time in the moment. He regarded the proclamation and nourishing effect of this eschatological event, and not of any statements about it, as the saving message of the gospel, which is open only to faith. The event of faith was therefore not open to historicist interpretations (as in Ernst Troeltsch) or even to objectivist interpretations (as in Barth), but depended entirely on the self-authenticating effect of existential experience. As he wrote in 1920, "The meaning of religion is the being, the life, of the individual."[14] It followed for Bultmann that the meaning of the cross, for example, depended entirely on one's individual experience of being crucified with Christ.

In *Theology of Hope*, and later in *Religion, Revolution, and the Future*, Moltmann criticized this existentialist approach from the standpoint of what he called a political hermeneutic of the gospel. When Bultmann distinguished between the person as a sociopolitical being and as a private individual, Moltmann argued, he privatized Christian experience into I-and-Thou situations that left theology with nothing to say about the meaning of life in its sociopolitical (historical) dimension. Moltmann wrote, "This faith is in the literal sense socially irrelevant, because it stands in the social no-man's-land of the unburdening of the individual—that is, in a realm which materialist society has already left free to human individuality in any case."[15] In this way, he insisted, Bultmann's existentialist hermeneutic trivialized the social meaning of Christian faith, since it was too private to challenge anything, including the rise of fascism.

It was precisely against this retreat from the world, which Moltmann had criticized since his repatriation, that he forged his own theological position. The name of the Christian God, he wrote, is not a cipher for the eternal present, but a "name of promise that discloses a new future."[16] God is the one who acts to liberate those who suffer and who promises them a new future. "The God spoken of here," he explained, "is no intra-worldly or extra-worldly God, but the 'God of hope' (Romans 15:13), a God with 'future as his essential nature' (as E. Bloch puts it), as made known in Exodus and Israelite prophecy, the God whom we therefore cannot really have in us or over us but always only before us, who encounters us in his promises for the future, and whom we therefore cannot 'have' either, but can only await in active hope."[17] Moltmann's position was thus based on the biblical notion that God is revealed primarily as the eschatological presence of the future.

It followed for Moltmann that eschatology is not the doctrinal epilogue of theology, but the essential medium of Christian faith as such, "the glow that suffuses everything here in the dawn of an expected new day." A living faith that is truly Christian must be characterized by a thoroughly eschatological consciousness, he asserted, "forward looking and forward moving, and therefore also revolutionizing and transforming the present." In this sense, *Theology of Hope* was a Christianized version of Bloch's ontology of the "not yet." Christian hope has a revolutionary orientation toward the future, he insisted, "for the good of the promised future stabs inexorably into the flesh of every unfulfilled present."[18] Moltmann concluded that the form in which Christ himself must be understood was not in the form of the Greek *logos* or of doctrinal statements based upon experience, but only upon "the form of statements of hope and of promises for the future."

Theology of Hope ended with a call for an "exodus church" that would reject every form of cultural domestication or trivialization of the claims of faith. "Only Christians who no longer understand their eschatological mission as a mission for the future of the world and of man can identify their call with the existing circumstances in the social role of their callings and be content to fit in with these," he declared.[19]

Moltmann's critique of bourgeois existentialism was deepened in his subsequent major work, *The Crucified God*, which argued that in Bultmann's theology the primacy of existential communication swallowed up the meaning of the cross on its own terms. By giving theological primacy to what is biblically a matter of secondary importance, Moltmann argued, Bultmann collapsed the historical significance of the cross into an existential experience of crucifixion with Christ. The meaning of the cross for the believer crucified with Christ is not first an exercise in historical interpretation through its repeated experience, Moltmann insisted, for in this view (Bultmann's) God's gift in the cross is logically preceded by someone's search for it. Rather, Moltmann asserted, "It is the revelation of God in abandonment by God, the acceptance of the godless by Christ himself taking on his abandonment, which brings him into fellowship with the crucified Christ and makes it possible for him to follow Christ."[20] Because he confused the relationship between grace and experience, Moltmann argued, Bultmann altogether failed to find any meaning in the cross except as an example of *conformitas crucis.*

The underlying problem with Bultmann's interpretation of the cross, in Moltmann's reading, was that it presented Jesus as an archetypal religious martyr. Bultmann once characteristically wrote, for example, that "we cannot tell whether or how Jesus found meaning in his death. We may not veil from ourselves the possibility that he suffered a collapse."[21] Moltmann conceded that this is correct from a strictly historical perspective, but argued that this is precisely why a Christian interpretation of the cross must be *theological.* That is, a Christian reading must take into account the Father whose being Jesus claimed to share, as well as the theological significance of Jesus's life-ending cry of Godforsaken abandonment.

The Crucified God insisted that a *Christian* understanding of Jesus must focus on Jesus's relationship with his Father and subsequently with Jesus's mission as a sacrifice for the sake of the coming kingdom. Jesus perceived divine reality, Moltmann asserted, in terms of his Father's historical initiative and promises. God was the redeeming power who "sets at liberty those who are oppressed" (Luke 4:18) and who promises them a new future. This was the overriding thesis of Moltmann's *Theology of Hope,* but in *The Crucified God* the same thesis was deepened by his reflections on the trinitarian implications of the death of Christ. Moltmann argued that most theologians since the Reformation have interpreted Christ's death primarily in terms of his exemplary suffering or as the proof of his faithfulness, and have therefore failed to connect the meaning of the cross to God's triune nature.

Moltmann countered, however, that it is uniquely in the cross that we perceive God's giving and receiving in Christ and the spirit of sacrifice that connected their relationship. The incarnational relationship of Godhead-Manhood in Christ is theologically secondary to the personhood of Christ as the Son of God. The death of Christ on the cross, Moltmann therefore concluded, was a death *in* God that connects divine affection, suffering, and death to our own.[22]

This conception of the interconnection between the trinity and the cross is achieved, in Moltmann's work, through the use of a dialectical method that transforms the dichotomies of subjectivity versus objectivity, knowing versus feeling, and revelation as history versus revelation as Word into an active tension of reconciliation. As he stated in his Hegelian conclusion to *Theology of Hope*, "a thing is alive only when it contains contradiction in itself and is indeed the power of holding the contradiction within itself and enduring it."[23] For Moltmann, dialectic reveals the active and ongoing in life in opposition to the static or fragmented approaches that compartmentalize life into essentialist faculties.

The dichotomy that Moltmann has worked most earnestly to bridge, however, is the apparent contradiction between the nature of Christian identity and the demands of political relevance. To the extent that one becomes involved in politics, he has observed, the loss of one's distinctively Christian identity seems to be risked; conversely, the more one seeks seriously to follow Christ, the more one seems irrelevantly idealistic in the harsh world of politics. Political involvement is unavoidable for those who seek to aid those whom Christ called "the least of these my brethren," but as Christians become drawn into political activity, Moltmann notes, they inevitably endanger their identity as Christians.[24]

Moltmann's preoccupation with this problem in *The Crucified God* marked a shift in emphasis from his earlier work. The hopeful tone of his previous books and his emphasis on the dialectic of promise and fulfillment seemed refuted by history itself in the later 1960s and early 1970s, as Soviet tanks smashed the democratic opening in Czechoslovakia, the United States waged a grotesque war in Vietnam, Martin Luther King, Jr., was assassinated, the Allende government in Chile was overthrown, and revolutionary movements brought new forms of slavery to Cambodia, Vietnam, and other third-world countries. Moltmann acknowledged that his earlier sense of hope had been chastened by these events, and he noted that Ernst Bloch had expressed the same experience of disillusionment.

It was not that world events had caused Moltmann to abandon his theological position. In his topical work of that period, *The Experiment Hope*, he reiterated his thesis that the future is the mode of God's existence in the world and argued that God "is not present in the same way that the things in the world are at hand. God, like his Kingdom, is coming and only as the coming one, as future, is he already present. He is already present in the way in which his future in promise and hope empowers the present.

He is, however, not yet present in the manner of his eternal presence. Understood as the *coming one* and as the *power of the future*, God is experienced as the *ground of liberation*, and not as the enemy of freedom."[25] This idea of God as the totally liberating power of the future is central to all of Moltmann's work. But the bitter disappointments of the Vietnam War era, especially the destruction of the democratic socialist experiments in Czechoslovakia and Chile, caused Moltmann to reconsider his understanding of the cross. "I can only speak for myself," he noted at the outset of *The Crucified God*, "but on my disappointment at the end of 'socialism with a human face' in Czechoslovakia and the end of the Civil Rights movement in the U.S.A., and at what I hope is only a temporary halt in the reforms in the ecumenical movement and the Catholic Church . . . the centre of my hope and resistance once again became that which, after all, is the driving force of all attempts to open up new horizons in society and the church: the cross of Christ."[26]

In *The Crucified God*, Moltmann thus argued that the cross is the center of Christian existence because it is in the cross that Christian identity and social relevance are finally integrated. The paradoxical dichotomy between identity and relevance can only be resolved for a Christian *in* the cross on which the Godforsaken Son of God took on *our* suffering identity. The suffering Christ himself reconciled our conflicts, Moltmann argued, and to be a Christian is to be crucified *with* Christ for others.[27]

The chief weakness in Moltmann's position, however, is that he has thus far failed to demonstrate how and why our present salvation is dependent upon an event (Golgotha) of the past. Though it is unassailably orthodox to assert that our wounds are healed in the blood of Christ, a theological explication of this confession needs to make clear how a religious event of the past can resolve, for example, the concrete problems that Christians face in the political field. Moltmann concedes that the crucifixion of Jesus can only be meaningfully distinguished from other executions in history by the fact that Jesus claimed special kinship with God and then suffered abandonment by God in his agonizing death. "Just as there was a unique fellowship with God in his life and preaching," Moltmann remarks, "so in his death there was a unique abandonment by God."[28] The clear intention of Moltmann's argument is to read the present meaning of Christ's suffering off the historical events at Golgotha. But this argument fails to explain the relationship between the historical events and the theological conception of the unity of dialectical history. That is, what is the *present* status of the events of Golgotha in the dialectical history? The few remarks that Moltmann makes in *The Crucified God* about living *in* God and participating *in* Golgotha merely suggest an answer, and even these suggestions are problematic when seen against his severe critique of Bultmann's doctrine of illumination.

Aside from the reasons he expressed at the outset, Moltmann also turned to a theology of the cross as a response to the criticisms that his earlier works had received. It was often asserted, for example, that his early works overemphasized the resurrection and that his futurism was too dependent on the vague notions of promise and hope.[29] In response to these criticisms, *The Crucified God* emphasized that the suffering and Godforsakenness of the *eschatologia crucis* not only breaks the false optimism of all utopian illusions but also vitiates the more popular inclination to obscure the reality of death. In the latter tendency, he observed, the death of Christ on the cross is usually regarded negatively, except as a necessary "setup" for the resurrection. Moltmann insisted that this perspective distorts New Testament theology, however, which never vitiates a negative cross with an all-consuming resurrection. In the New Testament, he argued, the glory of God is revealed dialectically in the cross of the resurrected Christ (the historical event) and the resurrection of the crucified God (the eschatological event). The resurrection of Christ was therefore not another corn-king resurrection myth, but the eschatological victory of the crucified. As Rebecca Chopp has noted, for Moltmann the cross and the resurrection are only comprehensible in dialectical tension. The history of Christian theology is marked with various attempts to sublate the cross into the resurrection or to separate them as wholly distinct modes of expression. Moltmann has argued, in contrast, that the meaning of the cross and the resurrection can only be revealed dialectically. The "scandal" of the cross that St. Paul described was not vanquished by the resurrection, but intensified by it.[30]

The Crucified God thus responded to the charge that Moltmann's futurism pulled history into the future and out of the concrete present, but the closing argument of the book exposed Moltmann to new charges of the same kind. Near the end of *The Crucified God*, in a section that contained a general discussion of modern social problems, Moltmann argued that theology must maintain a "critical function" that rejects the sacralization of any particular political ideology. After observing that the crucified God "is in fact a stateless and classless God," Moltmann proceeded to describe the "five vicious circles of death" (poverty, political force, social and cultural alienation, ecological destruction, and Godforsakenness) which he subsequently correlated with five "symbols of liberation" (socialism, democracy, emancipation, peace with nature, and faith in the crucified God).[31]

This discussion clearly explicated Moltmann's commitment to democratic socialism, arguing that the vicious circle of poverty "can be broken only through economic co-determination and control of economic power by the producers." To the liberationist theologians of Latin America, however, Moltmann's insistence on the "critical function" of theology replicated the traditional failure of bourgeois religious progressivism, since it seemed to undercut the theological arguments for socialism. Míguez Bonino asserted, for example, that it was timid and unfaithful for Moltmann to "draw back from materialization" and take refuge in a critical function that "is able to remain above right and left, ideologically neutral, independent of a structural analysis of reality." When Moltmann warned against the dangers of political sacralization, Míguez Bonino remarked, he should have reflected on the presuppositions that informed his own (bourgeois) notion of critical freedom.

The latter point was well taken, but the basic soundness of Moltmann's argument about sacralization was inadvertently confirmed when Míguez Bonino subsequently conceded that there is no such thing as a *divine* politics or economics. Since we lack a divinely revealed ideology, Míguez Bonino concluded, the best that liberation theology can do is use "the best *human* politics and economics at our disposal."[32] But this is exactly what Moltmann had done when he defended democratic socialism. Moltmann's arguments for worker control of economic power and his strictures against divinizing any form of politics were echoed, in nearly the same words, by Míguez Bonino. Referring to Míguez Bonino's *Doing Theology in a Revolutionary Situation* and to Rubem Alves's *A Theology of Human Hope*, Moltmann has ruefully observed that, "you first see yourself strongly criticized, to discover later, to your surprise, that the critic ends by stating the same thing that you had already said, even using the same words."[33] This is not to suggest that there are no actual differences between the positions taken by Moltmann and by the leading liberationist theologians, but the charge that Moltmann has failed to "materialize" his theological vision is unfounded. The irony is that this charge has been advanced by the same liberationists who have been most dependent upon Moltmann's work.

While he has occasionally complained that liberationist theologians have recycled his ideas without acknowledging their debt to his work, Moltmann's response to liberationist criticism has focused mainly on the nature and requirements of democratic socialism. Commenting on what he perceives to be an insufficient appreciation of the importance of democratic rights in liberation theology, Moltmann has declared that anyone who experiences political freedom "no longer believes the theories by which a dictatorship, be it rightist or leftist, tries to justify itself." Though he concedes that first-world progressives have no right to judge third-world revolutionary movements that seek "to overcome class rule and dictatorship," Moltmann has repeatedly argued that, in the end, only *democratic* socialism is *worth* fighting for. For anyone with an actual choice, he has insisted, the only authentic form of socialism is democratic socialism, which fulfills the human desire for self-determination in the political as well as the economic spheres of social existence. Moltmann has therefore criticized the liberationist tendency to assume that socialism can exist without democratic political entitlements, or that economic justice can be sustained in the absence of human rights.[34] For Moltmann, democratic socialism is primarily the faith that the fulfillment of the idea of democratic self-determination is an actual possibility.

But to hold that faith, he insists, is not to suspend one's critical judgment about revolutionary movements or the practical dilemmas of socialist planning. In his open letter to Míguez Bonino, Moltmann emphatically asserted that to support liberationist movements in the third world is not to be naïve about their short-term prospects. The hope for third-world revolutionary movements is not that they will institute some permanent form of proletarian class rule, but that they will establish democratic systems of collective self-government. Democratic socialism is the historical form that Christian hope *must* take, Moltmann has more recently argued, "given the present poverty of capitalism and its democracies as well as socialism and its dictatorial governments."[35] Though Moltmann concedes that democratic socialism extends the *liberal* notion of legitimacy, he argues that democratic socialism ultimately constitutes a "third way" between capitalism and Communism. This point is crucial to Moltmann, because it supports his vision of a world order that converges toward a single social-democratic model.

In his provocative work *On Human Dignity*, Moltmann observes that the cold war has been fueled for more than four decades by the rivalry between two economic systems struggling for domination over world markets. The hope for a new world order beyond the blocs, he therefore suggests, rests upon the prospects for democratic socialism on both sides of the bloc system. To the extent that the existing Communist and capitalist nations begin to converge toward democratic socialism, he asserts, the long-held hope for an end to the cold war will become an attainable possibility. "I do not think that I am thereby withholding anything from the freedom and the humanity of the people," he remarks. "In the end the only thing that is at stake in socialism and democracy is that the people become the subject of their own history of freedom and human beings attain their unhindered humanity."[36]

In his various writings over the past two decades, Moltmann has thus offered a clear and compelling argument for democratic socialism as the most worthy political form of Christian hope. He has promoted economic democracy as the most legitimate model of large-scale business ownership and as the ideal for any attainable form of world economic convergence. As an argument for a decentralized and fully democratized social vision, these writings have unquestionably explicated the vision that was implied in *Theology of Hope*. Because these same writings have repeatedly insisted on the centrality of the cross in Christian experience, however, the question naturally arises whether the military defense of democracy, or any violent struggle for it, can be justified on Christian grounds. If the cross of Christ, as Moltmann insists, is the center of Christian faith and the revelation of its meaning, can a follower of Christ ever rightly take up arms to prevent or overthrow political tyranny? If Christ taught that evil can only be redeemed through the power of sacrificial love, and therefore opened his arms to his enemies on the cross, can his followers ever choose violence instead?

For twenty years, Moltmann carefully avoided these questions in his major theological works and only briefly discussed them in his more topical writings. *The Crucified God* extensively examined the theological and sociopolitical meaning of the cross, for example, without ever connecting the way of the cross to the redemption of evil through nonviolence. Moltmann raised the subject only once, in his historical discussion of the concept of the "way of Christ" in biblical and later Christian traditions. "To suffer and be rejected signify the cross," he observed. "To die on the cross means to suffer and to die as one who is an outcast and rejected. If those who follow Jesus are to take 'their cross' on themselves, they are taking on not only suffering and a bitter fate, but the suffering of rejection." Moltmann noted that in the early history of the church the closest form of following the crucified Christ was to be a martyr, but he dismissively countered that this tradition mistakenly treated Christ's suffering as an *exemplary* sacrifice. The way of the cross is eschatological, he asserted, and not to be understood in a moral sense.[37]

In his topical writings of the same period, Moltmann's comments on the moral question of violence were similarly dismissive, notwithstanding his repeated claims for the importance of the cross in Christian experience. Moltmann's early assessment of the morality of violence rested upon the traditional distinction between the kingdom as *presently* known and the kingdom as *not yet* fulfilled. In *The Experiment Hope*, for example, he argued that the concept of nonviolence "belongs to the eschatological remembrance of faith in Jesus." The kingdom of Christian expectation is the realization of fellowship without violence, he observed, which explains "the Christian's deep horror of violence already in the present." Moltmann noted that a preference for nonviolent solutions to political disputes is therefore axiomatic from a Christian standpoint. But in the *domain of politics*, he asserted, the moral question automatically shifts to "a question of power, distribution of power, and participation in the exercise of power."[38] As he elsewhere explained, "It's not a question of knowing whether violence or nonviolence is immoral; rather, we face this other problem: How can we take a meaningful part in the exercise of legitimate political power?"[39]

On those occasions when Moltmann briefly addressed the moral question of violence, he thus implied that pacifism is irrelevant and ultimately irresponsible in the political realm. Though he asserted that the Christian concept of nonviolence is relevant as an eschatological remembrance of faith, Moltmann rejected any interpretation of the cross that prescribed a pacifist ethic for Christians. Following Dietrich Bonhoeffer, he argued that responsible political activity entails "the readiness to incur guilt," and that the refusal to accept such responsibility could make one responsible for even greater violence and "irredeemable guilt" through one's acquiescence.[40] As George Hunsinger has observed, Moltmann's early work repeatedly discussed the theology of the cross and the dilemmas of political violence, but never at the same time.[41] His reflections on the problem of force brought in the cross only to establish the principle that love must be ready to become guilty in order to be redemptive.

But the guilt accepted by Christ on the cross was not the guilt of violence.

Though the meaning of the cross is not reducible to a pacifist ethic, it is certainly a distortion of Christian theology to discard this element as irrelevant to politics. As Moltmann has amply demonstrated, the crucifixion of Jesus was a political execution. The founder of the Christian faith died as a political criminal of the Roman state. For nearly two millennia the cross of Christ has therefore symbolized to his followers the call to accept suffering rather than inflict it on others. Whatever else may be said about the theological significance of the cross, the call to redeem evil through self-sacrificial love must be the core of its meaning.

For twenty years, Moltmann interpreted this call as an eschatological rather than a moral reality. He traded on the traditional distinctions between the eschatological commands of Christ and the political realities faced by churches that live "between the times" of Christ's appearances. Since the church happens to exist during the historical interim when the kingdom has not yet been fulfilled, Moltmann argued that the church should not hold itself to the moral standards of the as-yet unrealized kingdom. In the kingdom of God, he asserted, freedom and harmony will be maintained without force; but in the unredeemed world of modern politics, freedom and community can only be attained and preserved through the use of force. Politics is about power.

This resort to dualism is a reasonable position on its own terms, but, as John Howard Yoder has shown, the New Testament presents a different concept of the nature of the kingdom. In the biblical idea, the peace of Christ *is* an eschatological presence, but not in the sense that it only fully exists at the edge of history or beyond history. Rather, as Yoder has explained, "These aeons are not distinct periods of time, for they exist simultaneously. They differ rather in nature or in direction; one points backwards to human history outside of (before) Christ; the other points forward to the fullness of the kingdom of God, of which it is a foretaste. Each aeon has a social manifestation: the former in the 'world,' the latter in the body of Christ."[42]

It was a sign of Moltmann's intuitive dissatisfaction with his position that for two decades he repeatedly returned to the question of violence, albeit briefly on each occasion. But instead of developing a position that followed directly from his theological vision, Moltmann excluded the question of the morality of violence from his theory of the significance of the cross. He defended the Christian right to resort to force on the ground that politics is a separate sphere of existence and that war is a means of politics, or the continuation of politics by other means. It is evident from his recent writings, however (as well as from personal conversations with the author), that Moltmann's intuitive dissatisfaction with his argument about violence, as well as with the unbiblical distinctions it rested upon, have driven him to a different assessment of the question.

While he refrains from making a universal judgment about the viability or morality of just-war theory, Moltmann has recently shifted to a more personal perspective on the question, asking what it means for a middle-class Westerner to follow Christ in the nuclear age. "We in the Federal Republic of Germany and the United States have to come to grips with the possession of nuclear weapons, and now quite specifically with the refusal of armament or disarmament," he asserts. "We must in this situation live out our service of peace as Christians and churches of Christ."

Moltmann reviews the classic Lutheran and Anabaptist arguments on the question, finding that neither position is acceptable as a Christian response to the threats of the nuclear age. Though he expresses admiration for the traditional Anabaptist insistence on love of neighbor, defenseless-ness, and readiness for suffering, he questions whether Christians are actu-ally meant to abandon their political responsibilities over creation. "If the community of Christ separates itself from society," he asks, "does it not then show only its own 'great refusal,' not the criticism of this violent world in light of the judgement and Kingdom of God?" That is, if Christians withdraw from society, how will the light and judgment of Christ ever reach the public world?

The Lutheran counterposition, as expressed in the sixteenth article of the Augsburg Confession, begins with the principle that "all established rule and laws were instituted and ordained by God." Given the assumption that all governmental authority is divinely instituted and ordained, the Augsburg Confession concludes that Christians have a moral duty to obey the commands of the state "to punish evil doers with the sword, engage in just wars, and serve as soldiers." The Augsburg Confession resolves the apparent contradiction between these precepts and the explicit commands of Christ by explaining that the gospel "does not teach an outward and temporal but an inward and eternal mode of existence and the righteous-ness of the heart." By this reading, the commands of Christ are interpreted as inward verities for Christians, but separate from the duties by which Christian citizens are bound. Since the gospel is not "outward and tem-poral," it does not promote social activism or sanction disobedience of civil authorities. The Augsburg Confession does assert that Christians should disobey civil authorities "when they command to sin," but Moltmann rue-fully notes that this exception has typically been given a narrow interpre-tation in Lutheran church history. In Moltmann's reading, the Lutheran dichotomy between the realms of "the gospel and the Spirit" and "the law and the sword" has effectively eliminated the prophetic element from the Lutheran theological tradition. "So just as the Anabaptists stand in danger of pulling themselves back out of the world quietistically and without crit-icism," he observes, "so the Lutherans stand in danger of going along with the world as it is and cooperating without criticism. The 'silent ones in the land' and the 'pious state underlings' thus in the end have little to contrib-ute to peace and justice in politics and economics in the world."[43]

Having rejected two contrasting forms of Christian witness that under-mine the social mission of the church, Moltmann offers his own position, which begins with an assessment of the morality of nuclear deterrence. "The peace of deterrence through mutual fear may technically be nonemployment of weapons, but it is not peace," he asserts. "Mutual deterrence through fear is a condition of extreme lack of peace, because it increases potential realities of violence. Even without nuclear war the stockpiling of armaments already destroys the life of human beings and the natural environment. The military-industrial complex spreads itself like a cancerous growth and infects all dimensions of life." Moltmann therefore declares his support for the *Ohne Rüstung Leben* (Life without Armaments) movement in Europe, which calls for gradual, unilateral nuclear disengagement leading to eventual nuclear and conventional disarmament. The fact that this program sounds utopian, he remarks, is proof that we have become prisoners of the superpower deterrence system. Moltmann observes that most European churches have justified the possession of nuclear missiles, on account of their deterrent value, while insisting that the actual use of nuclear missiles would be morally unjustifiable in any conceivable circumstance. But if a nuclear strike of any kind would be unquestionably immoral, he argues, then one is logically driven to the conclusion that possession of the missiles themselves is immoral, because these weapons must be designed and programmed for use. Moltmann therefore declares that he is personally prepared to live without them.

He distinguishes the personal from the political choice. As a follower of Christ who places loyalty to the kingdom over any political loyalty, he professes that he is ready to risk persecution and martyrdom rather than support political preparations for war. Moltmann acknowledges that the content of this commitment, which he calls simply "the way of faith," is meaningful only for Christians. He defends the religious integrity of this position, first, without regard for its political implications, but that does not cause him to forsake politics. Moltmann argues that Christians should be involved in the political process, but involved first *as Christians*. The church should not be disqualified from participating in the political process, he implies, if it takes the Sermon on the Mount seriously. Religious conviction should lead to social involvement, though he concedes that on the political level a larger set of factors must also be assessed.

Moltmann acknowledges that unilateral disarmament or appeasement could provoke aggression and could also make a nation subject to blackmail or extortion. Whoever advocates unilateral disarmament, he writes, must therefore consciously risk "the freedom, the rights, and the security of his or her own country in order to save the whole of life on this earth from nuclear death." Church officials and theologians have traditionally sought to avoid this decision by criticizing the arms race while accepting the presumed necessity of nuclear deterrence. Moltmann insists, however, that the two positions are irreconcilable. If the use of nuclear missiles would cause destruction out of proportion with whatever any given war could be said to be about, then not only their use, but also the readiness to fire them, is immoral.

"Up to now," he remarks, "both sides of this issue have made their calculations as if neither Christ nor the Sermon on the Mount had existed." The same charge could be leveled against Moltmann's own earlier writings about violence, but his recent work has attempted to bring together the *theology* and the *way* of the cross, by claiming that nonviolence is the heart of the Christian gospel. Moltmann argues that when we retaliate or threaten to retaliate against an enemy, we enter an inescapable vicious circle. Retaliation freezes the goodness that is within an enemy and within oneself. It causes one to be increasingly determined by the enemy and forecloses the possibility of bringing out the goodness in an enemy. We can be liberated from the vicious circle of fear and retribution only when something else becomes more important to us.

In Christian language, the "something else" is the love of Christ, which empowers the faithful to love their enemies and to repay evil with good. Whoever follows the way of Christ, therefore, no longer *reacts* to the enemy, Moltmann observes, "but seeks to create something new, a new situation for the enemy and for himself or herself."[44] Building on a Pauline theme, Moltmann asserts that God is not an idol that represents force, but the liberating power revealed through suffering and weakness. Just as Bonhoeffer realized near the end of his life that Christians must "participate in the sorrow of God in the world," Moltmann declares that the follower of Christ "seeks God in his own weakness, not at his edges, and not in his strength, but seeks God in the sufferings of Christ in the world." The usual way of religion, and certainly the way that religion is typically used for political ends, is to look to God as the source of strength and order. In this case, the search for God becomes a search for greater strength through God's power. "But if God reveals himself in Christ crucified," Moltmann argues, "then we must try to find God in his grief in the world, and seek communion with those who suffer most in the world."[45]

The latter argument is a recurring theme in Moltmann's earlier work, but it was only with the publication of *On Human Dignity* that Moltmann embraced the pacifist implications within it. For too long, he remarks, the Christian churches have framed the moral issues of war and deterrence in terms of the question of national security. But the commands of the Sermon on the Mount and the desire to experience God's love for our enemies should lead the church to ask different questions, such as: How can we bless those who curse us? How can we bring out what is good in our enemies? Moltmann argues that the relentless demand for national security is driven by a counterproductive fear of war, which rationalizes ever more absurd levels of overkill capacity in the name of safety. After four decades of failing to contain the arms race through negotiation, he remarks, it is clear that the spiral of military escalation will only be broken if one side unilaterally steps out in faith away from war. The choice to support unilateral disarmament must be personal before it can be political, but Moltmann contends that the most meaningful Christian response to the arms race is *both* personal and political. He advocates unilateral nuclear disarmament and gradual conventional disarmament as positions for Christians in all countries, beginning with his own. "The more the church moves from being a *church bound to the state* to a *free church*," he says, "the clearer can become its witness to peace and the less ambiguous its initiative for peace."

For Moltmann, this would not represent a move toward sectarianism, but a move toward a realization of the true solidarity of the body of Christ. Christians would stop killing each other in the name of politics or anything else. "It will become a peace church to the degree that it confesses *Christ* and Christ alone as its and the whole world's peace and shows the necessary consequences of this confession," he declares. To confess Christ as Lord is incompatible with killing other members of Christ's body, or killing *anyone* in whom the light of the Spirit dwells. The theological argument for pacifism is firstly an argument for religious integrity, but Moltmann argues that the pacifist option is politically realistic as well. "Pacifism is the only *realism* of life left to us in this apocalyptic situation of threatened world annihilation," he concludes. "Pacifists are the realists of life, not merely voices of utopia."[46]

In personal conversation, Moltmann has conceded that he only means the latter statements in a literal or absolute sense with regard to *nuclear* pacifism. "There is a contradiction in my life that I have never resolved," he acknowledges. "I am a pacifist, yet if I had a chance—like Bonhoeffer— to kill the tyrant who was killing others, I know that I would do it." Pausing to formulate a thought that is even more revealingly personal, Moltmann continues, "There is something morally unacceptable about Germans today calling themselves pacifists in the first place. For we Germans are indebted to those who liberated us, at enormous cost, from the madman, Hitler. I mean this very seriously. We Germans benefited—we were *liberated*— through the suffering and violence of others who fought against Hitler." He concluded that he cannot reconcile his deeply felt pacifism with his knowledge that violence sometimes serves the higher moral end.

Moltmann thus describes his position as a contradictory impasse, but I believe that his emphasis on the question of killing the oppressors who would otherwise kill others contains the beginning of the most morally worthy resolution. It is often assumed that the fundamental difference between the pacifist and just-war traditions is that the former serves the ends of love, while the latter only serves the ends of justice in a dualistic sense. This distinction was vigorously insisted upon by Reinhold Niebuhr and is widely repeated today by just-war theorists and pacifists alike. But the original Augustinian conception of the just war was not a dualistic theory in the Niebuhrian sense. Rather, it provided a method for determining when the ends of love could be served by the resort to force. "Faced with the fact of attacks upon the innocent," St. Augustine wrote, "the command not to kill must give way to the command of love, interpreted as the obligation to protect the innocent."

There are two authentically Christian traditions of moral theory on war because there are two legitimate and irreconcilable interpretations of the law of love. The first emphasizes that one cannot love one's enemies by trying to kill them. The second emphasizes that love compels one to protect the innocent from aggression. Stated this plainly, the former argument might seem to carry the greater moral force, but the refusal to defend the innocent can make one an accomplice to murder or genocide through one's acquiescence. Realism begins with that moral fact. For those, such as myself, who accept a narrowly defined just-war position *and* the kind of theological position expounded by Moltmann, the way of Christ is to mediate evil through love and to renounce, *so far as possible*, participation in war, violence, and all other forms of militarism.[47]

A second weakness in Moltmann's early thought has been more clearly resolved in his recent writings. Perhaps the key defect in Moltmann's early theological work was that it depended upon a deracinated logic of the future. To comprehend what is meant by such a statement as "God's being is future," for example, one must have some notion of what the divine reality *is* whose "being" is said to be future. As Langdon Gilkey and John Macquarrie have argued, theological statements are unintelligible if they cannot identify some situation *in experience* in which the word "God" should be invoked. Moltmann's early work failed to ground his theological assertions in experience, however, and in his zeal to base everything on the biblical logic of promise he repeatedly denigrated the epiphanic tradition in Christian theology. That is, he dismissively rejected the entire Christian theological tradition that has emphasized the importance of the experience of divine presence. This was a (characteristically Barthian) repudiation of a large theological heritage. In response to Moltmann's argument, Macquarrie sensibly replied that religion depends upon presence as well as promise, and argued that past and future can only be used to verify each other with reference to present experience.[48]

Moltmann first began to address these problems with his position in *The Crucified God*. Although that work retained his customary denigration of epiphanic language, Moltmann's interpretation of the cross as an experience within the triune life of God pushed him to attribute greater importance to the doctrine of the trinity and (at least for God) to the role of experience. This shift in Moltmann's theological perspective has marked all of his recent work, which is important to the present discussion because of its social implications.

One of the consistent themes in Moltmann's work is the argument that traditional Christian theism has sacralized monarchical images of religious and political authority. The futurist logic of *Theology of Hope* was offered as an alternative to religious and political monarchicalism, and *The Crucified God* suggested, in a different vein, that the authoritarian legacy of

Christian theology could be overturned by a deeper understanding of the doctrine of the trinity. Moltmann's recent work has developed the latter thesis. In *The Trinity and the Kingdom of God*, Moltmann argues that the monarchical conception of unity has been the foundation of classical Western monotheism and that a *nonmonarchical* concept of divine reality must conceive God as an interrelationship of persons. "The notion of a divine monarchy in heaven and on earth, for its part, generally provides the justification for earthly domination—religious, moral, patriarchal, or political domination—and makes it a hierarchy, a 'holy rule,' " he explains. "The idea of the almighty ruler of the universe everywhere requires abject servitude, because it points to complete dependency in all spheres of life."[49]

Moltmann therefore proposes that a modern, anti-imperialist theology of the trinity should not begin with the traditional, abstract concepts of substance and hypostasis, but *concretely*, through the history of God's triune self-revelation within the world. The starting point for trinitarian theology should not be with a theory of being, but with the concrete examples of divine suffering revealed through the life of Christ. Theology must begin with "the suffering of Christ as *the suffering of the passionate God,*" he writes, who is not the removed self-sufficient monarch of classical monotheism, but the triune mystery within and beyond creation who suffers for our sake. The final negation in Moltmann's characteristic series of "nots" is that the proper language of Christian theology is not the language of domination— of kingship, power, and possession—but the language of community, fellowship, mutuality, and love. Though the freedom of God was conceived in classical monotheism as a function of divine self-sufficiency, removed from the suffering of the world, Moltmann asserts that the freedom of God is God's vulnerable love. "God demonstrates his eternal freedom through his suffering and his sacrifice, through his self-giving and his patience," he asserts. "Through his freedom he waits for man's love, for his compassion, for his own deliverance to his glory through man."[50]

The implications of this conception of God for the doctrine of nature have been developed in the second volume of Moltmann's dogmatics, *God in Creation*. "We have begun to understand God in the awareness of his Spirit, for Christ's sake, as the triune God, the God who in himself constitutes the unique and perfect fellowship of the Father and the Son and the Holy Spirit," he writes.[51] God is not the absolute subject of traditional monotheism, but a triune fellowship of persons in which the Creator, through the Spirit, dwells *in* creation. Moltmann explains that the unifying idea of his "non-hierarchical, decentralized, confederate theology" is the notion of God as a triune unity that indwells and transfigures creation. This conception presupposes a pre-modern concept of reason as the organ of perception and participation, in opposition to the objectifying, dualistic assumptions of modern analytical philosophy.

Moltmann concedes that the organic theological cosmologies of the past (as in Schleiermacher, Rothe, and Heim) have been rejected by most contemporary theologians, partly out of fear of pantheism, but he asserts that it is essential "to take up the old ideas again."[52] The beauty of the organic (or integrative) theological models constructed, for example, by Karl Heim, is that they conceived the world as a manifold God-given creation that exists *within* God. While he disassociates himself from the mechanistic assumptions of the Heimian and process-theological systems, Moltmann argues that all relationships in creation that are analogous to God "reflect the primal, reciprocal indwelling and mutual interpenetration of the trinitarian perichoresis: God *in* the world and the world *in* God; heaven and earth *in* the Kingdom of God, pervaded by his glory; soul and body united *in* the life-giving Spirit to a human whole."[53] Against the Augustinian and Cartesian identification of consciousness with spirit, therefore, Moltmann assumes an organic metaphysical model in which consciousness is reflective *and* reflected spirit. Spirit is not only the conscious subjectivity of one's reason or will. Spirit comprehends the entire unity of body and soul.

Without rejecting his earlier conception of God as the divine power of the future, Moltmann has thus adopted a more inclusive understanding of divine reality as a triune fellowship of persons whose relationship creates and indwells history. Though his overriding purpose has been to conceive divine reality in a decentralized, nonmonarchical manner, and though he has essentially retained his methodological Barthianism, Moltmann's shift in content emphasis has also made his theology more meaningful in an existential sense by refocusing attention on the indwelling God of present experience. His work has thus profoundly revealed the modern relevance, as well as the limitations, of the neo-orthodox biblical vision. Rather than begin with some foundational notion of human need or experience, and then cut the biblical message to fit this construct, Moltmann has attempted to understand the modern world in the light of the biblical witness. His method is to absorb the world into his interpretation of the biblical world.

This method has its limitations. Moltmann makes a sharp distinction between biblical and cultural theologies, and typically disassociates himself from theories that are principally drawn from the latter.[54] His devotion to the Scripture principle of classical Protestantism also leads him to hold, in opposition to feminist criticism, that the patriarchal connotations of traditional Christian language can be removed without disposing of the terms themselves. He argues, for example, that Christian "Father" language has an emancipatory, nonpatriarchal meaning that can be recovered while the usage of this language is retained. Though he is sympathetic to feminism in other respects, he thus rejects much of the criticism of traditional Christian language that feminist scholars have offered in recent years.

Moltmann's attachment to a particular understanding of the biblical witness is also the source of a crucial difference between his theological method and the method used by liberationists. While I have argued that Moltmann is right in his dispute with liberationists about the social importance of *democratic* empowerment, I believe that the liberationists have made a compelling argument on the issue of theological method. To Moltmann, the liberationist method of beginning with human suffering is a new version of the anthropocentric mistake. He agrees that the reality of human suffering must be central to Christian theology, but he argues that suffering has theological significance primarily because God is in it. To Moltmann, it is axiomatic that theology must always begin with the divine object of faith rather than with the questioning or suffering human subject. As he asserts in *The Church in the Power of the Spirit*, "The church's first word is not 'church' but Christ."[55]

It follows for Moltmann that the suffering of the world is important to theology, first, because it is God's own pain. As he states in *The Future of Creation*, God "suffers with them, he suffers because of them, he suffers for them."[56] Whereas liberationists first reinterpret the meaning of Christian faith in light of the human experience of oppression, Moltmann interprets the meaning of suffering by beginning with the disclosure of God's being in creation. Rebecca Chopp has aptly explained that for Moltmann "Christianity interprets suffering, but suffering does not interrupt Christianity."[57] Though he gives a central place in his theology to the significance of suffering, Moltmann's methodological positivism precludes the possibility that suffering could ever "interrupt" or transform his preconceived theological structure.[58]

The main problem with this method (apart from the fundamental question whether theology can actually begin with the divine object) is that it makes history and suffering abstract. Moltmann's method gives theological primacy to the dialectic of contradiction rather than to the historical reality of suffering. That is, he begins with the idea of divine self-disclosure, understood through the dialectic of God and world. The consequence, as Chopp has noted, is that suffering becomes a vehicle for divine revelation. "God chooses self-revelation in the unlike (history) through the unlike of history (suffering)."[59] Moltmann's methodological assumptions thus prevent him from taking the experience of suffering seriously enough on its own terms. His dialectic falls short of the liberationist test of praxis, because it makes suffering an abstraction. In personal conversation, Moltmann has told me that he regards this critique as reflective of either the guilt complex of such first-world, middle-class academics as Chopp or myself, or of what he derisively calls the "social pietism" of Latin American liberation theologians— most of whom, he notes, are themselves middle-class professors. This is an effective argument, evoking the very guilt complex that Moltmann criticizes. As I will argue in chapter 7, however, the categorization of "middle-class" as an epithet is a longstanding Leftist tradition that deserves to be buried.

While I have registered several criticisms of his position, I believe that Moltmann has nonetheless offered the most generative, socially valuable, and suggestive theological work of the past generation. More than any other contemporary theologian, he has revealed the enduring power of the biblical witness. His interpretations of hope, eschatology, the cross, the trinity, panentheism, theopaschionitism, and the Kingdom of God have powerfully shaped the agenda of modern theology. In recent years, his growing concern with the worldwide ecological crisis and his development of an explicitly panentheistic conception of divine reality have broken new ground in the contemporary search for a satisfactory theology of nature.[60] Moreover, his theology has been influenced to an extraordinary degree by his engagement with Marxism, especially with Bloch's neo-Marxist philosophy of hope. For Moltmann, however, the hope of Christian faith is ultimately distinctive. As he states in *Diskussion ueber die "Theologie der Hoffnung,"* for him the future is *adventus*, the coming of God, whereas for Bloch the future is *futurum physis*, the coming-to-be of matter. Since Christianity posits the existence of an *adventus* that determines the process of actualization, Moltmann observes, Christian theology is inherently idealistic and ultimately irreconcilable with Marxism.[61]

Moltmann has since argued that it is possible for Marxists and Christians to share the same political hope, and that the most worthy goal of international political convergence would be democratic socialism. He is unfailingly clear, however, that neither the end of the cold war nor the fulfillment of democracy would signify the Kingdom of God. He has repeatedly insisted that it is always mistaken to identify the presence of the kingdom with *any* human endeavor, "since we cannot raise the dead." The actual presence of the kingdom would include the eschatological presence of all who have died. But because he regards liberation from oppression as an *anticipation* of the kingdom of God, Moltmann regards democratic socialism not as the presence of the kingdom but as the historical hope of those who struggle to gain the closest approximation of the Christian spirit within history.

5

Gustavo Gutiérrez and
the Theologies of Liberation

In the spring of 1977, when Gustavo Gutiérrez was completing his year as a visiting professor at Union Theological Seminary in New York, he was asked by a student in a seminar how it felt to have started a new theological movement. An awkward pause followed. Gutiérrez looked blank for several seconds and then squinted at the student, appearing not to have understood the question.

Since his grasp of English was rather weak, two students tried to explain the question to him while Gutiérrez sat in silence, indulging their assistance until he was ready to speak. Finally, he looked at his questioner and replied, "Is not a question I can answer. I start nothing." Another pause followed. Gutiérrez is a kindly, unassuming, unfailingly gracious man, not inclined to make dismissive pronouncements of any kind. He struggled for the precise words and tone. "Some of you have learned about theology of liberation through my writings," he observed, "but I did not start this theology. I only express what I learn from others, especially the poor." He explained that he saw himself as a conduit of the faith and struggles of the poor in Latin America, rather than as a creator or "father" of liberation theology. What made liberation theology distinctive among the schools and movements of modern theology, he asserted, also made it impossible for him to accept the assumption behind the question. It was a variation on an answer he is often required to proffer.[1]

His insistent denials notwithstanding, however, Gustavo Gutiérrez is the most influential figure in modern liberation theology, and arguably the most significant theologian of the past generation. No one has made a greater impact on the shape or direction of theological discussion in our time. Though his praxological vision has been limited in certain respects by his conception of the liberationist departure in theological method, I will argue that this conception is more generative and authentic than the major liberationist alternative to it. The meaning of the liberationist

101

departure in theology is epitomized in Gutiérrez's life and work.

He was born into a poor mestizo family (part Quechuan Indian) in Lima in 1928. His mother never attended school; his father was a lower-class urban worker. As a youth, Gutiérrez contracted severe osteomyelitis, which forced him to spend six years in bed and left him with a permanent limp. Gutiérrez spent his bedridden adolescence developing his intellectual interests, and following his graduation from high school he enrolled in the school of medicine at San Marcos university in Peru, where he became active in Leftist politics. Gutiérrez anticipated a career as a psychiatrist, but as he approached the end of his undergraduate program he began to question whether his personal desire to serve the needs of the poor would be satisfied in the psychiatric profession. The question eventually moved him to leave his medical program and enroll, for one semester, at the Roman Catholic theological seminary in Santiago, Chile, where he tested his religious vocation.

The following year (1951) he enrolled in the master's degree program in philosophy and psychology at the Catholic University in Louvain, Belgium. Gutiérrez finished this program in 1955 and moved into the theology program at Lyon, France, where he completed his master's degree in theology in 1959. He was ordained to the priesthood in Lima in 1959 and undertook a one-semester postordination program at the Gregorian University in Rome before returning to Lima, where he has since remained.[2]

This itinerary is significant, and worth recounting, for two reasons. The first is that except for his opening semester in Santiago, Gutiérrez's entire seminary education took place in Europe. As a beginning seminarian, he accepted the conventional assumption that theology was something one learned in European universities, in European languages, as a preparation for ministry in one's own country. It was further assumed that the religious needs and interests of Latin Americans would be met by the continued importation of European theologies.

Gutiérrez's earliest glimmerings of dissent from these assumptions, however, occurred during his training in Louvain, where he formed close friendships with Camilo Torres and Juan Luis Segundo. This is the second noteworthy aspect of Gutiérrez's seminary experience. During his programs of study at Louvain, Lyon, and Rome, Gutiérrez became friends with numerous Latin American *seminaristas* whom he would not have known in Latin America. The most significant of these friendships for Gutiérrez was his relationship with Torres, a student from a prosperous Colombian family who came to Louvain in 1953 to study sociology. Torres arrived at Louvain with mildly progressive political views and a gnawing sense of guilt over the privileges he had inherited as a son of the bourgeoisie. At Louvain, the latter feeling and his study of Marxism pushed him to the Left—a process that Gutiérrez observed, in friendship, with intense interest. As a lower-class Amerindian who had been victimized by the poverty and racial bigotry that Torres only imagined, Gutiérrez was deeply moved by his friend's political and moral conversion, but he was also more cautious than Torres in his attitude toward political ideologies, and less motivated by inner guilt. Several years later, after his radicalization had grown more desperate, Torres resigned from his university and clerical positions to join a Colombian guerrilla force. "When the people have nothing against me," he declared, "when they have carried out the revolution, then I will return to offering Mass. . . . I think that in this way I will follow Christ's injunction . . . 'Leave thy gifts upon the altar and go first to be reconciled to thy brothers.' "[3] Torres was killed in 1966, gaining posthumous fame throughout Latin America as the symbol of Latin American revolutionary Christianity. It is a symbol that Gutiérrez has struggled with — on personal, religious, and political levels — ever since the death of his friend.

Though his academic training and his friendships with Latin American students in Europe moved him to become more critical of his conventional religious assumptions, it was only when Gutiérrez returned to Lima, in 1960, that he began to recognize the need for an alternative theology. He has recalled that when he returned to Peru he was prepared to teach the kind of theology he had learned in Europe, which focused on the problems of historical criticism and modernity. Having spent the past decade grappling with the intellectual problems that consumed the attention of European theologians, he had come to identify with the reformist theological program of Yves Congar, Henri de Lubac, and Jean Danielou. Gutiérrez fully expected to spend his own career working within this theological tradition.

The break occurred, however, when he returned to Catholic University in Lima and tried to teach the *nouvelle théologie* of Congar and Lubac to Latin American undergraduates. It was an experience of cultural reawakening. What he came to realize, Gutiérrez has since recalled, is that because even the most progressive European theologies were the products of European thought and experience, it was imperialistic to impose them on Latin American students. What was needed in Latin America, he decided, was a decolonialized theological project that reflected the realities of indigenous Latin American experience. Latin American liberation theology was born in that realization.

This recognition coincided with a reawakening of Gutiérrez's political interests. After nearly ten years of separation from the grinding poverty and misery of his native country, Gutiérrez's re-exposure to the rows of single-room *tugurios* in Lima quickly restimulated his interests in political activism. From his base in Rimac (one of the oldest *barriadas* in Lima, where he still lives), Gutiérrez set out in the early 1960s "to unlearn my previous education" and reeducate himself in the realities of Latin American history and culture. This process required, by his own recollection, a total reeducation in the facts of Latin American history, the meaning of Scripture and theology, and the causes of Latin American oppression. He immersed himself in the lives of the poor in Rimac and studied a wide range of literature on the history of Latin American dependency, including the letters of a sixteenth-century Spanish bishop and the essays of an early twentieth-century Peruvian Marxist. The bishop was Bartolomé de Las Casas (1474-1566), who gave up his colonial estates and his luxurious life-style at the age of forty to work on the side of the Indians. Though Las Casas shared much of the worldview common to sixteenth-century Spanish missionaries, he was led by his experiences among the Indians to reject the church's supposedly "Aristotelian" supposition that Indians were "naturally inferior" to whites and therefore appropriate objects for slavery. This example of beginning the process of theological reflection with an experience of solidarity with victims, rather than with an abstract principle of doctrine, was instructive to Gutiérrez. He drew encouragement from the bravery of Las Casas's campaigns against the slave trade and was deeply moved by the accounts of Las Casas's opposition to the *encomiendas*, the colonial plantations given by the king to Spanish lords as land grants. Near the end of his life, Las Casas explained to his critics that he had seen the face of Christ, above all, in the faces of the Indians. "I leave Jesus Christ in the Indies with our God, beating him, afflicting him, insulting and slapping him, and crucifying him, not once but thousands of times," he wrote. For Las Casas, the problem with the church's theology was that it failed to recognize what he called "the scourged Christs of the Indies" through whom Christ himself was being revealed. Through the writings of this unlikely bishop, Gutiérrez first recognized the possibility of a liberationist theology.[4]

During the same period he became reacquainted with the writings of the legendary Peruvian social theorist José Carlos Mariátegui. Mariátegui was a Marxist theoretician and precursor of the Christian-Marxist dialogue who played a central role in the formation of the Peruvian Communist party in the 1920s. Though he rejected the institutional church, Mariátegui also rejected the scientistic dogmatism and atheism of the European Marxist parties, arguing that there was a generative core of truth in the religious traditions of the poor. Like such neo-Marxist mentors as Croce and Labriola (with whom he studied in Europe), Mariátegui understood Marxism not as a system of dogmatic principles but as "a method of interpretation in each country . . . which functions and acts on the general context, on the social medium, without disregarding any of its characteristics."[5] This contextualist reading of Marxism was highly instructive to Gutiérrez. His later insistence on the determinative importance of historical context, the value of popular religion, the role of the class struggle, and the usefulness of Marxist theory can be traced to the formative influence of Mariátegui's work upon his thought.

The first fruits of Gutiérrez's reeducation were presented at a conference on pastoral mission, organized by Ivan Illich, that convened in 1964 in Petropolis, Brazil. In a paper that prefigured the opening chapter of *A Theology of Liberation*, Gutiérrez argued that theology should be reconceived as a secondary act of reflection on the meaning of one's practical engagement in the world. Theology should be reconceived as critical reflection on praxis. By asserting the priority of praxis in the life of faith and theological reflection, Gutiérrez established the fundamental principle on which his subsequent reconception of theology was based.

This reinterpretation was worked out during a period when a new wave of revolutionary ferment, including guerrilla warfare, was spreading throughout much of Latin America. Gutiérrez struggled to develop a theological interpretation of the situation that was equally faithful to the needs of the time and to the historic integrity of the Christian theological tradition. He introduced the phrase "theology of liberation" in 1968 at the Encuentro Nacional del Movimiento Sacerdotal ONIS Conference in Chimbote, Peru. A month later, in August, Gutiérrez and several other priests from the ONIS organization arrived in Medellín, Colombia, for the Second General Conference of the Latin American Episcopate (CELAM). The purpose of the conference was to examine the overall situation of the church in Latin America in light of the teachings of the Second Vatican Council. Gutiérrez participated in the conference as a theological consultant, conferring with sympathetic bishops and working on several of the conference's sixteen documents. The most important of these statements—the historic Medellín pronouncement on peace—was written almost entirely by Gutiérrez. In ringing phrases, this statement condemned the structures of violence and oppression that afflict the majority of Latin Americans and called on the church to serve as an advocate for "global, bold, urgent and profoundly renovating transformations."[6] Although most of the Medellín documents were couched in the more carefully modulated prose of ecclesiastical jargon, three of them clearly indicated their support for a program of socioeconomic transformation "in objectives as well as in means."[7] These pronouncements amounted to a declaration of support for a theological current that was then only in its infancy.

Gutiérrez was acutely aware at the time, however, that the liberationist movement lacked a developed explanation of its theological and socioeconomic perspective. He therefore gathered and edited the materials he had written for the ONIS and Medellín conferences, amplified his theological arguments, and presented the resulting draft at a 1969 meeting of SODEPAX (the Commission on Society, Development, and Peace, jointly sponsored by the World Council of Churches and the Pontifical Commission on Justice and Peace) in Cartigny, Switzerland. The following year, he appeared at a theological symposium in Bogotá with a draft of *A Theology of Liberation* in hand. The book finally appeared (in its Spanish edition) in 1971, announcing that a new kind of theology had begun to address the needs and experiences of the underclass from their own perspectives. In this epochal work, Gutiérrez explained that liberationism marked a new departure in theology because it began not with the disembodied agenda of first-world theology, but with the experience of God's presence among the poor.

A Theology of Liberation declared at the outset that it was a theological reflection "born of the experience of shared efforts to abolish the current unjust situation and to build a different society, freer and more human."[8] The language of rupture and transformation was joined with a conception of theology as a "second act" of reflection on liberating praxis. Using a Hegelian expression, Gutiérrez remarked that theology rises only at sundown. Liberation theology reflected the irruption of the poor into Latin American history, he asserted, presupposing a new interlocutor of religious meaning.[9]

This shift in perspective was the crucial feature of Gutiérrez's project. It has often been noted by such critics as Moltmann and Lonnie Kliever that the theological and socioeconomic arguments in *A Theology of Liberation* were not original.[10] Other readers such as Alfredo Fierro and Dennis McCann have further observed that much of the language and scriptural exegesis in the book were precritical.[11] The elaborate discussion of historical and eschatological consciousness that was contained in Gutiérrez's section "Eschatology and Politics," for example, was clearly dependent on the Blochian and Moltmannian dialectics of hope, and Gutiérrez's discussion of the exodus motif in Scripture was largely derived from Gerhard von Rad's theology of the Hebrew scriptures.[12]

To press this point as criticism of the book, however, is to misconstrue the nature of Gutiérrez's project. Gutiérrez has acknowledged that most of the theological and exegetical arguments in *A Theology of Liberation* were dependent on the work of others. For him, however, the point was not to come up with theological formulations that no one had ever thought of before; the point was to synthesize and express the spirituality of the emerging liberationist movement. As he later explained, "We have no stake in a reputation for intellectual originality. . . . What we care about is not a matter of 'having our own theology,' the way the petit bourgeois used to dream of having their own house someday. Such a dream does haunt the intellectual world. No, our concern is to establish the fact that theologies arise out of concrete historical ambiences, and then to go ahead and produce a theology out of our own ambience. Having our very own theology is thus of no importance."[13]

A Theology of Liberation therefore presented its essential points in a collective voice. When Gutiérrez took up the question of the ownership of the means of production, for example, he filled the entire section with quotations from the Medellín documents, the ONIS *Declaraciones*, the statements of Colombian and Chilean priests, and the manifestos of other Latin American liberationist organizations.[14] His purpose was not to hide behind these statements, but to stand in solidarity with them. Because he had already rejected the individualistic conception of authorship, it was unnecessary for Gutiérrez to confirm that he agreed with the assertion he quoted from the ONIS pronouncement that "we must opt for social ownership of the means of production."[15] *A Theology of Liberation* owed its considerable power to the fact that it reflected more than the opinions of a single author.

Gutiérrez insists that this shift in perspective distinguishes liberation theology from the progressive theologies of the past or present. Liberation theology does not seek to add a "social dimension" to an assumed structure of disembodied thought. Rather, in his reading, liberation theology reconceives theology itself in light of the interests and experiences of the poor, who "want to be the active subjects of their own history and to forge a radically different society."[16] Because the poor of Latin America seek to eradicate their misery, Gutiérrez has elsewhere argued, "they choose social revolution rather than reform, liberation rather than development, and socialism rather than liberalization. These options, which seem to the ruling classes utopian, are utterly rational to the oppressed."[17]

The disjuncture between liberationist and progressivist theologies is revealed, for Gutiérrez, in the fundamental questions that these theologies address. Modern progressive theology, beginning with Schleiermacher, has been preoccupied with questions posed by the Enlightenment, historical criticism, science, and technology. The critical questions of unbelievers — as in Schleiermacher's addresses to the "cultured critics of religion" — have set the agenda for modern theological scholarship.[18] Gutiérrez does not criticize this intellectual tradition. His own work has been decisively influenced by the most progressive forms of modern European theology, especially the work of Moltmann, Johannes Metz, and Edward Schillebeeckx. He only observes that the problems of first-world theologies do not reflect the concerns of the marginalized people who have created liberation theology. For them, the fundamental theological questions are how to be a person and believe in a personal God in a world that grotesquely represses their personhood. "The question is not how we are to talk about God in a world come of age," Gutiérrez asserts, "but how we are to tell people who are scarcely human that God is love and that God's love makes us one family. The interlocutors of liberation theology are the nonpersons, the humans who are not considered human by the dominant social order — the poor, the exploited classes, the marginalized races, all the despised cultures. Liberation theology categorizes people not as believers or unbelievers, but as oppressors or oppressed."[19] Viewed from the perspective of the oppressed, he observes, the most cherished articles of the progressivist faith — including the liberal conception of democracy and the progressivist "opposition" to violence — often appear in a different light.[20] Gutiérrez's argument on the question of violence begins with the assertion that, contrary to its image, liberation theology is motivated by a profound abhorrence of violence. It is personally distressing to Gutiérrez that liberation theology is so often portrayed as a theology that advocates violence, and he is frequently challenged to defend his position by critics who presume that they "oppose violence" more than he does.

Gutiérrez counters that one of the goals of the liberationist movement is to break the vicious cycles of systemic violence that pervade Latin American societies. For Gutiérrez, the problem with the question of violence is that it is repeatedly framed in a way that places the burden of moral judgment on the victims of violence. He distinguishes among three types of violence, defining *institutionalized* violence as the structural oppression of existing social orders and *repressive* violence as the means by which oppressive regimes are maintained. The third form of violence in Gutiérrez's typology is the *counterviolence* of the oppressed.[21]

The idea of institutionalized violence is the key to this typology. Gutiérrez's native country provides a case study in the concept. Peru's small mestizo ruling class has hoarded the country's wealth for the past century, and more recently has buried its prospects for economic growth under $14 billion of modernization debts. Because most of the country's debt is structured like variable rate mortgages, with interest percentages tied to fluctuations in the U.S. prime rate, the compounding of inflated interest rates has run the national debt far beyond the original principal. In a country where half the population is hungry and lacking in medical care and where the infant mortality rate is 127 per thousand, nearly 70 percent of the nation's export earnings over the past decade have been used to pay the interest on modernization loans. The debt has become literally unpayable, amounting to more than four times the nation's annual export earnings. To Gutiérrez, the burden of debt repayment on the backs of the poor—who did not ask for skyscrapers or modernized airports—is the culmination of a long history of systemic violence under which the majority of Peruvians have worked to serve the interests of a privileged minority. The debt burden is a form of violence not only because it has materially impoverished the lives of millions of people already living at the edge of starvation but also because it has eviscerated any hope they may have sustained for economic development in the future.[22]

Gutiérrez has concluded that the possibility of redistributing the country's wealth by a program of economic and political reform "is no longer believable after the experience of many attempts at 'reform' in Latin America."[23] Now that economic modernization has exacerbated the maldistribution of wealth in Latin America and intensified the suffering of those whom he calls "the marginalized," Gutiérrez argues that the options have narrowed. Because the most vicious forms of violence are embedded in the socioeconomic structures of Latin American societies, he contends, and because these structures are reinforced by military and paramilitary violence, the right of the oppressed to resort to counter-violence must be upheld. While the decision to engage in revolutionary violence can only be justified if it represents a last resort, he explains, as a last resort it is nothing less than a moral right.[24]

Gutiérrez's rejection of theological progressivism extends to what he calls, with a touch of sarcasm, "the sacred principles of bourgeois democracy."[25] In response to Jürgen Moltmann's critique of liberation theology, which faulted the liberationists' apparent lack of concern for political liberty and democracy, Gutiérrez has insisted that the question of democracy is far more ambiguous from the perspective of the oppressed. On the one hand, he argues, the goal of the liberationist project is to obtain "real democracy and liberty" for the common people of Latin America; yet on the other hand, the historical record of North American and European conduct toward Latin America reveals that "democratic" rhetoric has often been a smokescreen for economic exploitation and even military intervention. Given that the United States is the great bastion of democratic values in the world, Gutiérrez declares, the historical Latin American experience of subjection to U.S. interests—and occasional invasions—has "made us wary of bourgeois society's lies" and skeptical of the sacredness of bourgeois democratic principles.[26]

Gutiérrez acknowledges that the bourgeois revolution was truly a movement for freedom in parts of the first world, and he therefore concedes that progressivist theologians are accurately describing their *own* experience when they celebrate the values of liberal democracy. But the problem with bourgeois civilization, he asserts, is that it was built upon, and continues to be sustained by, the exploitation of dependent countries. "Today we clearly see that what was a movement for liberty in some parts of the world, when seen from the other side of the world, from beneath, from the popular classes, only meant new and refined forms of exploitation of the very poorest—of the wretched of the earth." For the poor, he argues, what is needed today is nothing less than a complete break from the reformist palliatives of bourgeois politics. "For them, the attainment of freedom can only be the result of a process of liberation from the spoliation and oppression being carried on in the name of modern liberties and democracy."[27] Liberation theology does not cherish the political tradition of liberalism, because this tradition has promoted the predatory system of capitalism for the past two centuries in the name of freedom. "This is why only a class analysis will permit us to see what is really at play in the opposition of oppressed countries and dominating countries," he insists. "All this will lead us to understand the social formation of Latin America as a dependent capitalism and to foresee the necessary strategy to get out of that situation."[28]

Gutiérrez's reference to "dependent capitalism" is taken from the theory of economic dependency first developed by Fernando Henrique Cardoso and Enzo Falleto in their classic neo-Marxist study, *Dependencia y Desarrollo en América Latina*.[29] Writing in 1969, Cardoso and Falleto argued that because the historical development of the world market had "created relationships of dependence (and domination) among nations" the developmentalist economic policies of the 1950s and after mainly exacerbated the problems they were designed to solve. Taking this analysis one step further, Gutiérrez interprets the "social formation of Latin America" as a process in which the first-world economic powers have used the "periphery" coun-

tries of Latin America as a foreign proletariat. Because it is in the nature
of capitalism to exploit the natural and human resources of vulnerable
nations, he argues, it is self-deceptive to think that any program of liberal
reformism can succeed in the third world. With the downfall of the Allende
government in Chile most clearly in mind, Gutiérrez has observed that the
international capitalist class is clearly unwilling to relinquish its control over
foreign markets, and that "the most trifling attempts" to institute reforms
"will be met without fail, in most countries, by the removal of capital,
business boycotts, disinvestment, promotion of black markets, and political
sabotage." The lesson is that reformist strategies are counterproductive.
"It is clear that international capital seeks countries that offer submissive-
ness and cheap labor," he writes, "and that when it does not find those
conditions in one country it goes elsewhere in search of better conditions
for exploitation, thereby destabilizing the regimes that tried the reforms."
Like his longtime friend and colleague, the Jesuit liberationist Juan Luis
Segundo, Gutiérrez therefore insists that whenever democratic governments in the dependent countries attempt to institute socioeconomic
reforms "all the mechanisms of democracy breed its destruction."[30]

Gutiérrez thus rejects the strategy of economic modernization on both
economic and political grounds. Since his socioeconomic analysis is based
on a form of dependency theory that José Míguez Bonino has developed
in much greater detail, my assessment of the strengths and weaknesses of
this theory will be reserved for chapter 6. In light of his severe indictment
of bourgeois democracy, however, and his repeated insistence that socialism
is the necessary alternative to the capitalist system, it is important to inquire
at this point what Gutiérrez means by "socialism."

The answer is surprisingly vague. Though he has offered voluminous
criticisms of the capitalist system, arguing that a socialist alternative is
required, Gutiérrez's descriptions of that alternative are cursory at best.
The only programmatic statement on the subject that can be found in any
of his works is Gutiérrez's repeated assertion that socialism calls for the
elimination of private ownership of the means of production. In *The Power
of the Poor in History*, for example, he advocates the elimination of "the
private appropriation of the wealth created by human toil" and asserts that
this goal can be achieved "only by installing a political power at the service
of the great popular majorities."[31]

Gutiérrez is clearly aware that this kind of rhetoric has repeatedly rationalized the imposition of totalitarian governments throughout the world in
the name of revolutionary need. On several occasions he has pointedly
disassociated himself from these revolutions, claiming that Latin American
socialism is an indigenous project "that is well aware of the deficiencies of
many of its own concrete forms in the world today." Beyond the vague
assurance that liberationist socialism must be different from the existing
"socialisms" of the Soviet or Maoist type, however, Gutiérrez does not
elaborate. While insisting that liberation theology must be a socialist pro-

ject, he does not explain—beyond the terms of one vague and highly problematic slogan about eliminating private control of production—what he
means by socialism.

Gutiérrez's justification for this failing has taken two forms. He has
argued on occasion that because the various liberationist movements of
Latin America are spread across numerous countries and rooted in profoundly different social contexts it would be seriously mistaken to define
what "socialism" should mean within any of these variable contexts. This
argument is irrefutable on one level, but unsatisfactory and evasive on a
deeper level. It is unarguably true that liberationist strategies and goals
must vary according to the highly differentiated circumstances in which
liberationist movements find themselves. Gutiérrez's insistence on this
point marks a decisive improvement over the ideological dogmatism that
has characterized most revolutionary movements of the past century. Yet
if "socialism" is to mean anything other than one's own immediate, undefined moral ideal, the term must be defined at least as clearly as one defines
capitalism, modernization, or liberalism. To insist on the necessity of a
socialist alternative without providing a basic explanation of the term is a
serious failing.

Gutiérrez's second justification of this failing is that it is not the business
of liberation theology to provide such an analysis. In *Liberation and Change*,
he argues that liberation theology "does not aim to be a revolutionary
Christian ideology" or a theological rationale for any given ideological commitment. Liberation theology does not begin with *a priori* ideological positions, he explains; rather, it begins with one's engagement in the concrete
and collective struggle for liberation. "It seeks to rethink the faith from the
perspective of that historical praxis," he says, "and it is based on the experience of the faith derived from the liberating commitment."[32] Liberation
theology is therefore tied only to the struggle for liberation, he argues, and
not to any *a priori* ideological notions.

Like his first argument, though, this justification is simultaneously true
and evasive. It accurately describes Gutiérrez's theological method, but it
evades the fact that Gutiérrez's writings are filled with ideological judgments and assertions. Though his work is not based on ideological commitments, Gutiérrez's dedication to the emancipation of the poor has led
him to reject emphatically a series of ideological positions and embrace an
undefined form of socialism. In this respect, Gutiérrez is similar to Marx;
he vehemently criticizes all of the alternatives to socialism while failing to
provide an equally serious discussion of socialism itself. The parallel should
be instructive, for it was precisely this failing of Marx's that has allowed
several generations of totalitarians to call themselves Marxists.

The subject is especially serious because Gutiérrez, like Marx, has
repeatedly called for the elimination of private ownership of the means of
production. As the history of Marxism attests, this is a slogan that can
justify anything. It ignores the most basic distinctions between large and

small enterprises, as well as the differences among the various forms of economic socialization. Most important, it ignores the question of the relationship between democratic freedom and socialism.

These are weaknesses that Gutiérrez unfortunately shares with Segundo, the Uruguayan liberationist whose friendship with Gutiérrez dates back to their student days at Louvain. Next to Gutiérrez, Segundo is the most influential theologian that the liberationist movement has produced. In his frequently reprinted essay "Capitalism versus Socialism: Crux Theologica," Segundo has starkly defined capitalism as "a political regime in which the ownership of the goods of production is left open to economic competition," and socialism as "a political regime in which the ownership of the means of production is taken away from individuals and handed over to higher institutions whose main concern is the higher good."[33] He argues that these (actually outdated) definitions are clearer than the alternatives; but their use also serves his more subtle purpose of placing all social-democratic strategies within the capitalist camp.

Segundo declares, "Today the only thing we can do is to decide whether or not we are going to give individuals or private groups the right to own the means of production that exist in our countries." That, he asserts, is "the option between capitalism and socialism."[34] He offers no calculation of the amount of centralized planning, or the economic costs, or the implications for freedom that this program would entail. Nor does he draw any distinction between essential and nonessential means of production, or between large and small firms, or between centralized and decentralized forms of socialization. In sweeping, proto-Marxist fashion, he focuses on the necessity of collective ownership and assumes that socialism is fundamentally a program of economic nationalization.

The missing alternative in Gutiérrez's and Segundo's discussions of socialism is modern democratic socialism, which advocates decentralized forms of socialization and mixed economic ownership while accepting the necessity of the market system.[35] This omission is particularly curious in light of the fact that it is precisely the decentralized, cooperative form of socialism that the base communities of Latin America continually struggle for. The fundamental idea of modern democratic socialism is to fulfill the democratic revolution by struggling for popular sovereignty over all political, civil, and economic systems. The object is not to nationalize business and financial interests, but to attain democratic control over them through worker ownership, reorganized pension funds, expanded cooperatives, and collective capital funds. Though the praxis of communitarian socialism must take place on a comparatively primitive level in the third world, involving far lower levels of organizational, financial, and technological complexity than in the first world, the efforts of the Latin American base communities are struggles toward the same essential goal of economic self-determination. The unfortunate aspect of Gutiérrez's and Segundo's work is that, though they are deeply involved in the communitarian praxis of the base communities, their discussions of political economics do not reflect this engagement. They recycle the collectivist rhetoric of Marxism rather than defend the principles and ongoing praxis of economic democracy. In this area, though they have insisted that liberation theology must reflect the praxis of a prior personal commitment, their writings reflect the overriding influence of an ideological tradition more than the lessons of their own experience.

While they share similar conceptions of socialism, however, the differences between the theologies of Gutiérrez and Segundo are otherwise very considerable, marking the essential differences between the two primary forms of liberation theology. I will argue that the crucial question for the future of the liberationist movement is whether it will be Gutiérrez's or Segundo's conception of the project that will prevail as the liberationist viewpoint.

In his seminal work *The Liberation of Theology*, Segundo reinterprets the Bultmannian concept of the hermeneutical circle as "the continuing change in our interpretation of the Bible which is dictated by the continuing changes in our present-day reality, both individual and societal."[36] Like Moltmann, Segundo begins with and emphatically rejects Bultmann's individualistic program of theological interpretation, but Segundo goes well beyond Moltmann in interpreting "societal" reality in terms of political need. He criticizes the intellectual tradition of modernity from an explicitly revolutionary standpoint, arguing that the process of interpretation in Western social science has traditionally been "interrupted" by the Western academic devotion to ideological neutrality. Segundo pointedly criticizes Max Weber and Karl Mannheim for refusing to commit themselves to liberation as the highest value, and he argues that even Marx failed to sustain a liberationist hermeneutic when he examined the phenomenon of religion. Instead of considering how religion might serve the revolutionary ends of the class struggle, Segundo observes, Marx dogmatically assumed that religion should be abolished. Segundo argues that Marx allowed his own philosophical views to "interrupt" his engagement with the practical needs of the revolutionary struggle, and therefore failed to consider "whether a new interpretation favoring the class struggle of the proletariat might be possible or even necessary."[37]

"Even necessary" is Segundo's own thesis. Because atheism is alien to popular Latin American culture, Segundo argues that a reassessment of the religious issue *is* necessary for Marxist movements in Latin America. He implies that antireligious movements tend to be sectarian affairs, carried out by elites who speak for "the people," but whom most of the people distrust. Though he elsewhere defends the necessity of elite vanguards, on other grounds, within revolutionary movements, Segundo is sharply critical of the self-defeating atheism within Marxist ideology, which repels the very masses whom Marx sought to mobilize. Instead of asking himself how religion might serve the revolution, Segundo argues, Marx "interrupted" his commitment to praxis when he assessed religion, and disastrously dismissed the whole phenomenon as a haven for the heartbroken and as a drug for those in misery.[38]

Segundo's example of a fully liberationist interpretation of religion is the work of the North American theologian James Cone. The content of Cone's theology may or may not be true, Segundo avers, but in Cone's method Segundo recognizes an approach similar to his own in which the primary purpose of theology is to promote the social liberation of a particular community in the name of religion. For Cone, that community is the black race.[39] Without apology or equivocation, Cone declares that black theology is not accountable to any doctrinal criterion, authority, or organization except the black community. The only truth, as Segundo remarks, is "the truth of liberation itself as defined by the oppressed in their struggle."[40] The moral implication of this commitment is that a liberationist ethic must be specifically contextual in nature, for, as Cone explains, "The revolutionary situation forces Black Theology to shun all abstract principles dealing with what is the 'right' and 'wrong' course of action. There is only one principle which guides the thinking and action of Black Theology: an unqualified commitment to the black community as that community seeks to define its existence in the light of God's liberating work in the world."[41]

Cone therefore interprets the classical Christian doctrines of sin, redemption, grace, eschatology, and divine reality by their significance for the victims of history, especially the black race. His methodological liberationism leads him to reject the idea of universal truth, as well as classical creedal statements about divine universality, and leads him, further, to claim that black people are not meant by God to follow the way of the cross. Cone acknowledges that the concept of redemptive suffering is central to the postexilic and messianic biblical literature, which culminates in the Christian church's theology of the cross, but because he considers this concept hostile to the concrete interests of black people, he argues that it has no rightful place in a black theology. Asserting that blacks are "the chosen" of God, Cone declares that God "has chosen them not for redemptive suffering but for freedom. Black people are not elected to be Yahweh's suffering people."[42] In this way, Cone freely reinterprets the meaning of Christian ideas to serve the cause of black revolution.

While it is always a matter of judgment whether a given interpretation is *actually* the most useful or liberating one, Cone's work *is* methodologically consistent in subjecting every theological subject to a political test. Segundo therefore approvingly cites Cone's theology as an example of authentic liberationism, with one caveat. Segundo notes that he sometimes disagrees with Cone's interpretations of Scripture, but concedes that these are matters of individual judgment. The aspect of Cone's theology that Segundo finds unsettling is his outright rejection of the concept of redemptive suffering. He acknowledges that this idea has often served the interests of oppressors throughout church history, but because the way of Christ was unarguably the way of redemptive suffering, Segundo questions whether a theology of the *Christian* faith can plausibly dispense with the idea, for any reason. Segundo observes that Christ himself was chosen for freedom, yet also for redemptive suffering; thus, he asks, "What about Jesus himself?" Segundo implies that although Cone is on the right track methodologically, he lacks a theory that could deal with problems of this kind. Segundo's own solution is to argue that all ideologies, including the ideology of Jesus, are historically conditioned and relevant only to the circumstances within their own social and historical contexts. Thus, "turn the other cheek" is a relevant ideological maxim in some contexts, and an irrelevant or mistaken one in others. As we shall see, Segundo is prepared to press this argument to extraordinary lengths.

But the appeal to historical or ideological relativism does not dispose of the idea of redemptive suffering, for as even Segundo suggests, the cross of Christ has more than an ideological meaning. Even if one were to accept Segundo's argument that all of the teachings of Jesus are ideological and therefore relative in value to their context, the symbolic or doctrinal significance of the cross could not be relativized on the same ground. Segundo seems to have grasped this, in his expression of uneasiness with Cone's Christology, but he fails to acknowledge the implications for his own position. The redemptive way of suffering love, as revealed ultimately in the cross, is intrinsic to any authentically Christian theology. The meaning of the cross is always politically relevant, but it also transcends the importance of ideologies of all kinds, since Christ is more than the bearer of an ideology.

In his uneasiness with Cone, Segundo *seems* to have perceived that some limit on ideological criticism is necessary in theology, yet he fails to draw that conclusion, because such a concession would undermine his own method. Segundo raises the question of a limit on ideology and then summarily "leaves it aside," as he says, in order to conclude with an endorsement of Cone's thoroughgoing liberationism.[43] But the question he leaves hanging is the objection that undercuts his own hermeneutical argument. Segundo perceives that some limit on the politicization of theology is necessary if Christian theology is to remain *Christian* in any meaningful sense. But all limits that one might propose would be extrinsic norms or doctrines, which is exactly the idea that Segundo and Cone reject at the outset. According to their hermeneutic, in which "the only truth is liberation itself," Cone is fully justified when he reinterprets the faith according to a political criterion. Segundo raises an important question about this method and then abandons it, for to pursue the question would require him to either revise his method or to accept Cone's total politicization of theology.

But Segundo does neither. His (purely verbal) solution to the dilemma trades heavily on the concept of ideology, which he defines as "the system of goals and means that serves as the necessary backdrop for any human option or line of action." That is, ideology is "a concrete system conditioned by history" that must be distinguished from faith.[44] Segundo asserts that faith *is* distinct from ideology, and claims that this distinction can save liberation theology from being totally identified with or determined by revolutionary politics.

As an example of the total politicization that liberationists should avoid, he has repeatedly cited the work of the Brazilian liberationist Hugo Assmann. In his foundational study, *Opresión-Liberación: Desafío a los cristianos*, Assmann argued that the political significance of faith is not something additional to faith, but is rather the "act of faith as such in its concrete context of historical praxis."[45] Segundo first criticized this position in his early work *Masas y minorías en la dialéctica divina de la liberación*, arguing that Assmann had reduced Christian theology to his own ideology of revolution.[46] In his subsequent writings, Segundo has aptly observed that the relationship between faith and ideology is the fundamental theoretical problem for liberation theology, which the liberationist movement continually faces in multivarious ways. He has bitterly observed, for example, that although the Vatican constantly criticizes liberation theology for its ideological character, the worldview of the church hierarchy itself is deeply ideological, even in the narrow political sense of the term. The most ironic contradictions in the church's official pose have been effectively noted in Segundo's polemical response to Vatican criticism, *Theology and the Church*.[47]

Segundo takes the underlying issue too seriously, however, to content himself with easy polemical victories. In *The Liberation of Theology* he notes that various liberationists have conceded the point that "faith is not an ideology" — and then insisted that what is *needed* is a liberationist ideology. As Segundo rightly observes, however, the crucial question for any of these theologians concerns the *content* of faith. Most liberationists still operate within the mainstream of the Christian theological tradition. Jon Sobrino's doctrinal arguments are so traditional, for example, and his references to revolutionary conscientization are so incidental, that Dennis McCann has classified him as a "European" theologian who happens to live in El Salvador.[48] Here, as elsewhere, McCann exaggerates, but he has correctly identified the dispute over politicization ("conscientization") as the fundamental dilemma of liberation theology. The question, which is crucial for both theological and political reasons, is whether liberation theology is to remain a movement within the mainstream of the historic Christian churches or become a sectarian movement outside of them. More than any other liberationist, Segundo represents the cutting edge of the question, which ultimately asks whether liberationism can accept any external limit on its ideological redefinition of faith.

Although McCann and others have portrayed Segundo as a Leninist who rationalizes the mendacity and violence of revolutionary vanguard organizations, Segundo has always rejected the equation of Marxism with faith, and in recent years he has pointedly criticized the self-delusions of those whom he calls "the high priests of the guerrilla movement."[49] He has strongly criticized guerrilla strategies on practical grounds, noting especially that guerrilla warfare destroys the very network of social relationships that all civilized societies, including postrevolutionary societies, require. Thus, McCann's portrait of Segundo is somewhat overdrawn, since Segundo is outspokenly critical of the ravages of guerrilla violence and of those who assume that only Leninist strategies are viable or worthwhile. Segundo relies heavily upon Lenin's *What Is To Be Done?* in his analysis of the problem of inertia among the Latin American masses, but, as his recent writings confirm, that does not necessarily make him a dogmatic advocate of Leninist tactics, or even of a Communist interpretation of the Christian faith.

It is also true, however, that Segundo's theological position is substantively and programmatically sectarian, and that it effectively rationalizes a form of ecclesiological and political vanguardism. While he protects his claim to orthodoxy by disassociating himself from Assmann and by invoking the distinction between faith and ideology, Segundo defines *faith* in a way that completely subjects it to ideological control. That is, his concept of faith is too empty to impose a limit on anything.

Segundo distinguishes between the substantive *content* of religious ideas and the *learning process* implicit within these ideas. The former he calls ideologies, which are historically conditioned and relative, and therefore authoritative only within their own specific contexts. The latter he calls faith. Faith has no content of its own, but is rather the unending process through which ideologies are created and developed. He explains, "Faith, by contrast, is the total process to which man submits, a process of learning in and through ideologies how to create the ideologies needed to handle new and unforeseen situations in history."[50] For Segundo, the problem with traditional concepts of faith is that all of them presuppose that faith must have some substantive content, which is based on some version of a "deposit" or foundation of doctrine. His alternative rejects all forms of doctrinal foundationalism. Faith is not bound to any idea except the idea of liberation. To have faith, therefore, is to commit oneself to the process of historical transformation, through which appropriate ideologies are created and developed. "While faith certainly is not an ideology," Segundo explains, "it has sense and meaning only insofar as it serves as the foundation stone for ideologies."[51]

Faith is foundational, however, only in the sense that it is the name given to the human desire for useful ideologies. Rejecting the traditional presupposition that religious faith should be *about* something, Segundo emphatically asserts: "What, then, does the faith say to me in the concrete? What is its truth *content*? If I remain logically consistent in deducing conclusions from the above principles, then my only response can be nothing."[52] Faith cannot possibly limit or control the politicization of theology, since faith only exists within ideologies as the generative desire for the best ideology.

Segundo's interpretation of the function of the Holy Spirit exemplifies his overall theological program. Because he defines faith as the process of learning to learn the most appropriate ideologies, his Christology emphasizes the role of Christ as teacher. The mission of Christ, in his interpretation, was primarily pedagogical. But after the church lost its teacher, Segundo asserts, under historical circumstances in which the actual teachings of Christ were no longer entirely meaningful or appropriate, the church's loss was compensated by its experience of the Holy Spirit. Throughout the subsequent course of church history, Segundo explains, the Spirit of Christ has educated human hearts through an internal process of illumination, without providing new information, "as the pupil confronts reality with new ideologies." According to Segundo, the purpose of the Spirit has always been to energize and direct the human movement toward liberation, using the only effective means that exist. "And those means are nothing else but a succession of ideologies vis-à-vis the concrete problems of history."[53] The mission of the Spirit, therefore, is always to direct human faith (the contentless desire for appropriate ideologies) toward the most contextually useful ideologies.

Segundo thus identifies liberationist theological interpretation with the ends of conscientization. Most liberationists, such as Gutiérrez and Míguez Bonino, continue to assume that liberation theology must attempt to correlate the socioeconomic and spiritual themes of the Christian scriptures and tradition. For Segundo, however, liberation is everything. He does not correlate historical liberation and spiritual salvation, or move from scriptural text to historical situation. He identifies salvation with liberation and rejects any aspect of Christian scripture or tradition that does not appear to serve the ends of his ideological program. Just as he insists on a completely ideological interpretation of faith, he argues that the entire content of Scripture is ideological. The value of Scripture for liberation theology, in his reading, is therefore limited to the pedagogical intent of the whole scriptural process.[54]

Faith is thus reduced to a "pedagogical interest" that can only be discovered through the process of ideological construction and engagement. Since faith is nothing without an ideology and the church contains many ideologies, Segundo concludes that "a common faith does not exist within the church. The only thing shared in common is the formula used to express that faith. And since the formula does not really identify anything, are we not justified in calling it a *hollow* formula vis-à-vis the decisive options of history?" He concedes that faith may bring us to a given understanding of divine reality, but Segundo argues that the "empty space" between our religious ideas (which are ideological) and the problems of the real world can only be bridged by an adequate ideology.[55] Faith itself is literally meaningless except insofar as it facilitates the development of worthwhile ideologies.

Segundo contends that most liberationist theologies are overly theocentric. In his view, this criticism applies even to the extreme historicism of Rubem Alves and the theology of revolution advanced by Richard Shaull, which both take refuge in some form of Lutheran dualism as soon as one asks: through whom or what is the Kingdom coming? For Alves and Shaull, he claims, as for most liberationists, only God is ultimately the subject of the new future in process. In the name of "faith," most liberationists refuse to identify any specific movement or ideology with the work of the Spirit.

Segundo argues that the same religious caution has been displayed by the Roman Catholic bishops of Chile under the Pinochet regime. While Chileans have suffered the unspeakable abuse and contempt of the Pinochet government, Segundo observes, the Chilean bishops have proclaimed themselves to be on the side of "the risen Christ." They have hidden behind the self-deception that faith exists outside of ideologies and have therefore evaded their apostolic mission under a regime that deserves prophetic criticism and opposition. In the same way, Segundo unfairly argues, for all of their impassioned theorizing about the dawn of a new messianic humanism, Alves and Shaull have failed the test of authentically liberationist criticism, because they have refused to identify any particular historical movement with the inbreaking kingdom. This kind of evasion, he laments, "can only produce despair in the Latin American."[56]

Segundo offers an alternative. Liberation theology can only liberate *itself*, he argues, if it first renounces the "verbal terrorism" by which the term "sect" has acquired a negative connotation. He notes that the New Testament used the word *sect* to designate the nascent Christian church, which was, after all, originally a sect within Judaism. But as the Christian church eventually became integrated into the culture of the Roman empire, it took on the features of a "world religion," which were subsequently enshrined by Catholic dogma. The church increasingly assumed the identity of a universal religious and even political institution, and conceived its mission as a call to protect and propagate the universal deposit of revelation with which it was entrusted. One ideological consequence of this shift, Segundo observes, was that successive generations of Christians came to associate the characteristics of a world religion with the *church*, even though the biblical concept of the church was sectarian. "The unconscious power of language affected people's outlook. Since 'the church' was viewed as the direct opposite of a 'sect,' it would have to possess just the opposite traits."[57] Thus the process of catholicization completely inverted the original meaning of the term *church* and effectively condemned any movement or idea that could be called sectarian.

Segundo recalls all of this in order to reclaim the sectarian heritage of Christianity, with which he identifies. He claims that the actual "tradition of Christ and his message" are preserved in this heritage, but his main argument for sectarianism is not staked on biblical grounds. Dissenting from the liberationist Christologies of Gutiérrez and Sobrino, among others, Segundo remarks that one *could* build a theological position on a liberationist reading of Scripture, but only if one were willing "to go in for a great deal of abstraction" and a "terrible process of mutilating" the scriptures. He implies that liberation theologies are often based upon precritical exegeses of Scripture and are therefore easily shredded on historical-critical grounds.[58] Not wishing to add to this kind of literature, Segundo bases his argument for ecclesiological sectarianism on political grounds.

The reason why the original, biblical image of the church is relevant for our times, he argues, is that "the masses" have been integrated more or less successfully into the culture of technological civilization. Segundo conceives the Christian base communities as potential seedbeds of revolt against this system, which has stripped periphery nations of their scarce resources and forced them into new forms of dependency. Unlike churches of the "universal religious" type, which are integrated (and therefore co-opted) into the socioeconomic systems of the superpowers, sectarian churches are less dependent upon the system's economic interests or its capacity to confer institutional or cultural respectability. By virtue of their relative independence and their alienation from the dominant socioeconomic system, Segundo argues that sectarian communities are strategically positioned to agitate for a revolution "that will thoroughly and radically humanize the social structures" of the dependent countries. He contends that because Latin America is on the periphery of modern capitalist civilization the continent itself is strategically positioned to become the "fermenting ground" for a new conception of the mission of the Christian church.[59] Elsewhere he insists that wherever the church commits itself to revolutionary praxis the church *itself* must become transformed in the process, because it surely cannot be an agent of liberation in the modern world while working with "the same concept of God, sin, sacrament and church membership that was part of a church centered around the quest for extraterrestrial salvation."[60]

Just as the Western church of the fourth century adopted a new identity to accommodate the political challenge of its time, Segundo argues that churches of the modern age must face up to a similar crisis of identity brought about by the contradictions in liberal civilization. In the modern age, however, the kind of transformation that the church needs is wholly dissimilar to the Constantinian settlement. He asserts that the institutional churches are largely failing to confront the political challenge of our time, mainly because they are deeply integrated into the modern system and therefore too compromised to oppose it. What is needed, in this situation, are communities of faith that have assumed the identity and mission of revolutionary vanguards. Segundo does not fudge the meaning or implications of his vanguardist language. Quoting Shaull, he emphatically asserts that, as in revolutions of the past, the liberationist revolution "will depend upon a vanguard that is free to see what is happening, discern the shape of the future, and accept a new vocation over against the system."[61]

This is a position on the far side of the liberationist movement. Segundo is unlike the "high priests of the guerrilla movement" in his willingness to criticize *all* ideological strategies, but in his advocacy of ecclesiological and political vanguardism, as well as in his reductionistic definition of faith, he has promulgated a deracinated and ultimately sectarian vision of the church. In his mind, his extremism is the only realistic approach in a revolutionary situation. He believes that most liberationists have indulged in illusions about the authority of Scripture and tradition, the "deposit" of doctrine, the complementarity of liberation and salvation, the prospects for political change, and the function of the base communities.

His extreme theological relativism leads to the historicist agnosticism of Rubem Alves—whom he incredibly charges with theocentrism—except for one claim. Like Alves, Segundo relativizes the import of all theological precepts in order to establish a single absolute, which is revolutionary need. Unlike Alves, however, Segundo makes univocal religious claims for this absolute. In his early work, *A Theology of Human Hope*, Alves acknowledged that all liberationist claims are historical and therefore relative, and further lamented that the future, "once it is brought about by the revolutionaries, tends to become closed, because it is believed that it is the presence of the *eschaton*." Alves thus argued that a critical liberation theology must be critical of all religious claims, especially those that promote revolution, because otherwise liberation theology is easily reduced to rationalizations for left-wing authoritarianism. Christian revolutionaries who identify the presence of the kingdom with some form of historical liberation, he asserted, eviscerate their critical sensibility at the very time it is most needed. "That is why revolutions that were once the bearers of new hopes become crystallized, rigid, and dogmatic, a veritable resurrection of the sins of the conservative," he wrote.[62] Alves thus insisted that the relationship between revolutionary praxis and the movement of the Spirit must be assessed from the same critical viewpoint by which liberationists criticized capitalism or traditional theology.

It is axiomatic within modern critical theology that all religious language is symbolic. The relationship between praxis and the kingdom has therefore been interpreted symbolically in modern theology as an "anticipation" (Moltmann), or "analogical image" (Rudolf Weth), or "outline" (Johannes Metz). Unlike these theologians, Alves unfortunately adopted an extreme version of historicism, which, as his recent works confirm, has undercut his faith and his attempt to make religion politically meaningful.[63] But his work has nonetheless had the virtue of methodological consistency, because he has used the razor of historical criticism across the range of theological subjects.

The same cannot be said of Segundo, who uses an equally extreme form of historicist explanation in his theology, only to drop the razor altogether when he discusses the relation of the Spirit to revolutionary praxis. That is, Segundo offers an extremely critical, historical interpretation of religious ideas, insisting that all theological concepts are historical and therefore ideological, until he arrives at the question of revolutionary need. Then, for the sake of revolutionary ends, he makes univocal religious claims, explicitly identifying the kingdom with revolutionary praxis. "For who dedicates their life to an analogy?" he asks. "Who dies for an outline? Who motivates a human mass or a people in the name of an anticipation?"[64] Segundo thus insists that liberationist theologies must not be based upon symbols. Christians will fight and die for a cause, he asserts, if that cause is identified with the will of God; but no one will fight for an analogy. Segundo concedes that to equate the will of God with revolutionary praxis is not to claim that the kingdom is *fully* revealed in praxis. The eschatological kingdom is only revealed in a "partial, fragmentary" way in revolutionary praxis, he explains; but for the sake of revolutionary need, which is the only absolute, liberation theologies must identify concrete, revolutionary movements with the kingdom.[65]

For Segundo, the contradictory shift from historicism to precritical univocalism is made necessary by the logic of revolutionary need. The only kind of theology that can actually serve revolutionary need, he asserts, is one that sacralizes revolutionary action. By this logic, submission to any other kind of consistency is idolatrous. While he defends this position on practical grounds, one practical problem with his argument is that "a human mass" of Latin Americans will not likely "dedicate their lives" to a religion that has been reduced to revolutionary politics. To reach a critical mass of Latin American Christians, liberation theology must represent more than the political strategies of an educated vanguard. Against the kind of position that Segundo has promoted, therefore, Gutiérrez has repeatedly insisted that liberation theology must not reduce itself to "baptizing political revolutions."[66]

Though the theologies of Gutiérrez and Segundo are similar in their appeals to experience and solidarity, their rejection of liberal reformism, and their conceptions of socialism, Gutiérrez does not share Segundo's sectarianism or his theological reductionism. While Segundo has insisted that the "manipulative influences" of revolutionary elites are central to the praxis of liberationism, Gutiérrez has avoided both religious and political vanguardism. Arguing that it is a mistake to sacralize any political ideology or strategy, Gutiérrez has asserted that "there is close relationship but no identification" between authentic liberationist praxis and the inbreaking reign of God.[67]

For Gutiérrez, the purpose of liberation theology is not to sacralize or rationalize any particular form of political engagement. Rather, he has explained, "Our concern is only for a deep, fruitful fidelity to a way of living the faith in the midst of the struggle of the poor for their liberation." Rejecting Segundo's insistence on the necessity of "manipulative influences" that will "further the reflective progress of the community," Gutiérrez has repeatedly argued that theology must *reflect* and learn from the praxis of existing communities. Unlike Segundo, Gutiérrez has avoided the rhetoric of manipulation and conceived liberation theology as a project within the mainstream of the Christian theological tradition. And unlike both Segundo and Míguez Bonino, Gutiérrez has never scorned popular Latin American religion or assumed that the faith of the masses is too backward to be socially generative. He has tirelessly insisted that liberation theology must emerge directly from the experience of the oppressed, and has thus observed that, unlike academic theology, liberation theology "will not sound nice, and it will not smell good."[68]

Gutiérrez's pietism does not prevent him from engaging in political organizing. In the Peruvian national context, he is aligned with the United Left, a coalition of Marxist parties that represents the second largest electoral constituency in the country. As an electoral force in national Peruvian politics, the United Left has vied for power in recent years with the American Popular Revolutionary Alliance (APRA), the social-democratic party founded in 1924 by the populist writer and contemporary of Mariátegui, Victor Haya de la Torre. While Gutiérrez is ideologically identified with the United Left, he has worked to promote a more populist, grass-roots strategy within both the APRA and United Left movements. "In the United States, I am called theologian," he has observed. "In Peru, I am activist."[69]

Like most liberationists, however, Gutiérrez rejects the notion that a commitment to revolutionary praxis requires a totally politicized theology. Henri Nouwen has aptly noted that Gutiérrez's theology is based upon his profound experience of the ever-gracious love of God, revealed in Christ through solidarity with the poor. "As one who has been exposed to many styles of theological liberalism," Nouwen remarks, "I am struck by the orthodoxy of this Christ-centered spirituality."[70] Gutiérrez has characterized the liberationist project as a collective effort to follow Christ in a world of oppression. Because the Latin American church never went through a modernistic phase, he observes, it has been possible in recent years for the church to produce figures like Oscar Romero, who rediscovered the meaning of his faith while retaining a rather traditional theology. Gutiérrez notes that it was Romero's religious faith—his deep commitment to the way of Christ—that gave him the courage to denounce the exploitation and oppression of the Salvadoran people. In his recent meditation on what it means to follow Christ in the modern world, Gutiérrez repeatedly cites the life and thought of Romero as exemplary for the modern church. "The world of the poor teaches us the form Christian love must take," Romero once remarked, "that it must indeed be gratuitous but that it must also seek to be effective in history."[71] This statement expresses Gutiérrez's own spirituality as well, which is fed, as Nouwen has observed, by his devotion to Christ and by the religious experiences of the saints.

In his recent writings Gutiérrez has plainly described, without referring to Marxism or sociological theory, the spiritual characteristics of liberationism. "It may seem somewhat reckless to speak of a spirituality taking shape amid the Latin American poor," he has written, "but that is precisely what is happening as I see it. . . . The process of liberation is a global one that affects every dimension of the human. . . . What is happening among us today represents a departure from the beaten path; it also forces us to realize that the following of Jesus is not along a private route but is part of a collective enterprise. . . . It is a collective, ecclesial spirituality that, without losing anything of its universal perspective, is stamped with the religious outlook of an exploited and believing people."[72] Gutiérrez therefore insists that it is no longer sufficient for liberationists to talk about joining the poor in their struggle. The ecclesial objective of liberationism is no longer to be the church of the poor, but to become the poor church. As long as the church preserves its stake in the existing social system, he argues, it will be prevented by its own material and cultural self-interests from *actually* joining the oppressed in their struggle for liberation. Liberationism needs a theology of relinquishment. Just as Dietrich Bonhoeffer argued that the church must give away its holdings and become the servant of the world, rather than a principality ruling over it, Gutiérrez contends that the church must relinquish its desire for power and respect if it intends to collectively follow Christ.[73]

Critics of liberationism frequently assert that liberation theology represents a new form of Constantinianism, rationalizing a left-wing merger between politics and religion.[74] Unlike his more sectarian colleagues, Gutiérrez has always taken this critique seriously, conceding that it reflects an existing threat within the liberationist movement. He asserts that the most effective response that the liberationist movement could make to this threat, however, would be to *actually join* the poor in their struggle and become a poor church. "We believe that the best way to achieve this divestment of power is precisely by resolutely casting our lot with the oppressed and the exploited in the struggle for a more just society," he writes. "The groups that control economic and political power will not forgive the Church for this. They will withdraw their support, which is the principal source of the ambiguous social prestige which the Church enjoys in Latin America today."[75]

The standard objection to this prescription is that it forces the church to choose sides in a political struggle. In 1978, when the Preparatory Document for the 1979 CELAM III Conference in Puebla, Mexico attempted to avoid the issue of political choice, Gutiérrez was forced repeatedly to explain why the question of political choice was, in reality, unavoidable. His arguments on the subject, which were reprinted in *The Power of the Poor in History*, were first outlined in *A Theology of Liberation*. "It is not a question of whether the church should or should not use its influence in the Latin American revolutionary process," he wrote. "Rather, the question is in what direction and for what purpose is it going to use its influence: for or against the established order, to preserve the social prestige which comes with its ties to the groups in power or to free itself from that prestige with a break from these groups and with genuine service to the oppressed?"[76] The question that liberation theology poses to the church, in this reading, is not whether the church should take sides in the class struggle, but whether the church should *change* sides. The common argument that the church should be politically neutral, Gutiérrez has insisted, is functionally an argument for the status quo. The church does not actually avoid politics when it avoids making pronouncements on the subject of politics. "When I discovered that poverty was something to be fought against," Gutiérrez has recalled, "that poverty was structural, that poor people were a class and could organize, it became crystal clear that in order to serve the poor, one had to move into political action."[77] To avoid that commitment, he implies, is to abet the existing system of injustice from which the church presently derives indirect benefits.

It is a mark of Gutiérrez's own profound commitment that he continues to live and work in Rimac. He could easily spend the rest of his life giving well-paid lectures at universities around the world. He chooses instead to work as a pastor and activist in a Peruvian slum, taking instruction in the spirituality of liberation from those around him.

Like one of his mentors, the Peruvian novelist José María Arguedas, Gutiérrez has spent his adult life "struggling against death"; but, unlike Arguedas, Gutiérrez has been sustained in the struggle by his experience of grace. The novels of Arguedas (which are famous in Peru) are filled with riveting descriptions of the social and personal ravages of Latin American oppression. More than any other Peruvian author, Arguedas captured the complex mixtures of despair, resentment, dignity, and fraternity that mark the lives of the Peruvian underclass — as well as the overarching system of violence that enforces their conformity.[78] Near the end of his life, as he was writing his last novel and simultaneously planning his suicide, Arguedas read one of Gutiérrez's lectures and made arrangements to meet him.

They formed an unlikely friendship. The elderly anticlerical Arguedas recognized his own burning compassion for the poor in Gutiérrez, and thus allowed the young priest to be a pastor to him, despite his lack of faith. Near the end of his life, in 1969, as he was completing his final novel, Arguedas thanked Gutiérrez for his friendship and remarked what a blessing it had been to him "that we understand and see each other, together enjoying a light that no one can extinguish."[79] In the opening pages of his novel, however, Arguedas inserted an explanation of his suicide, which he fulfilled upon completing the manuscript. "I have struggled against death," he wrote in that book, "or at least I believe I have struggled against death, very straightforwardly, by writing this broken and querulous account."[80] Gutiérrez was devastated by the loss of this tortured friend, and, as in his earlier friendship with Camilo Torres, he was left with a powerful sense of appreciation and gratitude for his friend, while feeling as well that he needed to resist in himself the conclusion that Arguedas had reached.

In his work we see the liberationist option in its original and most unadulterated form. While others have equated liberationism with given ideological commitments, Gutiérrez has been resolute in his insistence that liberation theology must reflect the ongoing practice of solidarity with the poor without identifying liberation with any particular theory or programmatic strategy.

This approach has its limitations. Though he has vehemently expressed his rejection of capitalist modernization and liberal reformism, he has failed thus far—because of his wariness of ideological theory—to describe the "socialist project" he repeatedly commends. The result is a theology that is long on political criticism and moral eloquence, but short on the vision of what it is, within history, that is worth striving for.

Gutiérrez is aware of this shortcoming, but to those who raise it in criticism he responds, with a touch of sarcasm, that even the poor have the right to think. In his conception, it is not the task of liberation theology to offer a theory of socialism or to address the questions raised by historical criticism or by modern science.[81] The task of liberation theology is to reflect on the meaning of the effort to overcome oppression and to build the church from below. When Michael Novak journeyed to Brazil in 1985 to lecture against liberation theology, a protester in São Paulo held up a sign that read "Liberation theology is ours." That is the point.[82]

The Christian religion, as Gutiérrez has recalled, has been tied through most of its history to a culture, the Western culture; to a race, the white race; to a sex, the male sex; and to a class, the ruling class. Its history has therefore been written largely by the hands of white, western, bourgeois males. To regain the memory of what it means to follow Christ, Gutiérrez has asserted, the church "must regain the memory of the 'beaten Christs of the Indies' as Bartolome de Las Casas called the Indians of the American continent. . . . It is a memory of Christ present in every person who is humbled, thirsty, hungry, in prison, present in the despised races, in the exploited classes."[83]

In this memory of Christ, he concludes, we find the basis for the liberationist option for the poor, which is rooted not in ideology or even in human compassion, but in God's own goodness.[84] If Gutiérrez has left much of the socioeconomic work to others, including José Míguez Bonino, it is because he is ultimately preoccupied with the recollection of Christ in the spiritual struggles of the exploited.

6

José Míguez Bonino and the Underside of Modernity

One of the most active participants in the Christian-Marxist dialogue, the French Marxist Roger Garaudy, has asserted that dialogue between Christians and Marxists is not an end in itself, but a project that leads to concrete cooperation in the modern struggle against capitalism. José Míguez Bonino has observed, however, that in Latin America the sequence has been reversed. Dialogue has not led to concrete cooperation; rather, revolutionary cooperation between Christians and Marxists has led to a subsequent mutual interest in formal dialogue. That observation is also an apt summary of Míguez Bonino's own journey as a liberation theologian.[1]

Born in Santa Fe, Argentina, in 1924, Míguez Bonino studied in Rosario and Buenos Aires before taking degrees at Emory University and Union Theological Seminary in the United States. He was ordained a Methodist minister in 1948, in Argentina, and served pastorates in Bolivia and Argentina. Since 1954, he has been professor of systematic theology at the Higher Evangelical Institute for Theological Studies in Buenos Aires.

His conversion to liberationism began in the seminary's cafeteria, the year after his academic appointment, when Argentine president Juan Domingo Perón was overthrown in a military coup. As a Protestant professor and a product of liberal North American schools, Míguez Bonino thought of himself as a progressive Christian in a reactionary, predominantly Catholic world. He disapproved of most Latin American military governments, as well as of the efforts of the Roman Catholic hierarchy to confer legitimacy upon them. He considered the Methodist church an enlightened segment of Argentine society, and regarded himself, by extension, as a friend of the poor, who constituted the vast majority of Argentines.

The Protestant churches in Argentina had opposed Juan Perón during his tumultuous first reign, and when Perón was overthrown in 1955 Míguez Bonino immediately joined the celebration in the streets. It seemed self-evident to him that the downfall of the demagogic military strongman was a redemptive event, since it opened at least the possibility that Argentina could become a liberalized nation. But when Míguez Bonino returned to the seminary from the celebration in the streets, he found the cooks in the cafeteria weeping over the fall of Perón.

The scene stunned him. For the first time, Míguez Bonino realized that his liberal education and professional advancement had alienated him from the very people he wanted to serve. "I asked myself at that point," he recalls, " 'with whom have I been during these past years? Have I really been looking for democracy? Have I been with poor people or with an elite?' "

That was the turning point. "I realized then that the Protestant church, through social advancement, had lost touch with the large majority of the people."[2] Míguez Bonino did not become a Perónist, but he eventually accepted the fact that a progressive political movement in Argentina must come to terms with Perónism. Though he had assumed that his acquired liberalism made him an ally of the poor, he came to realize that the Protestant churches were too removed from the poor to be a progressive force among them. "We had thought we were in the avant-garde," he recalls, "but we had actually been helping the project of economic and intellectual elites." The events following the fall of Perón convinced him that he had to find his way back to the world of common Argentinean people, among whom he had been born. "That was a very decisive experience in my life," he remarked. "After that came this whole movement in the churches of social concern and theology of liberation."[3]

At the outset of his recent book on liberation ethics, Míguez Bonino cites the words of an anonymous paper, which came in the mail "without date or place of origin, like so many similar writings in Latin America today."[4] The paper observes that the base communities of Latin America have thrown thousands of politically unsophisticated Christians into politics, "where they have had to learn how crudely ambiguous and dirty political life is." *Toward a Christian Political Ethics* is not about that struggle, and Míguez Bonino confesses, with apologies, that his book moves in the realm of theory. "Many friends who have staked their lives in the struggle will be impatient with it," he admits. But just as politics is necessary for Christians, he implies, because people suffer from politics, so is theory necessary if one's political commitment is to be adequately grounded. In both politics and theory, he asserts, a considerable amount of ambiguity is warranted, and probably inevitable, for the liberation movement is "a school of humility."[5] This assertion is typical of Míguez Bonino, not only in its emphasis on the primacy of concrete praxis, but also in its tacit expression of solidarity with the Latin American revolutionary movement, which is tempered by his sense of humility and the realization that politics is inherently ambiguous. These qualities and his acute perception have made him the outstanding Protestant exponent of Latin American liberation theology.

Several years ago, Míguez Bonino noted in an autobiographical essay that colleagues and students sometimes identified separate stages in his thought. The underlying premise of these theories was always that he had moved from a conventional church-centered theology to a militantly liberationist, world-centered theology. He good-naturedly allowed that the stage theories could be right, but he preferred the assessment of his wife, who contended that he had always been a preacher bound to his text, interpreting the meaning of Scripture for current circumstances. Though the circumstances had changed continuously over the past thirty years, he liked to think that his vision and evangelical method had remained constant through the changing times.[6]

Indeed, perhaps the most disarming aspect of Míguez Bonino's liberationism is that, although he has made an intensive study of Marxism and appropriated much of Marx's analysis, he uses traditional evangelical language alongside his Marxist dialectics. He opens his treatise on Marxism, *Christians and Marxists*, for example, with the confession that he accepts Jesus Christ as his Lord and Savior, and further explains that the witness of Holy Scripture is the foundation of his understanding and hope.[7] He has elsewhere defended the objective historicity of the resurrection of Christ and has explicitly criticized such liberal theologies as Bultmann's for their reductionism or faithlessness.[8] In his numerous works, an essentially Barthian theological perspective is mixed with a case for "basic and revolutionary change," which he understands as a Christian imperative illuminated by Marxist social analysis.

He has observed that like most of his fellow liberationists he was trained (and presumably destined) to become a second-rate theologian. He explains that this is neither an accusation nor a sign of humility, but simply a recognition that the time, cultural environment, and academic infrastructure that are necessary for serious scholarship have not existed in Latin America. Unlike Segundo, who insistently rejects the notion that authentic liberation theologies can be dependent on first-world theologies, Míguez Bonino acknowledges his profound debt to modern European theology, and emphasizes that most liberationists build upon Gerhard von Rad's salvation-history interpretation of the Hebrew scriptures and the Moltmannian theology of hope.[9] To him, it is axiomatic that the liberation movement, which is a school of humility, must work out its distinctive theologies in conversation with other modern theologies.

Though he is one of the original proponents of liberation theology, for many years Míguez Bonino was primarily known in first-world academic and church circles as an ecumenical theologian. He served on various boards of the World Council of Churches while writing his early books: *Concilio abierto*, an assessment of the Second Vatican Council; *Integración humana y unidad cristiana*, an evaluation of Latin American ecumenism;

and *Ama y haz lo que quieras*, an interpretation of Christian ethics. With the emergence of liberationism as a major theological movement, however, (heralded by Gustavo Gutiérrez's *A Theology of Liberation* of 1971) Míguez Bonino finally offered his own major work, *Doing Theology in a Revolutionary Situation*. This book is perhaps the most lucid and illuminating explication of liberation theology yet written.

He remarked at the outset that liberation theology had only become a new consumer good in the time since he began to write the book and that he was therefore, at the moment, somewhat reluctant to add another volume to the menu. As a new "school" of thought, he asserted, liberation theology would have its day and then disappear, like other schools. By one reading, liberation theology is a distinctive new set of theological positions, but Míguez Bonino argued that these were transient, and only of relative value. He was not especially interested in defining or reviving liberationist positions. He claimed that liberation theology has enduring worth solely to the extent that it serves and reflects the concrete Latin American struggle for revolutionary transformation, "a long road strewn with suffering, sacrifice, and death." Long after liberation theology has lost its market value as an interesting consumer commodity, the necessity of the liberationist project will be as urgent as ever. It is only as a participant in that project, Míguez Bonino explained, that he presented his theology, "under the conditions of dependent and dominated Latin America."[10]

He begins with a historical analysis of Latin American dependency. There is no such thing as Christianity "above" or "outside" its concrete historical configurations, and in Latin American history two predominant configurations have appeared: Roman Catholicism, via Spanish colonialism, and Protestantism, via North American and northern European neocolonialism. Míguez Bonino declares that Latin Americans today can only grow into self-understanding by comprehending the colossal impact of these two historical projects upon Latin American societies. For him, the lesson of Latin American history is the need for a project that breaks away from the paradigms of colonialism and neocolonialism. That is the purpose of liberationism.

His account of the legacy of Spanish colonialism emphasizes that for the conquistadors (both political and clerical) the campaign for conquest and evangelization constituted a "single project." Though the Spanish dream of complete Latin American submission to the king of Spain (and, therefore, to the King of Heaven) was never fulfilled, mainly because of the cultural and geographical complexities of Latin America, the Spaniards did manage to impose a form of their own semifeudal society upon most of the region. The conquerors were not pilgrims. The basic pattern of ownership, which still exists in many Latin American countries, ceded 80 percent of all fertile land to approximately 5 percent of the population, who developed plantation-model slave economies. This system was given crucial ideological support by the church hierarchy, which in turn often obliged Latin American oligarchs to cut church officials, as well as army officers, into the deal. The price of class empowerment for these groups, however, was their total subservience to the demands and interests of the ruling class. By transplanting the Spanish ecclesiastical model to Latin America, the colonizers ensured that the church would monopolize education, exercise the right of patronage, and hold access to social authority and power, but all of these privileges were contingent upon the church's support for the colonial system.

Míguez Bonino emphasizes that the imposition of the Spanish Catholic model on Latin America, and the consequent subordination of the church to the ruling class, produced a colonial church riddled with distortions distinctive to Latin America.

> It meant that a chasm appeared between the popular—sometimes mixed or syncretistic—religion, which developed among the poor, the Indians, later on the peasants, and the hierarchical structure brought wholesale from Spain. It meant that, while the masses became deeply committed to Catholicism, they always felt the official Church as something foreign to them, as a part of "those above" as popular speech calls the small oligarchy who decides their destiny. It meant, finally, that the Church knew no other way of influencing the people— no other pastoral method—than the use of the institutions of society.[11]

The colonial church, he concludes, was inextricably dependent upon the social structures of the colonial system.

Míguez Bonino laments the profoundly reactionary impact of this arrangement, and he notes that the ravages of institutional Catholicism's pact with the Spanish and Portuguese empires still decisively marks every Latin American country, but he attributes equal historical significance to the development of new forms of dependency under capitalism. To many of the intellectuals in Latin America during the nineteenth century, the specter of Anglo-Saxon achievements elsewhere seemed to offer a new hope. The Anglo-Saxon ideology of free minds and free markets first came to Latin America, Míguez Bonino recalls, "in the holds of the triumphant British navy." Subsequently, through commerce and books, the Anglo-Saxon combination of capitalist economics and Enlightenment philosophy appealed to Latin American intellectuals as a godsend in their struggle against aristocratic and clerical domination. Domingo Faustino Sarmiento, the renowned publicist of liberalism and president of Argentina, drew the contrast with the strokes of a master pamphleteer: "Yankee civilization was the product of the plough and the primer; ours was presided [over] by the cross and the sword. There, men learned to work and read, here they learned to idle and to repeat prayers."[12] For such intellectuals as Sarmiento, or the Chileans Andrés Bello and Francisco Bilbao, the religion of the

Anglo-Saxon countries seemed to offer an alternative to the Catholic fixation with ritualism and the next world.

Few of these intellectuals actually became Protestants. They were not attracted to Protestantism as a personal religion, but the characteristic Protestant emphasis on individual freedom, enterprise, and moral seriousness seemed to them to offer the kind of ethos that Latin America desperately required. Bilbao's slogan summarized their convictions: "Either Catholicism or Democracy." Protestant missionaries in Latin America encouraged this sentiment by specifically targeting the professional-class Latin American elites for evangelization. They shrewdly calculated that the growth of a liberal intelligentsia in Latin America would open the continent to larger Protestant missions.

In the nineteenth century, Míguez Bonino argues, the crucial political effect of the Protestant challenge was retrogressive. Because the Catholic church was unprepared to live in a world where religious ideas and customs were freely debated, it dismissed modern scientific and Protestant criticisms on dogmatic grounds, and retreated to its own self-enclosed ghetto. In Latin America, that retreat drove the Catholic church hierarchy into an even more deeply sycophantic relationship with the ruling class, as the church struggled to retain religious hegemony over societies in which its authority was objectively waning. Míguez Bonino observes that the church's pact with the oligarchs did not drive large numbers of peasants into the Protestant churches, but it did exacerbate the already well-founded estrangement between the hierarchy and the poor, and gave further impetus to the growth of an anticlerical folk-Catholicism among the poor. Modern liberation theology derives, in part, from that disaffection.

Although the Protestant faith was proscribed in most Latin American countries until the middle of the nineteenth century, by the end of World War I the number of Protestants in Latin America exceeded two hundred thousand. Pentecostal revivals in subsequent decades brought millions of peasants into the charismatic churches, but the more telling prewar and postwar development, in Míguez Bonino's interpretation, was the emergence of a much smaller, but influential, sector of predominantly professional-class Protestant denominations. To become a non-Pentecostal Protestant, in the late nineteenth or the early twentieth century, was often to make a social statement that one favored freedom, culture, democracy, and progress. "Protestantism is thus already linked with the whole North Atlantic ideological, cultural, economic, and political thrust beginning with the nineteenth century and up to the present," Míguez Bonino remarks. "Protestantism, in terms of its historical origin, of its introduction to Latin America, and of its ethos, came into our world as the religious accompaniment of free enterprise, liberal, capitalist democracy."

While the Roman Catholic church fought against the intrusion of modernity, Protestantism, and democracy with all the institutional means at its disposal, Míguez Bonino observes that eventually the economic interests of its sponsors led to concessions by the church. As the economic interest of the Latin American ruling class became increasingly dependent on obtaining credit, assistance and export trade with North America, the oligarchs became less interested in sustaining their fight against Protestantism and republicanism. Though they still relied upon the Catholic church to rationalize and legitimize their social rule, the alliance between the ruling class and the church hierarchy weakened as the oligarchs became more dependent upon their economic ties to North America. The church, having failed to repel the logic of modernity, was left holding the bag.

Míguez Bonino argues that the Catholic church, in Latin America and elsewhere, only began to enter the modern world when it realized that it could not defeat capitalism. The Second Vatican Council, in the early 1960s, marked the church's eventual point of arrival in the modern world, which had taken a hundred years of slow travel to complete. For the past generation, he notes, the long conflict between Catholicism and Protestantism over *politics* has seemed anachronistic. Today, all modern, nonfundamentalist churches use similar political language, and all of them invoke similar political ideals: democracy, equality, freedom. The transformation of Roman Catholicism in this century has produced an apparent ecumenical consensus on political ideology, along the lines traditionally espoused by Protestants.

Míguez Bonino originally learned this history as a rather self-satisfied Protestant. The schools and churches in which he was educated took pride in their connection with the "right side" of Latin American history, having stood for the past century for democracy and modernity. Míguez Bonino presumed himself a friend of the victims of Latin American history, by virtue of his association with its more enlightened religious tradition. But the tears of the seminary cooks after the overthrow of Perón moved him, eventually, to a quite different reading and self-understanding.

For him, as for most of the original liberationist theologians in the 1950s, the breakthrough in consciousness began with the realization that economic modernization had created new forms of Latin American enslavement. "The fundamental element in the new Latin American consciousness," he had explained, "is the awareness that our political emancipation from Spain was—however justified and necessary—a step in the Anglo-Saxon colonial and neocolonial expansion. Our independence from Spain made us available as suppliers of raw materials first and of cheap labor and manageable markets later on."[13]

He does not comment upon the technical arguments within dependency theory, or specifically align himself with any of the several versions of this theory, but Míguez Bonino's analytical perspective is founded upon the moral imperatives of the Bible and upon the basic claims of dependency theory. The fundamental postulate of dependency theory is that developed capitalist states create "centers" that dominate the more vulnerable nations in their "periphery," causing the peripheral nations to become disproportionately dependent upon external economic decisions. While there are several analytical variations within the family of dependency theories, all emphasize the effects of unfavorable trade agreements, aid to corrupt and repressive military governments, the promotion of cash crops for export, the existence of protected markets in the developed countries, and the exploitative policies of transnational corporations as important examples of the dynamics of dependency. As the Roman Catholic bishops of Peru proclaimed in 1969, "Like other nations in the world, we are the victims of systems that exploit our natural resources, control our political decisions, and impose on us the cultural domination of their values and consumer civilization."[14] In all of its several forms, dependency theory attempts to explain why economic modernization schemes usually reinforce the dominant position of developed countries, at the expense of poor nations. The basic mechanisms of modern export dependence were established during the colonial era, when relatively diversified and self-sufficient Latin American economies were converted into monocultures designed to serve the needs of developed markets. Míguez Bonino recounts that "Argentina was supposed to supply corn and meat; Brazil, coffee; Chile, saltpeter and copper; the Central American countries, bananas; Cuba, sugar; Venezuela, oil; and so on. Railways and roads were built not in order to serve internal or Latin American communications but as a two-beat mechanism in order to pump the production of the country into the large chosen port and to pump it out to the overseas metropolis."[15] During the period when this classically imperialist system of infrastructure and trade was organized, a British politician enthused that Argentina was not only "our least expensive colony" but also a remarkably agreeable one, inasmuch as it financed even its own occupation army.

In Latin America, this system of social organization has outlasted the colonial empires. During the 1940s in Guatemala, for example, the United Fruit Company owned the country's only major port (Puerto Barrios, the sole outlet to the Caribbean), the only railroad (which, for a time, charged the world's highest freight rates), and the only telephone and telegraph services. The treatment and wage rates offered to peasants by United Fruit amounted to slavery, yet, when the democratically elected government of Jacobo Arbenz Guzmán instituted a moderate land-reform program and legalized all Guatemalan political parties, the CIA organized its overthrow. Míguez Bonino ruefully observes that U.S. military aggression in Latin America has reaped its own bitter harvest, but he argues that the fundamental social evil in Latin America is the neocolonial economic system that the U.S. Marines have so often been sent to defend. Even in modern times, he avers, military intervention is a secondary issue, because interventions are merely "necessary maneuvers" for those who have large economic interests at stake in the current system. Though there were meaningful historical differences between the British and North American phases of the neocolonial process, he argues, the bedrock fact is that Latin American economic decisions and structures have been determined for more than a century by "liberal" nations that formed alliances with Latin American oligarchs and their governments.[16]

The latter fact generates the second half of Míguez Bonino's critique of modern capitalism, which he calls "the exposure of the hoax of democracy." In the past century, he argues, the cruelest and most insidious forms of enslavement have been imposed upon Latin America by those who justified themselves with the rhetoric of democracy. Although the formal norms of democratic theory were incorporated into virtually all Latin American constitutions during the era of "decolonialization," the rights presumably guaranteed in these constitutions have, in fact, throughout most of Latin America, existed only as the privileges of elites. The vast majority of Latin Americans in this century have been condemned to unremitting exploitation, malnutrition, and illiteracy, often backed up by military terror, while the elites who govern in their name have rationalized their policies under the flag of progress. They have immensely profited from the conversion of their countries into cash-crop monocultures, while restricting the "democratic" rights to education, medical care, and political authority to themselves. Today they purchase high-technology weapons, build networks of modern airports, and acquire billion-dollar telecommunications systems, often in countries where most people have never driven a car or used a telephone. In the past decade they have mortgaged the future of Latin America by running up utterly fantastic external debts in pursuit of urban modernization. As these debts have become unpayable, Latin American currencies have been debased and economic austerity programs imposed, the latter mainly upon the backs of the poor.

Míguez Bonino argues that despite its more elevated rhetoric the neo-colonial project of modern international capitalism has subjected the poor to even more vicious forms of oppression than the old colonial system. The "gigantic fallacy of the whole modernizing attempt," he contends, is the carefully nurtured and endlessly repeated myth that North American economic progress has been a moral achievement. The myth is that North American economic success was morally deserved, because of the relatively equitable distribution of North American wealth and the early establishment of democratic norms and values. The social function of this myth, in his estimation, is to reinforce the idea that the United States is the exemplary model of modernization, and that Latin American nations should therefore adopt its ideology of modernization.

Míguez Bonino does not pursue the fact that North American capitalism has never been as equitable or as democratic as the Latin American myth about it suggests. What *is* important to him is the evidence that North Americans have lived off the largesse of a system that has effectively underdeveloped Latin America. Those who point to the United States as the model for Latin American modernization, he argues, overlook the fact that "the rise of the Northern countries took place at a particular moment in history and was built on the possibilities offered by the resources of the dependent countries." North American growth did not occur on its own, but at the expense of socially backward Latin American nations.

"Development and underdevelopment are not two independent realities," he asserts, "nor two stages in a continuum but two mutually related processes: Latin American underdevelopment is the dark side of Northern development; Northern development is built on third-world underdevelopment." Míguez Bonino implies that Latin American nations would need to exploit a vulnerable continent of their own if they intended to take the North American developmentalist road. In the real world, however, where there are no more new worlds to resettle, it is self-defeating for Latin American officials to tie their countries to modernization schemes. "The takeoff point in Northern societies was dependent on the relation to the then colonized societies," he declares. "That situation does not obtain today and the process therefore cannot be repeated."[17]

Because modernization schemes have already reinforced the maldistribution of wealth in Latin America and have left the largest Latin American countries with unpayable external debts, Míguez Bonino concludes that even the most well-intentioned schemes of capitalist modernization should be regarded as instruments of domination. "For the growing Latin American masses, undernourishment, slavery, illiteracy, and later on forced migration, unemployment, exploitation, crowding, and finally repression when they claim their rights—these are the harvest of one century of 'liberal democracy,' " he explains.

He acknowledges that the emergence of capitalism in Latin America undermined the "stranglehold" of the earlier feudal arrangements, and he emphasizes that the extremely concentrated composition of Latin American wealth made the continent especially vulnerable to foreign manipulation. That is, he concedes that the cultural and political backwardness of Latin America were highly determinative factors in its modern history. The early Protestants in Latin America were right to criticize the lack of a democratic ethos in Roman Catholicism, as well as the reactionary effects of Roman Catholic polity upon Latin American culture and politics. But after decades of priding themselves on their own comparatively enlightened modernity, Míguez Bonino remarks, modern Protestants must confront the fact that their role in Latin America's history of enslavement was much more ambiguous than they had thought. It was Protestant ideology that provided a religious sanction for neocolonialism and Protestant rhetoric that propagated idealized images of the neocolonial powers. Míguez Bonino contends that Latin American Protestants can only overcome the oppressive limits of their tradition by joining the liberationist movement, which is, in part, a movement for a postmodern expression of the Christian faith. Though the split between Protestantism and Catholicism has been a marked feature of the Latin American church in its colonial and neocolonial phases, liberationism is inherently an ecumenical project in which the denominational disagreements of the past are no longer considered crucial or definitive.

I have noted that Míguez Bonino adopts a wholesale version of dependency theory without identifying himself with any particular variant of dependency analysis. This approach allows him to describe the ravages of economic modernization in Latin America without cluttering his argument with in-house debates. The problem with this approach is that it makes claims that are based upon the least credible forms of dependency theory. The range of dependency theory is represented by the unicausal neo-Marxist economism of Andre Gunder Frank at one end and the more culturally-oriented and multicausal analysis of Fernando Cardoso at the other end. The differences among the various forms of dependency analysis are significant. Unfortunately, several of Míguez Bonino's fundamental claims are based upon one-dimensional, Frankian-style arguments that oversimplify the dynamics of Latin American dependence. Because the facts of dependence are so evident and determinative in Latin America, it is crucial that liberationists make the most credible use of dependency theory.

The core of dependency theory is the argument that undeveloped countries in the periphery are often disproportionately dependent on external economic decisions made in the developed, "center" nations. The comparatively enormous economic and military power of the United States makes Latin American dependence, to some extent, inevitable. Small cuts in North American commodity prices, for example, can be devastating to Latin American nations dependent on their cash-crop income. Latin American countries have been further damaged by protected markets in the developed world and by the repeated U.S. resort to military force to protect its economic interests. The North American domination of Latin America has been further served by the influence of the United States government and business interests over the policies of the World Bank and the International Monetary Fund.

Multinational corporations have further reinforced the dependent inferiority of Latin America by taking advantage of the continent's cheap labor markets and low tax rates, often to make products useful only in first-world markets. By assuming control over third-world finance capital, natural resources, production, and marketing, multinational firms have repeatedly undermined Latin American prospects for economic self-determination. As the Latin American Roman Catholic bishops asserted in their historic statement at Medellín in 1968, "In many cases, these foreign interests exercise unchecked control, their power continues to grow, and they have no permanent interest in the countries of Latin America."[18]

In his exhaustive study for the United Nations, *Estrategia Industrial y Empresas Internacionales*, Fernando Fajnzylber has documented the exploitation of Latin American resources by multinational firms. Between 1960 and 1968, for example, U.S.-based multinational corporations reported taking, on average, 79 percent of their net profits out of Latin America. When critics of this arrangement argue that multinational firms should be required to reinvest their profits in Latin America, it is frequently asserted, in rejoinder, that such requirements are self-defeating. Multinational firms owe their primary moral responsibility, it is argued, to their own shareholders, and it is usually further asserted that multinational investment is needed in the third world because multinational firms generate economic growth through their investment of capital in their own enterprises.

The Fajnzylber study reveals, however, that multinational enterprises in Latin America have typically financed more than 75 percent of their investments from *local* capital. Between 1957 and 1965, for example, only 17 percent of the capital investments of U.S.-based multinationals were brought in from outside the poor countries themselves.[19] Numerous other investigations, commissioned by the United Nations and other institutions, have confirmed the same pattern. One of the most detailed studies, conducted by the Argentine economist Aldo Ferrer, reveals that from 1960 to 1970 approximately 78 percent of the manufacturing operations of U.S.-based multinationals in Latin America were financed from local capital.[20]

Latin American economic dependency has intensified in the past twenty-five years largely because of the promotion of urban modernization, which has incurred crushing external debts and given multinational firms disproportionate control over Latin American resources. The structures of dependency have grown even more insidious during the same period, however, because of the eagerness of Latin American governments to purchase high-technology weapons from first-world defense contractors. The volume of debt and the distortion of Latin American economic priorities have therefore worsened in the past generation. In Venezuela, the rapid process of modernization has eliminated millions of jobs for farmworkers, many of whom cannot find work in the cities, and exacerbated the country's grotesque levels of malnutrition and disease, while raising the national external debt to $37 billion. This absurd volume of debt has damaged Venezuelan prospects for new investment and economic growth, yet, in recent years, the Venezuelan government has purchased F-16A supersonic fighters and F-16B trainers from U. S. defense contractors. As I have argued elsewhere, it is the most recent and perverse stage in third-world dependency that sales of advanced weapons contracted by governing elites are impeding the development of third-world societies worth defending.[21]

One of the more telling examples of this phenomenon in recent years has been the Honduran government. Honduras is the second-poorest country in the Western hemisphere, yet in 1986 this brutally impoverished nation was encouraged by the United States government to use its military credits to purchase eight F-5E advanced jet fighters from the Northrop Corporation. Honduras presumably needed new, high-technology attack aircraft to go with its eight shiny new military airfields, also built by the United States. This country, which has essentially been turned into a U.S. military base, has become a pathetic example of how a dependent relationship can be reinforced by militarization.

The structures of Latin American economic dependency have been further deepened by the economic effects of United States military spending. While the Reagan administration dramatically increased appropriations for defense in the early and middle 1980s, the federal government was forced to borrow foreign capital to finance its expenditures. During the same period, unprecedented U.S. trade deficits and high interest rates kept the dollar overvalued. This combination of factors badly damaged Latin American capacities for economic growth, since the annual interest owed on their enormous external debts often exceeded the fresh credits they were able to attain, while high interest rates increased the amounts that were owed. The net result is that over the past decade the "modernized" Latin American nations have been unable to attain enough credit to finance their existing debts, while the debts have grown for external reasons outside their control.

Míguez Bonino and other liberationists are therefore entirely justified in basing their call for a postmodern social order on the claims of dependency theory. By focusing upon the center-periphery dynamic within modern capitalism, dependency theorists have offered a powerful explanation for the fact that not a single Latin American nation has been able to climb the ladder of economic development described by Walter Rostow in *The Stages of Economic Growth*, despite a hundred years of trying.[22] It is true, as corporate apologists insist, that the construction of skyscrapers, luxury hotels, modernized airports, and microwave communications systems have all promoted "development" of a sort in Latin America. It is even true that modernization programs have occasionally played a progressive role in the third world. For the most part, however, capitalist modernization and military-rearmament programs have distorted the economies of Latin America by channeling scarce domestic resources into highly concentrated, capital-intensive projects that do not serve the interests or needs of most Latin Americans. Thus, to such liberationists as Míguez Bonino, the fundamental breakthrough in consciousness that is needed in Latin America is the realization that "the efforts to prolong, consolidate, and carry through this project can only mean greater misery and tragedy for our continent."

It is also true, however, that Míguez Bonino, like Frank, overstates the historic dynamics of "domination and dependence" between North and Latin America. While the most exhaustive studies of the subject confirm that Latin America is dependent upon North American economic interests and in turn exploited by them, Frankian theory does not provide a totally sufficient explanation of underdevelopment. Some of the poorest countries in the world have had little or no contact with the developed world. Furthermore, and more important, such liberationists as Míguez Bonino have undermined their own arguments when they exaggerate the role of economic imperialism in North American history. Míguez Bonino flatly argues, for example, that North American economic development was *built* on third-world underdevelopment, but, according to figures compiled by the

U.S. Census Bureau, the value of total U.S. investments in Latin America in 1929 was $3.5 billion; in 1950, it had grown only to $4.6 billion. Current United Nations studies of foreign investment reveal that, even today, approximately 1 percent of total U.S. investments go to Latin America. These investments have had a seriously destabilizing impact on Latin American societies, but the total amounts are not enough to support the claim that North American economic development has been *based* on foreign exploitation.[23]

A similar problem with Míguez Bonino's appropriation of Frankian-style analysis is his tendency to discuss democratic norms and values only in connection with what he calls "the capitalist project." It is one of the more absurd (and self-serving) staples of conservative rhetoric that political democracy is compatible only with a capitalist economy, yet Míguez Bonino often appears to make the same assumption. He routinely associates the democratic political process with liberal modernism and, like Segundo, he discusses democracy only in connection with first-world capitalism (which he rejects as imperialist), or with Latin American constitutions (which he calls hoaxes), or with "third-way" Latin American social democracy (which he rejects as reformist). The problem here, as with Segundo, is that Míguez Bonino writes about socialism as though democratic socialism did not exist, and therefore fails to offer a vision of a democratic alternative to third-world dependency and tyranny. In his various writings, democracy is discussed only in connection with movements or ideologies that he rejects.

I do not believe that Míguez Bonino has *actually* rejected democratic principles or values as irrelevant to the Latin American revolutionary struggle. Unlike Segundo, his work does not promote vanguardism or any kind of ecclesiological or political sectarianism. In his overall tone, in his identification with "humanistic socialism," in his emphasis on being "with the people" and discerning their will, and in his eloquent critique of violence, Míguez Bonino's work is profoundly democratic in spirit. But because he lacks an operative theory of democratic socialism, he fails to offer an explicitly democratic vision of the postmodern, postcapitalist society that he seeks.

As he implied in his open letter to Míguez Bonino, Jürgen Moltmann was disturbed by the same failing in Latin American liberation theology. Though he did not raise the subject in specific criticism of Míguez Bonino's work, Moltmann vigorously asserted that *democratic* socialism is the most worthy vision of human liberation, because it fulfills the universal human desire for self-determination in the political as well as in the economic spheres of social existence. "Socialism without democracy" Moltmann declared, and "economic justice without realization of human rights are not hopes among our people."[24]

In response to Moltmann, several Latin American liberationists, including Gutiérrez, have argued that Moltmann's position may be relevant in the first world, but is largely irrelevant in Latin America. Gutiérrez has eloquently described the situation as a split between "theology in the modern spirit" and "theology in a world of oppression," and explained that Moltmann's work is a notable example of the former.[25] For this defense of his position against Moltmann's criticism, Míguez Bonino has thanked Gutiérrez and expressed his agreement with Gutiérrez's assessment.

For the most part, I also agree with Gutiérrez's analysis of the differing agendas in modern theology, and I have therefore argued that Moltmann's vestigial Barthianism unfortunately leaves him outside the liberationist theological paradigm, which begins with the experience of oppression. It does not seem to me, however, that a liberationist praxis should be divorced from the struggle for democratic self-determination; rather, I believe that Moltmann was right to insist on the primacy of the democratic ideal in any liberation movement worthy of the name. At the end of a century in which previous "liberation" movements have driven tens of millions to their deaths and imprisoned hundreds of millions under totalitarian regimes that they have not been free to criticize or leave, it is unacceptable for modern liberationists to wave aside the question of democracy. Contrary to the assurances offered by a chorus of third-world liberationists, the issues raised by Moltmann are not irrelevant outside the first-world context. Democratic alternatives are as desperately needed in Latin America as anywhere. The principles and values of democratic socialism are therefore as relevant in the Latin American situation as anywhere else.

One consequence of his lack of a positive theoretical orientation is that, after he has criticized the ravages of capitalism, Míguez Bonino has only the most vague formulations to offer about the "socialist" alternative. While he is too chastened by historical experience to embrace Marxism, he fails to describe or defend any other kind of socialism. For all of his emphasis on praxis, then, his own indiscriminate use of dependency theory leads him to become more and more abstract as he begins to confront the implications of his critique of modernization.

In his two central works, for example, he rightly criticizes the liberal developmentalist schemes of the past thirty-five years, which prescribed for Latin America a system of capital accumulation and the introduction of technology and economic planning, and which therefore rationalized the creation of such organizations as the International Development Bank (IDB), the International Monetary Fund (IMF), and the International Aid for Development (IAD). Míguez Bonino notes that these organizations were founded in the first wave of developmentalist enthusiasm that followed World War II, and were reinvigorated by the creation of the Alliance for Progress during the Kennedy administration. The history of these efforts, however, is a chronicle of failure. Míguez Bonino recalls that foreign interests used local capital to finance their enterprises and took more out of Latin America than they reinvested. Unfair trade policies, the effects of protected markets in the developed world, exorbitant user fees for patented North American technology, and accelerating debts combined to create more oppressive and maldistributed forms of dependency than had existed before the coming of the "developmental" agencies. Though the infusion of modernization and foreign capital created small sectors of new prosperity, the same growth inexorably occurred at the expense of the disenfranchised peasant and working-class majorities. In theory, modernization required reforms in Latin American tenure, at least some redistribution of wealth, and relatively stable political conditions in order to succeed. In fact, however, over thirty-five years of modernization schemes have utterly failed to break down the oligarchical class structures of most Latin American societies. Modernization programs have had little effect upon Latin American patterns of ownership or wealth, but with the increase in the number of foreign interests in Latin America a particular kind of concern for "political stability" *has* accompanied modernization. Míguez Bonino observes that with the growth of foreign interests to protect, and the simultaneous worsening of income maldistribution, social unrest has become increasingly intense on the continent "and populist regimes have been replaced, with the aid and support of the USA, by repressive governments which can guarantee the stable conditions required by foreign investment."[26] The most revealing example of this phenomenon, from either side of the argument, is Brazil, for it is in Brazil that multinational firms have made their most extensive third-world investments. Míguez Bonino notes that Brazil originally emerged as the showcase model of economic modernization in the mid 1950s, when the nation's bourgeoisie was "co-opted" by the specter of foreign investment, and when police repression was therefore applied with new vengeance "in order to avoid any unrest which might interfere with economic growth."[27] He concedes that Brazil *has* subsequently grown into the most economically advanced society in Latin America, but, writing in the early 1970s, Míguez Bonino observed that what is often not acknowledged "is that 41.6 percent of the total Brazilian industry is in foreign hands (94 percent in the chemical industry, 100 percent in the automotive industry, 82 percent in the rubber industry, and 71 percent in railways.)"

> The purchasing value of the salary has fallen 23.5 percent. The repatriation of profits to the centers of investment has multiplied in four years (1964-1968) by 4.2 percent and keeps rising. The naked truth is that Brazil has become, not even a colony of a foreign power, but a factory of multinational corporations; the Brazilian population, a reserve of cheap labor; and the Brazilian government, army, and police, foremen and wardens of these corporations.[28]

More recently, he has observed that in Brazil and elsewhere in Latin America governments operated or dominated by the military have repeatedly wrapped themselves in nationalistic garb, posing as the defenders of national sovereignty against North American manipulation. But in fact, he declares, "the nationalistic rhetoric of the military governments is in practice clearly undermined by the total sellout of their own national economies to the transnational interests."[29]

Faced with the spectacle of Brazilian debasement, which is advertised as successful modernization, Míguez Bonino calls for a liberationist project that rejects the logic of modernization. He insists that this project cannot be based on moral criticism alone. After noting the crucial role that the United States government has traditionally played in training and supporting Latin American military rulers, Míguez Bonino characteristically remarks that these military officers have not been especially wicked people. It is even a mistake, he contends, to regard their savage repression as the "cancerous outgrowth" of a system that can still be restored to decency. For Míguez Bonino, moralistic approaches to the Latin American situation are superfluous, because the economic ravages of modernization and the human agonies they have engendered are the normal products of this particular system. Thus, he concludes, "We are simply facing the normal and unavoidable consequences of the basic principles of capitalist production as they work themselves out in our global, technological time. The concentration of economic power, the search for higher profits, the efforts to obtain cheaper labor and to avoid higher costs are of the very essence of the system."[30] A meaningful response to the structural misery of Latin America will therefore go beyond moral or reformist criticism and embark on a socialist transformation of capitalism.

Within Latin America thus far, only Cuba has broken away from the U.S.-dominated system of corporate collectivism. Though I will argue later that Míguez Bonino is overly sympathetic toward Communist movements, he does not present Cuba as a model for other Latin American revolutions. He observes that the Cuban revolution has an enduring significance for Latin Americans, mainly because it symbolizes the possibility that a Latin American country *can* actually break away from the United States, but he concludes that the Cuban revolution does not offer a model that should be reproduced.

The problem is that Míguez Bonino is trapped between his extreme appropriation of dependency theory and his rejection of the Cuban model. His outright repudiation of modernization leads him to advocate the overthrow of capitalism, but in a situation where *any* conceivable revolutionary state will require international economic assistance, emergency and security aid, trade agreements, and other forms of assistance, liberation theology must face the implications of the fact that *some* form of modernization (and therefore of dependency) is a necessity. Castro himself, therefore, repeatedly urged the Sandinistas in Nicaragua not to burn their bridges with the World Bank and the International Monetary Fund. Among other considerations, he was surely moved to such counsel by the fact that the Soviet Union could not afford another Latin American client state, since it already provided $3 billion in annual subsidies to Cuba.

Míguez Bonino weakly asserts that, just as Latin American nations must develop their own appropriate forms of socialism, the theorizing of liberationists must also be adapted to particular national realities. This is unassailable as a high-ground generalization, but, curiously, like so much of the liberationist literature, his argument fails the test of concrete praxis. To serve the ends of praxis, liberation theology must criticize the consequences of modernization, as Míguez Bonino does, while offering an alternative that does not just reject modernization, or turn to Communism, or take refuge in abstract generalizations. Liberation theology needs a praxis of democratic socialism, which seeks not to abolish economic modernization but to *transform* it by achieving democratic control over economic planning and investment. The Mexican writer Octavio Paz has shrewdly observed of most liberation theologians that "they want to rescue the poor from their poverty, but at the same time they reject the conditions of an economy of expansion."[31] There is a tendency even within the mainstream of liberationist theology to adopt extreme versions of dependency theory, to equate modernization with capitalism, and to ignore or reject the alternatives offered by democratic socialism. The goals of democratic socialism are unachievable without a productive, modernized economy, but the realization of democratic-socialist goals in any nation would be more revolutionary than the alternatives to them.

Míguez Bonino's definition of the "Latin American socialist project of liberation" is typical of most liberationist writing on socialism, which is substantially compatible with a democratic-socialist perspective but overly dismissive of modernization and vague about the political and organizational design of socialism. He asserts that a Latin American socialist project must break away from the domination of "the empires" and their developmentalist schemes and launch a *parallel* revolution within the existing social structures of Latin America. Though capitalism has sustained semifeudal social systems throughout much of Latin America, Míguez Bonino emphasizes that these structures existed before the emergence of modern capitalism, and that today they are as much an obstacle to Latin American popular self-determination as the policies of multinational corporations. The underlying fact is that capitalist modernization and semifeudal tyranny have reinforced each other for decades in Latin America as "two dimensions of one single historical movement," but Míguez Bonino stresses that the liberationist struggle must be fought simultaneously on two fronts. Because the foreign and local capitalist interests invariably oppose and attempt to destroy the social gains achieved by liberationist movements, Míguez Bonino asserts that a socialist project requires a strong centralized state.

While he cautions against the dangers of old-style Socialist rhetoric, which tends to glorify the state and indulge in naïve illusions about the effects of nationalization programs, he insists that for the sake of realism the gains of popular movements can only be protected by a centralized socialist state. He equally insists, however, that socialism is not primarily an economic strategy, but a historical project that requires, for its success, a transformation of consciousness among the poor. Socialism for the common good is only possible if the vast majority of the oppressed become aware of the necessary costs of liberation and become awakened to a solidaristic sense of participation in the struggle as a *common* effort. It follows, for Míguez Bonino, that in a liberationist project all economic, social, and cultural considerations must be subordinated to the political struggle, which is "primary and determinate." The liberation movement is essentially a struggle for power for the sake of the common good.[32]

In his autobiographical essay "For Life and against Death: A Theology That Takes Sides," Míguez Bonino declares that while he has never felt a personal attraction to Marxism as a system he has also never felt compelled to oppose Marxism, partly out of a sense of solidarity with those in the liberationist movement who are Marxists.[33] In various writings he has remarked that while he generally avoids all ideologies, including Marxism, he also believes that certain elements of Marxist economic and social theory are correct. He explains, "I have more and more come to think in terms of a long humanist-socialist tradition, with early Christian and Hellenic roots, which has developed in the modern world, in which Marx has played an important — even decisive — part, but which he has neither created nor fulfilled."[34]

This is an attractive description of Míguez Bonino's political sensibility, which is clearly of a democratic-socialist type, but because he is committed to a united-front strategy the question arises whether his humanistic ideals are consistent with his advocacy of revolutionary alliances with Communists. Though he repeatedly argues that Latin American revolutionaries should not attempt to reproduce the Soviet or Cuban models, he does not address the implications of the fact that certain revolutionary factions in Latin America are fighting for a Soviet or Cuban-style dictatorial state. He occasionally notes that Communist parties are prominent forces within the existing Latin American revolutionary coalitions, and he lists these parties among the advocates of "socialism" in Latin America, but he repeatedly offers the assurance that these movements are pluralistic coalitions — as though that assurance settled the question.

I am suggesting that Míguez Bonino avoids the hard questions about Communist ideology, as well as the implications of making revolutionary alliances with Communists. His argument in *Christians and Marxists*, for example, is revealing. He begins that work with the declaration that, as a Latin American, he will not indulge in the criticisms of Communist oppression that are typical among first-world intellectuals. He notes with disdain that Solzhenitsyn's *Gulag Archipelago* has been lauded by European intellectuals who were apparently shocked by its revelations. But in Latin America, he remarks, the terrors described by Solzhenitsyn are everyday realities. The citizens of the "most Christian" nations of Brazil, Uruguay, and Chile are well acquainted with the mechanisms of state terror, he observes, even if they happen to know nothing about the Soviet Union. Míguez Bonino thus declares that he will refuse to examine or denounce the legacy of Communist terror, because Latin American governments have equally terrorized their nations over the past century.

This is a stunning misuse of the idea of moral equivalence, which, in its proper form, is a powerful argument for a social-democratic perspective. The claim that Communist terror has been approximately matched in this century by the violence and oppression of right-wing governments is a fundamentally important (and justified) argument. Míguez Bonino undermines his own basic contention, however, when he asserts that, because of this approximate equivalence of evil, liberationists should refrain from criticizing Communist oppression and even "Stalinist terror."[35] For the legacies of state repression, torture, and genocide in the Communist Soviet Union and China are hardly made more acceptable by the fact that Latin American governments have committed the same crimes. The relative equivalence of rightist and Communist evil does not reduce or excuse the degree of evil on either side. It points, rather, to the necessity of a democratic alternative.

Unfortunately, despite his knowledge of twentieth-century history, Míguez Bonino adopts a rather sympathetic attitude toward the various Communist movements in the world. This sympathy is largely a product of his closer acquaintance with Latin American dictatorships, but it also owes something to his friendships with Latin American Communists. In *Christians and Marxists* he claims that China and Cuba are more advanced and humane, today, than the other dependent countries near them, and he further claims that Marxist socialism has proved to be a "powerful and efficient motor of social change, economic development, and scientific progress," especially in the Soviet Union. He concedes that Communist countries have paid a high price for their social and economic achievements, especially in the area of human rights, yet even here he argues that the human costs of *Western* economic and social development have been at least equally severe. The difference in the case of Western economic development is that, under modern capitalism, the ravages of modernization have been disproportionately inflicted upon vulnerable nations in the economic periphery. That is, while Communist governments have rationalized repressive systems of domestic collectivism in order to promote their own versions of social and economic development, for Míguez Bonino the greater evil has been perpetrated by liberal capitalist nations that have forced weaker countries to bear the burdens of Western development. He is therefore more sympathetic toward Communism, since it is presumably less imperialist. He asserts that, whatever our misgivings about its record on human rights, it is difficult not to feel "a sense of admiration and gratitude" for the worldwide Communist movement, which, "in less than a century, through its direct action in some areas and through indirect influence in labor movements and other social forces in others, has raised to a human condition the life of at least half of the human race."[36]

The most serious problem with modern Communism, he asserts, is not the endlessly publicized issue of human rights but the "fact" that the existing Communist nations are not Communist enough. He notes that despite its official adherence to the goal of a classless society organized for the sake of the common good, the Soviet Union has actually reinstituted a market economy, private material incentives, and a system of enterprise administration, while often pursuing its own imperialist interests in the third world in ways that are indistinguishable from those of the United States. Both imperial powers routinely vote against fair terms of trade for dependent nations in UNCTAD or FAO meetings, and both struggle for peaceful coexistence between themselves while fighting proxy wars in the third world. Like the directive of the mythical Latin American president to his chauffeur, Míguez Bonino remarks that the actual policy of the Soviet Union has been to signal left and turn right. In the mid 1970s, Míguez Bonino believed that under the "extraordinary leadership" of Mao Zedong, China had created a far more dynamic and humane form of Socialism. He was moved to rhapsodize about the greater sense of participation and deeper feelings of "dignity and moral determination" among the Chinese, mainly because he knew less about China, but even in his absurdly idealized portrait of Chinese Communism, Míguez Bonino noted a lack of concern for the poor of the third world. He concluded that the existing Communist nations revealed the need for collectivist revolutions on a world scale, for which he found a mandate in the "scandalous collectivism" of the Bible.[37]

The claim that runs through all of Míguez Bonino's work is that Scripture commands an option for the poor. Unlike Gutiérrez, who interprets the option for the poor as the founding *experience* of liberation theology, Míguez Bonino adopts a more typically Protestant emphasis upon the priority of biblical proclamation and response. Gutiérrez has developed a theology of the "epiphanic vision," which is rooted in the assumption that because God dwells especially among the poor, solidarity with the poor *is* the fundamental religious experience. Grace is experienced through one's solidarity with those who suffer. The assumption that God is revealed through those who suffer is itself a biblical notion, of course, but Gutiérrez's approach is biblical in a different way from Míguez Bonino's, since Gutiérrez ascribes theological primacy to the manifestation of God's presence among the poor. For Míguez Bonino, by contrast, the liberationist option for the poor is not based upon experiential claims, but upon obedience to the Word of God, which calls believers to justice and righteousness. In agreement with Bultmann, Míguez Bonino emphasizes the importance of the *preunderstanding* that every reader differently brings to Scripture, but he contends that Bultmann only examined the phenomenon within the limits of his European, individualistic worldview.[38] Like most Christian theologians since the second century, Bultmann assumed that the truth claims of theology must be expressed, for the sake of intelligibility, in the language of a given philosophical system or hermeneutic. His own reinterpretation of theology was grounded in Martin Heidegger's existential phenomenology. Like most theologians, Bultmann assumed that theology must be rooted in some philosophical system in order to establish or defend its truth claims, which were conceptual in nature.

But the age of philosophical systems has passed. Míguez Bonino observes that modern philosophers have abandoned the ancient metaphysical project, in which their predecessors attempted to interpret history through pure concepts. As modern philosophers have rejected the search for pure concepts, modern theologians have accordingly begun to relinquish the notion that religious truths must be rooted in some conceptual relationship to a philosophical ontology. Modern and postmodern theologies, especially liberation theology, seek a fundamental reorientation in praxis, and have therefore turned to the social sciences. Míguez Bonino insists that this reorientation is a revolutionary development in theology, which raises problems that are "totally unknown to classical theology."[39] He argues that it is only through the theological use of the social sciences, however, especially Marxist economic analysis, that a deepened and more concrete understanding of the biblical message for our time can be found. The theory of preunderstanding that we need is not restricted to an abstract philosophical analysis of being, but includes the concrete conditions of people who belong to a given time, nation, and class, as well as the implications of these conditions. The meaning of the Christian faith cannot be abstracted from its historical embodiments. Míguez Bonino observes that although the theologies of the past have often found refuge in a conceptual firmament of abstractions the biblical witness itself is relentlessly concrete in its theological narratives and in its moralizing. He claims the same purpose for liberation theology. "We are not concerned with establishing through deduction the consequences of conceptual truths but with analyzing a historical praxis which claims to be Christian," he explains. "Historical praxis overflows the area of the subjective and private. If we are dealing with acts and not merely with ideas, feelings, or intentions, we plunge immediately into the area of politics."[40]

Míguez Bonino takes the plunge into politics with Scripture in hand, which he regards as the authoritative witness to God's redemptive acts in history. While he concedes that in the present time God acts in various modes that are not found in Scripture, he insists that the fundamental mode of God's agency connects all biblical and postbiblical history.[41] The meaning of history is that history is being transformed by God into the kingdom. Míguez Bonino asserts that although God acts in a plurality of modes, most of which are unknown to us, the biblical theme of the kingdom of God is the single constant that connects biblical and postbiblical experiences of the divine self-disclosure. Yet this crucial and most fundamental of all biblical themes has been repeatedly misconstrued in Christian theologies. Míguez Bonino argues that in the history of Christian thought the question of the relation between history and the kingdom has most often been answered with some version of dualism, though in overreaction against dualistic theories some theologians have advocated monist solutions.

He clearly regards the dualistic solutions as more damaging and less biblical. Dualistic interpretations typically distinguish between sacred and secular history, while associating the Kingdom of God especially with the former. The classic formulations of this position are found in the works of Augustine and Luther, but Míguez Bonino contends that most Christian theologians, including even Moltmann, have resorted to some form of two-kingdoms theory in order to preserve the sacredness of at least some dimension of history. In *Toward a Christian Political Ethics* Míguez Bonino stringently criticizes the social legacy of Luther's distinction between the kingdom of the "law and the sword" and the kingdom of the "gospel and the Spirit." Though he acknowledges that, for Luther, the sovereign purposes of God were fulfilled in *both* kingdoms through their different means, he argues that this dichotomy effectively sanctioned the acquiescence of Lutherans during and after the time of Luther to any secular order that happened to hold power. "History, unfortunately, offers all too many painful illustrations of what this can mean," he remarks, "and not always among Lutherans."[42] The reactionary implications of two-kingdoms theory were most perniciously revealed during the Nazi era in Germany, when, as Karl Barth expressed it, the Lutheran doctrine of the two kingdoms "established, confirmed, and idealized the natural paganism of the German people instead of limiting and restraining it."[43]

Like Barth, Míguez Bonino traces the Lutheran and Augustinian concept of the two kingdoms back to the "deeply unbiblical" conception of redemption found in pre-Christian gnostic and mystery religions.[44] He argues that this fundamentally pagan idea has constantly afflicted the church in part because it has seemed Christian to those who did not know the Bible, and further because it has offered a thoroughly domesticated revision of the biblical doctrine of the kingdom, which served the institutional interests of the Catholic and Protestant churches. Two-kingdoms theory has invariably spiritualized the biblical message, turning Christianity into a religion that is preoccupied with heaven and the interior life of the soul. Dualistic theories produce a "religious and otherworldly version of the faith" in which concrete, human history "becomes little more than a general framework of episodic events without any eschatological significance."[45] Míguez Bonino conceives liberation theology as a return to the biblical conception of the relationship between history and the kingdom, in which the creative, redemptive, and transformative purposes of God are constantly revealed, in a variety of ways, *within* ordinary history.

He concedes that certain classical theologians, such as Irenaeus and Origen, went too far in their repudiation of dualism, and thus formulated monistic theologies that reduced the divine kingdom to human history. More recently, the same monistic identification of the kingdom with history has been promulgated by Gutiérrez, who repeatedly asserts in *A Theology of Liberation* that there is "only one history."[46] For Gutiérrez, the history of faith is not a sacred narrative separate from ordinary history, but an energizing dynamism *within* history that is ultimately, eschatologically, a "transforming invitation."

Míguez Bonino argues that the monistic solution is more biblical than any version of dualism, yet he asserts that Scripture does not identify the kingdom with history, because the kingdom is within but also beyond history. The problem with monistic formulations is that they are logically immanentistic and therefore inevitably deify human history. In explicit disagreement with Segundo and Gutiérrez, Míguez Bonino contends that divine redemption must never be reduced to, or identified with, instances of historical liberation. The God of the Bible is, unarguably, immanently constitutive of all reality, and the divine purposes are constantly revealed within history, but in the Bible the transcendence of God beyond history is also unfailingly assumed. Míguez Bonino therefore asserts that the biblical conception of the relationship between history and the kingdom is best understood dialectically, as unity-in-difference.

He conceives the relationship between history and the kingdom as analogous to the Pauline concepts of the earthly and the resurrected body. Míguez Bonino notes that when Paul refers to living human beings, he uses the same eschatological concept—"body"—that he uses to refer to the resurrected life. For Paul, the "body" of a historical person continues beyond history. The identity of a person is continuous, yet there is a crucial discontinuity between the mortal, historical body of a person and the transformed, perfected body of the same person in the resurrection. "The transformation does not 'disfigure' or 'denaturalize' bodily life," Míguez Bonino explains, "instead, it fulfills and perfects it, eliminating its frailty and corruptibility." In the same way, he argues, history is continuous with the divine kingdom, yet history is only finally redeemed through its transformation into the kingdom. Just as the events of a mortal life only have eternal meaning in relation to the resurrection, the events of history are ultimately meaningful only in relation to the divine transfiguration of history. Just as the purpose of the historical body is only fulfilled by its transformation into the resurrected body, history itself is only fulfilled in the eschatological perfection of the kingdom. The Kingdom of God is therefore not the negation of history, Míguez Bonino insists, "but rather, the elimination of its frailty, corruptibility, and ambiguity. Going a bit more deeply, we can say it is the elimination of history's sinfulness so that the authentic import of communitarian life may be realized."[47]

Míguez Bonino's position on the relationship of history and the kingdom thus places him between Gutiérrez and Moltmann. Though he agrees with Gutiérrez that liberation theology must not reduce itself to "baptizing" revolutionary movements, he disassociates himself from Gutiérrez's monistic identification of history with the kingdom, and he rejects Gutiérrez's experiential interpretation of the option for the poor. To Míguez Bonino, the biblical starting point does not begin with one's experience of God's presence among the poor, but originates, rather, in the declarative command of the Word of God, which is in but also always beyond the world.

On the other hand, Míguez Bonino criticizes Moltmann for taking refuge in the notion that theologians serve a "critical function" by adopting a standpoint above ideological politics. Moltmann wrote in *The Crucified God* that "the crucified God is really a God without a country and without [a] class. But he is not an apolitical God; he is the God of the poor, of the oppressed, of the humiliated."[48] It is elementary that God should not be identified with a particular country or class, any more than God should be identified with a given race or sex or religion. Míguez Bonino criticizes Moltmann, however, for failing to go beyond this fundamental truism, and for therefore failing to deal with the fact that those who are poor, oppressed, and humiliated are members of a *class* and live *in countries*. He asks, "Is it really theologically responsible to leave these two sentences hanging without trying to work out their relation? Are we really for the poor and oppressed if we fail to see them as a class, as members of oppressed societies?"[49] The problem with Moltmann, he concludes, is that in order to avoid the sacralization of any particular ideology or movement he draws back from identifying any "materialization" of the divine presence in history. Míguez Bonino concedes that there is no divine politics or economics. "But this means," he says, "that we must resolutely use the best human politics and economics at our disposal."

As we have seen, in his response to Míguez Bonino, Moltmann explicitly defended democratic socialism as the best human politics and economics at our disposal. The remaining disagreement between Míguez Bonino and Moltmann, therefore, is not a dispute over political concreteness in theology; it is, rather, ideological. As Míguez Bonino has observed, Moltmann's devotion to the importance of critical freedom is entirely consistent with "the liberal social-democratic project which progressive European theologians seem to cherish particularly." He suggests, however, that *this* is the conception that Moltmann and other European theologians need to desacralize, since it is the product of a political ideology, just as "our own option for socialism and a Marxist analysis" will generate its own social values.[50] Desacralization implies that neither critical freedom nor class consciousness can be identified with the kingdom. The remaining difference between Míguez Bonino and Moltmann, then, is the difference between a Marxist and a social-democratic conception of socialism.

This difference has important implications for ethics. One problem with the "liberal social-democratic project," in Míguez Bonino's estimation, is its invariable tendency to produce an idealistic ethics that makes moral judgments on the basis of external ethical ideals. His central example is the neo-Kantian liberal social ethics promulgated by such neo-Protestants as Adolf von Harnack in the latter part of the nineteenth century. Harnack is an excellent example of liberal idealism, he argues, in part because Harnack eloquently epitomized the bourgeois worldview of liberal Christianity, and further because the tradition he represented was a precursor of the North American Social Gospel. For Míguez Bonino, the fundamental problem with the Social Gospel was that it, also, traded on an idealistic ethics.

He focuses on Harnack's essay "The Evangelical Social Mission in the Light of the History of the Church," which explicated Harnack's version of the "ethical ideals of Christianity." This essay included the assurance that Christian morality must avoid economic subjects. "It has nothing to do," Harnack intoned, "with such practical questions of social-economics as the nationalization of private property and enterprises, land-tenure reforms, restrictions of legal hours of work, price regulations, taxation, and insurance."[51] Harnack explained that the church should "interfere" in public policy discussions only when such "serious moral evils" as dueling or divorce were raised in debate. He argued that the social vocation of the church was otherwise to promote mutual trust and peace, to "draw together" the rich and the poor, and to "help break down mischievous class prejudices."

Míguez Bonino respectfully observes that the power and wisdom of the liberal tradition are thoughtfully expounded in Harnack's ethical writings, as well as the limitations of this tradition. Though the advocates of the North American Social Gospel later sought to transcend these limitations by offering a moral assessment of economic subjects, Míguez Bonino contends that the decisive limitation of liberal theology in all of its varieties is that its ethical principles invariably belong to a different world "from that in which the actual structural decisions are made."[52] Liberal theologies of all kinds feature ethical systems that begin with abstract moral questions, such as whether violence or theft can ever be justified. The fallacy of this approach, he charges, is that it presupposes a socially *neutral* standpoint from which an objective discussion of morality can be conducted.[53] But the neutral standpoint is an illusion. Every theory or discussion of ethics has social implications, especially those that are presumed to be objective or socially neutral. Míguez Bonino claims that liberal ethical systems are nearly always conservative in their social function because they operate at a level of abstraction that effectively justifies existing conditions, rather than changing them.

Míguez Bonino takes this criticism of liberal ethics from Marx, who violently rejected the ethics of Christian liberalism and even of Christian socialism because he regarded Christian moral principles as fantasized projections that were, at best, useless in the real world. Marx observed that in Christian theology, love is the source and criterion of moral value. But in the modern capitalist world where Christians actually lived, Marx argued, it is not love but *money* that determines and confers value on human relationships. "Human individuality, human morality, has become both an article of commerce and the form in which money exists."[54] As long as human relationships are mediated by the alienating "fetish" of money, Marx insisted, it is idiotic for Christians to go on prating about the primacy of love, since true love, in the modern world, "is a fantasized expression of the real world." He conceded that the Christian socialists of his time focused on the same problem, and even sometimes advocated "overthrowing Mammon," but he asserted that because they were bound by their Christian ideals and its love language they were incapable of overthrowing anything. Marx argued that Christian morality is not only inherently idealistic, but a functionally reactionary form of idealism as well. Though Christian theology is filled with expressions of concern for justice and the needs of the poor, the church has also historically inculcated among the poor the virtues of "cowardice, self-abasement, resignation, submission, and humility." What the proletariat needs, Marx continued, is an ethos of courage, pride, and independence, which even the most progressive churches cannot affirm. "The social principles of Christianity are sneaking and hypocritical while the proletariat is revolutionary."[55]

As a Christian liberationist, Míguez Bonino naturally believes that the Christian faith can and must be revolutionary in the exact sense that Marx considered impossible. Here as elsewhere, however, he uses Marxist criticism to purge Christian theology of its obscurantist and counterrevolutionary elements, as well as to assert the social primacy of the class struggle, which he calls "a war prompted by greed and power."[56] He embraces Marx's accusation that the church has traditionally inculcated reactionary values among its faithful. The spirituality of a liberationist movement, by contrast, must repudiate every counterrevolutionary form of Christian experience, and cultivate among the faithful a mode of spiritual existence that is equivalent to the Marxist idea of *militancy*. Míguez Bonino asserts that the various Communist movements of this century have produced "innumerable examples of heroic and selfless devotion" that exemplify his ideal of liberationist militancy.[57]

For a true militant, he observes, party discipline is not an external imposition, but the core of his or her spirituality. He cites as an example the Italian Communist Antonio Gramsci, who bravely fought his slow death in Mussolini's prisons and concentrated "his last ounces of strength and lucidity to the cause of the proletariat of his country, without bitterness, totally consecrated to a future which he would not see." He pays similar tribute to Che Guevara, who forsook his "well-earned place of privilege and power" in the Cuban revolutionary government to risk his life and eventually die in the Bolivian jungle for the sake of peasants who, for the most part, did not answer his call. Míguez Bonino argues that although Gramsci and Guevara are among the most admirable examples of Marxist militancy, even at its worst the Communist movement has displayed a profound depth of militant purpose that liberationists must also find. He asserts that even Joseph Stalin, an admittedly "perverse example," possessed the deep sense of commitment and purposefulness that subjectively defines a militant. Though Stalin could be callous, hateful, and cynical, and was at times driven by "inhuman motivations," Míguez Bonino remarks that even here "one feels always in the presence of a man who, in his innermost being, has given himself to a cause." The depth of Stalin's revolutionary commitment, as with any true militant, was made possible by the fact that the commitment mastered his entire lifetime. He lived in complete subjection to the revolutionary cause and its discipline. In his life there was "no frivolity, no equivocation, no possible relativising of this commitment."[58] Míguez Bonino adds that this is the spirit the liberationist movement requires.

His admiration for those whom he calls "red heroes" is mainly based, however, on Latin American experience. Referring to the various Latin American revolutionary movements of the past sixty years, Míguez Bonino recalls "the tortures, the suffering, the deaths of thousands of communist revolutionaries" throughout the continent, and applies to them the saying of Christ, "Greater love has no man than this, that a man lay down his life for his friends" (John 15:13). He asserts that although Communists throughout Latin America have been forced to exclude all that is superfluous or distracting from their lives for the sake of revolution, and have therefore at times appeared ruthless or unfeeling, most of these militants have been primarily motivated, as Guevara claimed, by deep feelings of love. Guevara acknowledged that such an assertion could only be offered "at the risk of sounding ridiculous," but the note of irony is missing in Míguez Bonino. After the terrors of the past generation in Chile, Argentina, Brazil, Guatemala, El Salvador, and elsewhere, he does not temper or conceal his admiration for the revolutionaries, or question their motives.

Míguez Bonino's own militancy is his chief asset as a writer. His various works convey a deep sense of revolutionary solidarity and an insistent conviction that justice must be the ground and goal of Christian social ethics. He argues that the problem with the traditional types of Christian ethics is that all of them have ultimately elevated some other concern, such as social order or moral purity, to preeminence rather than justice. To struggle for justice, he concedes, is to confront the hard reality of power, which "refuses to submit to general principles or moral norms." He therefore rejects pacifism as a moralistic retreat from the essential struggle. "Politics reveals an autonomy that has to be recognized and respected," he explains, "unless one is willing to forgo efficacy altogether."[59] He elsewhere argues, on the same grounds, that Christian criticisms of Communist vengeance and enmity are usually moralistic, if not hypocritical. He notes that the Bible itself attributes vengeance and enmity to the founders of the faith, and even to God, when matters of justice are at stake. Because the biblical dialectic of solidarity and hatred is inherent, to some degree, in every liberation movement, Míguez Bonino asserts that modern Christians must avoid moralistic criticism on the subject of Communist tyranny. Moralistic judgments on this subject are hypocritical.[60]

Míguez Bonino further contends that Christian moral norms, and the revolutionary means that Christians may require, do not substantially differ from the norms and means that Communists uphold. Though it is commonly claimed that Communists eschew morality, Míguez Bonino argues that most Communists only reject the external, idealistic mode of ethics that liberationists also reject. Lenin's formula that the moral good is "that which serves the revolution" is typically interpreted as a repudiation of moral discourse, but Míguez Bonino asserts that, rightly understood, it merely summarizes the way in which an ethic of justice confers moral value. Liberationism and Marxism-Leninism are in agreement, he implies, in assuming that moral value cannot be disengaged from concrete revolutionary praxis. He contends that Lenin himself was sensitive to moral considerations, even in the ordinary sense of the term, and argues that this assertion is "easy to prove" in the literature.[61] It does not seem to give him pause that even Stalin could be defended in the same way.

During his reign, Stalin signed more than forty thousand death warrants and was directly responsible for the deaths of untold millions, yet along the way he delivered humanitarian speeches and pronouncements and personally assured visiting Westerners of his liberalism. This was also Lenin's approach, though Lenin occasionally dropped the pretense when such Western pilgrims as Bertrand Russell solicited his assurances. When Russell gently inquired whether Lenin's wholesale slaughter of suspects and enemies was actually necessary, Lenin gave him an abrupt reply. Russell later recalled, "His guffaw at the thought of those massacred made my blood run cold."

That is the missing element in Míguez Bonino's assessment of the historical legacy of Communism. In his sincere desire to avoid self-righteousness he refuses on principle to examine the implications of Communist terror, totalitarian rule, and economic bankruptcy. What is missing is any acknowledgment of the meaning of Lenin's guffaw or the mass graves of Cambodia or the hatred for Communism shared by all of the otherwise differing countries of Eastern Europe.

Míguez Bonino's work is more constructive when he turns to the question of liberationist ethical content. His method moves, in his terms, from praxis (history) to theory (ethics) to praxis (strategy). Since he rejects the notion that liberationist ethics should be based on abstract principles, he grounds his own position on a series of middle axioms that he calls "historical mediations." The axioms move in three concentric circles that become increasingly specific or concrete. The first is the idea of a universal human sense of fairness or obligation, as postulated in natural law and Kantian moral theories. Míguez Bonino asserts that a "virtually universal consensus" exists on the moral values of just distribution, equal opportunity, liberty, and truthfulness. The implications and requirements of these principles become more concretely specified in the political sphere, where systems are organized to serve the public welfare, preserve social peace, protect individual freedom, and ensure equality of opportunity. In the third concentric circle, Míguez Bonino observes that "the application of these four criteria requires a recognition of their interrelatedness, analysis of the correct circumstances, and the correct use of available means."

To the objection that these axioms are rather vague, and even compatible with conservative ideologies, Míguez Bonino replies that they can become more concrete only in specific situations. That is, the specific implications of these maxims can only be determined within particular social situations, because any other definition or interpretation would represent another form of externalized, idealistic ethics.

There are, however, natural-law and Kantian versions of this model with which liberationism is definitely incompatible. Míguez Bonino notes that conservative proponents of his model typically assume that the public good is served by preserving "peace" and the existing social order. But to view the question from the underside of history, from the perspective of its victims, is to learn that only a social transformation will serve the public good. Throughout the third world, liberationists find that to serve the public welfare, freedom, and equality of opportunity they must call for "a radical shift in power, a mobilizing vision (ideology), a total commitment (praxis), and a concrete historical focus (contextuality)."[62]

He observes that in every struggle for freedom and self-determination liberationists inevitably confront a conflict between the human costs of liberation and the human costs of its postponement. This dilemma is unsolvable, he argues, in the realm of theory. Moral axioms can only inform one's praxis, as one attempts to minimize the human costs on both sides, while seeking to maximize the possibilities for liberation.

> Revolutionary change, it is said, sacrifices human lives. But how many lives are sacrificed by prolonging for a century or two a form of production or distribution of goods that has ceased adequately to serve the needs of the people? Crash programs, it is said, sacrifice a generation. But how many generations are sacrificed in the hope of gradual change? Such questions can be multiplied. I am *not* necessarily arguing at this point in favor of revolution or crash programs. I *am* arguing against the verbal terrorism of an ideologically inspired fallacy.[63]

Within the latter, he includes the verbal terrorism of those who relentlessly warn against "violence," as though the social systems of Latin America were not already riddled with the violence of military terror and economic oppression.

For nearly a century, Míguez Bonino laments, the promise of economic modernization was sold to Latin Americans as salvation itself. He ruefully recalls that the homegrown evangelists of this faith were the liberal elites and Protestant churches of Latin America. Today, he remarks, their harvest is evident: "We sowed democracy and reaped the national security state." To the variable extent that they have become integrated into the Western system of monopoly capitalism, Latin American nations have become debt-ridden, low-tax, cheap-labor havens for transnational firms, and Latin American governments have become wardens for these firms. "The new military rulers are no longer the individualistic colonels or generals of the traditional *cuartelazos*, but a technocratic-bureaucratic elite," he remarks. "Educated in the American military academies, they act as guardians of the transnational corporations." Míguez Bonino argues that although their use of terror to enforce conformity is widely feared, these guardians of monopoly power will eventually be overthrown by their enemies—their victims.

> Here is the crux of the problem: an underprivileged minority can be accommodated in a relatively affluent economy. Or it can be repressed violently—even the genocide of a tribe or ethnic group has been envisioned as "justifiable." But it is not possible permanently to repress or eliminate the large and growing majority of the people. As the economy abroad, in worldwide crisis, continues to export inflation, insecurity, and unemployment to the Third World, and as the domestic conditions of appropriation and distribution compound the crisis, social unrest and conflict are bound to escalate. A regime that has nothing but sheer repressive force on which to rely is ultimately doomed—even if in the short run it manages to create untold misery, suffering, and death.[64]

Míguez Bonino bases his hope for the future on that assessment of the prospects and costs of revolution. In his work, we encounter a sympathetic and compassionate figure who represents, as well as anyone, the mainstream of the liberationist movement. His method does not reduce theology to politics, or submit faith to a political test, or identify the socialist movement with the Kingdom of God. He does assert that Socialism is "really and continually related" to the kingdom, and therefore also "related" to his hope as a follower of Christ. With characteristic propriety, however, he explains, "The gospel does not stand or fall with the correctness of this view. But my theology does."[65]

His theology is the product of a faithful reading of Scripture "in a revolutionary situation." While his theology is based upon a liberationist reading of Scripture, he does not claim that this is the only legitimate way to interpret the Christian faith, or that the meaningfulness of the faith stands or falls with his reading of it. Míguez Bonino does not reduce theological doctrines to the ends of revolution, but argues that liberationism is the most accurate expression of the historic Christian faith.

Like Gutiérrez, however, Míguez Bonino also identifies liberation with the Socialist movement. He thus places great emphasis upon his programmatic commitment to Socialism, which he defines, like Gutiérrez, as the "social appropriation" of the means of production, political management, and human freedom.[66] He declares that the Socialist project "concretely defines my Christian obedience in the world," but the problem with his definition of the project is that it *isn't* very concrete. It largely avoids, for example, questions about centralization of authority, market freedom, and political rights. The result is that his formulations are compatible with every type of socialization. Though he repeatedly asserts that "the socialist option" is fundamental to liberationism, he fails to examine the stultifying problems of economic inefficiency and bureaucratic authoritarianism that have characterized the various command economies of the past century. He adopts an extreme version of dependency theory, and therefore writes time and again about the need for a "socialist" alternative, but he never assesses or even considers the arguments for decentralized modes of socialization. In this area, he frequently identifies his position with that of Gutiérrez, but there are similar problems with the outlook of Gutiérrez, who has envisioned as his goal a society "in which private ownership of the means of production is eliminated."[67] Gutiérrez has explained that he believes the *masses* must appropriate the means of production and political management, but, like his other formulations, this argument is compatible with state collectivism.

This is not to say that Gutiérrez and Míguez Bonino have actually advocated such a system. It is to say that, despite their repeated insistence on the necessity of a concrete socialist project, their own writings on the subject are vague. If some version of socialism is the most worthy goal of the liberationist movement, as I believe it is, then it is imperative that liberationists define the vision of socialism that they uphold and explain how it is different from other forms that share the same name. The ideology of state socialism, for example, is not new or historically innocent. Liberationists should not pretend that it is either.

Míguez Bonino has repeatedly dismissed this kind of criticism as a vestige of European liberalism, but the decentralized, cooperative vision of economic democracy that I am advocating is as desperately relevant in Latin America as anywhere. It is the operative vision for hundreds of thousands of base communities in Latin America today. Míguez Bonino has argued that "all we have today in Latin America are reactionary, reformist, or revolutionary engagements, and therefore reactionary, reformist, or revolutionary readings of what we have called 'germinal events of the Christian faith.' "[68] This assertion is true. The key question that it raises, however, is whether "revolutionary" must mean the praxis of centralized collectivism. If the answer is affirmative, then it is clear that revolutionary praxis— whatever else it may be called—cannot be called a means to liberation. Too many liberation movements have already taken this road to collective slavery.

Liberation theology must insist, rather, that *liberation* implies freedom, self-determination, economic democracy, and peace. These are revolutionary ideals. They have inspired and sustained base communities, cooperative associations, and unions throughout Latin America. The alternatives to them inexorably lead to some form of dictatorship. Liberation theology, therefore — as Míguez Bonino has eloquently argued — must struggle to represent the faith and concrete interests of the poor with the best politics at our disposal.[69] That describes nothing less than the politics of democratic socialism.

7

Toward a Theopraxis
of the Common Good

The central irony of the democratic-socialist tradition is that while social-ism has always been dismissed by its critics as utopian, the various socialist movements in Europe and the Americas have often failed to take even progressive (much less utopian) positions on issues outside their industrial focus. As we have seen, for example, Walter Rauschenbusch retained ves-tiges of the racism and sexism of his cultural background while urging socialism upon the churches. During the same period, the Socialist Party in the United States regarded racism as largely an epiphenomenon of the class struggle. Eugene Debs fought for the rights of blacks within the trade unions, but when he was asked what the socialist movement offered blacks, he routinely answered, "Nothing—except socialism." Like his party, he saw black workers as workers, but not as blacks.[1]

The historical limitations of democratic socialism have also been illus-trated in the work of Paul Tillich, whose neo-Marxist conception of social-ism was so narrowly Eurocentric that he virtually ignored the third world and later shied away from politics after he came to a country that lacked an organized proletariat. As in the cases of Rauschenbusch and Debs, it is reasonable to assume that Tillich would have adopted a broader conception of socialism if he had lived in the present age of feminist, black, ecological, and third-world liberation movements. Today, as a consequence of these developments, it is increasingly agreed within the progressive movements of the first world that socialism requires a feminist, racial, ecological, and international consciousness that earlier movements for socialism lacked.

Unfortunately, this development does not necessarily promote agree-ment on ideological or praxological questions among the various factions of first-world progressive movements, much less between these movements and the liberationist movements of the third world. Speaking as the product of a liberal-democratic culture, for example, Jürgen Moltmann has identi-fied socialism with democratic empowerment and declared that all forms of vanguardism and authoritarianism are repugnant to him. While he has claimed to withhold judgment on the efficacy of vanguard strategies in the third world—on account of the enormous differences in context between first- and third-world societies—Moltmann's clear implication has been that third-world liberationists should take the social-democratic path rather than some version of revolutionary Marxism.[2] As we have seen, this recommendation has been disputed by liberationists, who assert that in much of the third world Moltmann's liberal socialism is either a nonexistent alternative or an already discredited form of co-optation.

The existence of this kind of disagreement within contemporary religious socialism has raised the question whether it should be possible to agree upon the basic elements of a common liberationist social vision. In her provocative work *Communities of Resistance and Solidarity*, Sharon Welch has argued that the discontinuities within modern liberationism preclude the possibility and even the desirability of a common social vision. Welch contends that all universalistic moral claims are inherently ahistorical and functionally oppressive. Though she concedes that human rights language has been useful, at times, as a means of expressing minimal standards of moral accountability, Welch argues that even the concept of human rights is an ideological notion that masks the historical causes of oppression. Following Michel Foucault, she insists that all forms of moral discourse (including her own) contain rhetorical strategies designed to secure power. She thus advocates an intentionally marginalized and "intrinsically relative" liberationism that respects the "integrity of the particular" without appealing to common moral values or precepts.[3]

Because praxological questions are always contextual, I find Welch's argument convincing on a programmatic level, where the specific needs and conditions of given historical circumstances must always be addressed on their own terms. To accept Welch's entire assessment of moral language, however, would be to undercut the meanings of moral terms that Welch herself uses repeatedly. It is self-defeating to declare one's opposition to "oppressive" economic systems or the "inhumanity of torture" or the "evils of sexism" if one simultaneously relativizes all moral language on historicist grounds. Without some basis of common moral reference, the moral criticisms of modern societies advanced by liberationists are unintelligible to those outside the liberationist fold. This is not to overlook the problems with universalistic moral language outlined by Welch, Foucault, and others. The project I am describing does not rest upon or require ontological claims about the universality of moral norms. It does require enough common moral ground to make an intelligible appeal to those who are not already converted. Liberationist criticism needs to be rooted in traditions of moral discourse that are larger and more inclusive than the discourses of countercultural vanguards. What is needed, in other words, is a perspectivistic socialist discourse that clears the widest possible path between moral absolutism and moral relativism.[4]

Like most of the figures I have examined thus far, I believe that the most regenerative and humane forms of social praxis embody the moral values of prophetic religion and democratic socialism. In its most representative forms, religious socialism has unified these two streams of moral discourse, holding up a normative social vision that draws upon common traditions of religious and cultural values. The fundamental appeal of religious or democratic socialism within the first world is to move beyond the welfare state, through democratic empowerment, while preserving the gains of liberalism. Rather than retreat into some form of sectarianism, democratic socialism struggles for democratized forms of social organization and authority on the basis of democratic principles.

In political cultures that lack traditions of democratic entitlement, religious socialism must draw upon fewer resources. Latin American liberation theologies have traded heavily, for that reason, on the social implications of biblical and patristic teaching. These limitations should not be taken, however, as a negation of democratic socialism as a political vision for the third world. If the social-democratic parties of Latin America have often compromised socialism beyond recognition, that does not invalidate the goals of authentic democratic socialism. The socialist vision is relevant even in societies that feature weak or nonexistent democratic traditions, because the character and direction of liberation movements are partly determined by their operative vision.

To defend democratic socialism as the most worthy form of liberationism is to assume that this tradition can become more inclusive than it has been in the past. In recent years, the racial and ideological limitations of historic democratic socialism have been criticized most significantly by Cornel West, who has argued that democratic socialism, like liberal theology, is an outmoded historical project. West has observed that socialism today must include Marxist, feminist, Garveyist, ecological, and antimilitarist elements to provide the new emancipatory vision that is needed. In his estimation, however, democratic socialism has been too compromised by its historic identification with middle-class electoral reformism to provide this alternative. Like liberal theology, he has argued, democratic socialism represents a creative project of the past that should be viewed today, at best, as a "crucial stepping-stone" to the revolutionary alternative that is needed.[5]

West's assessment of the alternatives within socialism has been offered in his typological analysis of Marxism. He has distinguished among the Stalinist, Leninist, Trotskyist, Gramscian, Bernsteinian, and Councilist traditions, dismissing the first three as authoritarian distortions of socialism. West argues that Stalinism is the Ku Klux Klan of Marxism, representing (like the Klan) a total perversion of its founding symbols. Continuing with the religious analogy, he equates the Leninist and Trotskyist traditions with fundamentalist theologies, "which give self-serving lip service to truncated versions of the major norms." West is more respectful toward the Gramscian tradition on account of its democratic elements, but he concludes that because it defends freedom on the grounds of strategy rather than principle the Gramscian tradition is ultimately Leninist in spirit. Like neo-orthodox theology, he explains, Gramscian Marxism represents "an innovative revision of dogmas for dogmatic purposes."[6]

Of the two remaining types of Marxism, West equates Bernsteinian democratic socialism with the Social Gospel and the Councilist tradition with liberation theology, arguing that only Councilism provides an adequate social vision. Like the Social Gospel, he asserts, the democratic-socialist tradition has typically tied a powerful critique of capitalism to an "abortive" praxis. West acknowledges that democratic socialism retains the Marxist concepts of the class struggle and the dialectic of history, but he argues that because democratic-socialist parties have historically emphasized electoral reformism and anti-Communism this tradition represents a "regressive Marxist praxis" in the modern world. What is needed, he concludes, is a pluralistic revolutionary vision that democratic socialism is too compromised to provide.

West has identified himself with the Councilist Marxism of Rosa Luxemburg, Anton Pannekoek, and Karl Korsch, which he conceives as a "left-wing Marxist" position between democratic-socialist reformism and Leninist authoritarianism. From the Councilist perspective, he explains, the underlying problem with democratic socialism is that it has historically promoted class collaborationism through its emphasis on anti-Communism and its tendency to view workers primarily as wage earners, voters, and consumers. By contrast, the Councilist tradition regards workers primarily as collectively self-determining producers who (at least ideally) prefigure the coming Socialist order. The Councilist position is revolutionary rather than reformist, insisting that workers must focus on seizing power through revolutionary organizations that already prefigure a Socialist society. Because Councilism is anticollaborationist and internally democratic, West identifies this tradition as the progressive stream within Marxism. "Councilism is to Marxism," he asserts, "what liberation theology is to Christianity: a promotion and practice of the moral core of the perspective against overwhelming odds for success."[7]

The problem is the overwhelming odds. As a revolutionary alternative to the social-democratic preoccupation with electoral reformism and trade unionism, I regard Councilism as a valuable tradition that has made important contributions to modern socialist theory. The problem is that while the democratic-socialist tradition has, at least, organized actual parties and worked in solidarity with existing trade unions, the Councilist tradition has existed mainly in the minds of neo-Marxist intellectuals. West has derided the compromised praxis of democratic socialism, but the praxis of Councilism is solidarity with an imaginary movement. The organizations imagined in the past century of Councilist theory still do not exist. To argue that they should exist, as West has done, is commendable, but under the given circumstances it is politically self-defeating to declare that alternative strategies are "abortive" or unworthy of support. As Michael Harrington reluctantly concluded thirty years ago, it is more revolutionary to be in solidarity with actually existing unions than to be in solidarity with a fantasized proletariat.[8]

It is not my point that the Councilist position is theoretically or even praxologically mistaken. The Councilist tradition is an important resource for modern socialism. One of the most valuable resources for the theory of decentralized socialism, for example, is the work of G. D. H. Cole, the Fabian theorist who attacked Fabian state socialism on guild-socialist grounds. I believe that any serious conception of socialism for the future must appropriate the major elements of Cole's theory of guild socialism, which was, in part, a product of the revolutionary Councilist tradition that West has embraced.[9] The Councilist emphasis on revolutionary prefigurativism is especially relevant in third-world societies that lack a tradition of trade unionism. My objection to West's discussion of Councilism is only that it derides democratic socialism and the Social Gospel, while identifying liberationism with a *single* form of Marxism. This approach overlooks the historical failures of Councilism as a form of praxis, as well as the enduring value of the democratic-socialist and Social Gospel traditions. While his criticisms of the democratic-socialist tradition are largely justified, the vision of socialism that West has advanced is unattainable on Councilist terms alone. The Councilist tradition needs democratic socialism in the same way that liberation theology needs to be shaped, informed, and limited by the theology of the Social Gospel.

Without explicitly acknowledging any shift in his position, it is evident from his recent essays that West has begun to move toward the same conclusion. While he continues to define his social ideal in Councilist terms, West's recent work has promoted what he calls a "democratic and libertarian socialism" that draws its operative social vision more from the writings of Branko Horvat, John Kenneth Galbraith, Wlodzimierz Brus, and, especially, Alec Nove than from the Councilist literature. In these essays, West has begun to work out a more pluralistic conception of socialism that assumes the need for market discipline, price mechanisms, and decentralized economic planning.[10] Rather than reject economic democracy and electoral reformism on Councilist grounds, West has begun to identify himself (at least strategically) with the kind of market socialist position outlined by Nove in *The Economics of Feasible Socialism* and by Brus in *The Economics and Politics of Socialism*.[11] From this perspective, which is also my own position, the immediate economic goal for the Left is to create a form of socialism that is more pluralistic in its mixture of ownership forms than the socialism of the past.

The vision itself is not entirely new. The structural elements of what is today called market socialism were suggestively discussed nearly a century ago in the debates over syndicalism and were incorporated into socialist theory, at a high level of socioeconomic sophistication, in Oskar Lange's

classic book of 1931, *On the Economic Theory of Socialism*.* The pluralistic
nature of this social vision was effectively summarized in C. A. R. Crosland's epochal 1957 work, *The Future of Socialism*. "The ideal," Crosland
asserted, "is a society in which ownership is thoroughly mixed-up — a society
with a diverse, diffused, pluralist, and heterogeneous pattern of ownership,
with the State, the nationalized industries, the Co-operatives, the Unions,
government financial institutions, pension funds, foundations, and millions
of private families all participating."[12] This statement summarizes the economic vision of modern democratic socialism if one adds, in the words of
the Frankfurt Declaration (1951) of the Socialist International: "and private ownership in agriculture, handicraft, retail trade, and small and mid-
dle-sized industries."[13]

As I have argued in detail elsewhere, I believe that certain innovations
in contemporary democratic socialism have made the social vision of Crosland and the Frankfurt Declaration more attainable than in the past. The
turn toward decentralized forms of socialization within the modern socialist
movement has created the possibility of attaining market-oriented forms of
democratic control over the investment process. In Sweden, for example,
the ruling Social Democratic government has enacted the Meidner Plan
for Economic Democracy, which imposes an annual twenty percent tax on
major company profits payable in the form of stock to a series of mutual
funds controlled by unions and the public. The tax can only be paid in the
form of shares, not cash, and it remains within each firm as a new form of
equity capital for investment. As their collective proportion of stock ownership grows, workers are increasingly entitled to representation on company boards. Voting rights of the employee shares are jointly held by locals
and branch funds, with the first forty percent split between the locals and
the national unions. As I have argued in chapter 2, market socialism is a
strategy not only to empower workers in large firms, but also to empower
all wage earners, as well as those who do not earn wages. The Meidner
Plan thus requires public representation on the governing boards of the
wage-earner funds and stipulates that all wage earners (not only those
employed by the contributing firms) are entitled to vote for board representatives. Dividend income is used for collective purposes, and at present
rates of growth the largest two hundred Swedish firms should become
worker-controlled within thirty years. Within sixty years, most of the equity
capital in Sweden will be collectively owned.[14]

The Meidner Plan offers a way to attain democratic control over the

---

* The crucial difference between the market socialism of Lange and contemporary market
socialism focuses upon the question of centralized ownership and planning. While Lange's
model allowed greater room for the role of the market than traditional state socialism, his
conception of socialism was still essentially statist, featuring state-owned firms run by managers
hired on profit-bonus arrangements. Contemporary democratic socialism is pluralistic and
decentralized, emphasizing, wherever possible, the construction of networks of cooperative
ownership.

economy while retaining the discipline of the market. It requires no program of nationalization, and investors still seek the highest rate of return.
Because it uses a decentralized, market-oriented strategy to gain democratic control over the process of investment, I regard the kind of strategy
represented by the Meidner Plan as the essence of modern democratic
socialism. This approach retains the historic socialist insistence on collective
empowerment while reflecting, as well, the recent turn in the socialist movement toward market realism. It therefore materially advances the vision of
democratic transformation advocated by most of the figures we have examined, including West, who has recently asserted that the fundamental issue
for the socialist movement is the extent to which it will become possible to
establish "public accountability of limited centralization, meritorious hierarchy, and a mixture of planned, socialized, and private enterprises in the
market along with indispensable democratic political institutions."[15] That
summarizes the socioeconomic vision of modern democratic socialism.

Most books on socialism, including my own, have emphasized socioeconomic arguments that criticize capitalism or defend the viability of socialist
theory. One of the problems with this analytical focus, however, as Robert
Dahl has observed, is that the preoccupation with theory has often subtly
reinforced the notion that the struggle for socialism is essentially a matter
of working out the socioeconomic arguments.[16] The same shortcoming in
socialist theorizing has been noted by Dorothee Sölle, whose writings on
religious socialism have shifted the focus toward more subjective factors.
Sölle has especially emphasized the subjective struggle of will that middle-
class people almost invariably face when they confront the prospect of
breaking neutrality in the class struggle.

She argues that most middle-class people are fatalistic as a result of their
education and their position in the class system. Although most middle-
class people are sufficiently educated to comprehend the ravages of racism,
sexism, and imperialism, Sölle observes that their desire for success and
financial stability in the existing system restrains their desire for justice.
This attitude is reinforced by an educational process that emphasizes ambiguity. For reasons that are defensible in themselves, the educational systems
in modern bourgeois societies tend to promote and reward reflection, skep-
ticism, and ambiguity. These systems therefore produce students who
become offended—as Kierkegaard observed—whenever they are confronted with an either/or choice on a question of substantial or transcendent
importance.[17] The consequence is an irresolute wavering between the "one
hand and other hand" of every important question, including the interests
of the poor. Sölle concedes that the bourgeois process of socialization is
positive insofar as it makes people sensitive to the ambiguities of life and
gives them a sense of distance on the choices they face. Because middle-
class people are not totally defined by their immediate needs and interests,
they are comparatively free to make decisions. The problem is that this
freedom, in the context of an objectively ambiguous class position, often

binds the same people to an endless wavering between contradictory possibilities.[18]

My point is not to denigrate the middle class. Because of their relative well-being and security, middle-class people are often more capable of generosity, sensitivity, tolerance, and intellectual objectivity than those who are oppressed. While it is often assumed that middle-class sensibilities are incompatible with socialism, modern Christian socialism (including Latin American liberation theology) has thus far largely been a product of middle-class thought and experience. The point obtains even for those liberationists, such as Hugo Assmann, who have emphasized the "epistemological privilege of the poor."[19] Because liberation theology has often been presented as the direct irruption of the poor, the middle-class elements in the movement have frequently been regarded as an embarrassment. Assmann has confessed along these lines that "as a Westernized Latin American . . . I don't feel happy with the fact that my theological dissertation was written in German. I have a psychological necessity to say to you in Western language that I am not Western. . . . If you look in my library you will find books by German authors, French authors, Italian authors, Marx, Moltmann, etc. There is something false in this."[20]

The shrewdest critics of liberationism have repeatedly exploited this supposed weakness in liberation theology, but there is nothing "false" in a Latin American theologian learning the history and languages of Western thought. It is only false (or mistaken) to accept the taunts of the Right that liberation theology is discredited on account of its middle-class elements. It is true, as Assmann implies, that Latin American liberationists have needed to adopt more critical perspectives on Western theology in order to develop more indigenous theologies of their own. It is also true, as Gutiérrez and Míguez Bonino have poignantly recalled of themselves, that many liberation theologians have needed to purge themselves of their acquired habits and assumptions in order to enter into solidarity with the poor. But as the cases of Gutiérrez and Míguez Bonino confirm, it *is* possible for those who have enjoyed middle-class privileges to form alliances with the poor. For liberation theologians, the value of middle-class acculturation is that one attains a voice to speak for those who cannot speak for themselves. The middle-class origins of democratic socialism only represent a judgment on socialism if one begins with romantic assumptions about the poor as a messianic force. To affirm the liberal bourgeois elements within democratic socialism is to reject the ultraleft romanticization of the proletariat, as well as the Rightist assumption that liberationism is necessarily tied to such notions.

While I have thus far developed the argument about the connection between liberalism and socialism by focusing on the arguments for economic democracy, the same relationship also obtains in other areas. Liberal feminism is a crucial example. In her valuable study *The Radical Future of Liberal Feminism*, Zillah Eisenstein has argued that any serious pursuit of liberal feminist goals must eventually outstrip the limitations of liberalism itself.[21] The same point has been made by Rosemary Ruether and by such opponents of feminism as Michael Levin and George Gilder.[22] While feminist demands for equal rights, federally funded child care, parental leaves of absence, flextime, work sharing, and income equity can all be promoted as liberal reforms, the accumulated impact of such measures would transcend the limitations of welfare-state reformism. Taken seriously, feminist demands for social and economic equity contain redistributive implications that amount, as Levin has charged, to a feminist road to socialism.

The North American feminist case for comparable-worth legislation, for example, is a variant of the European democratic-socialist argument for solidarity wage policy. Such feminist scholars as Ronnie Steinberg and Lois Haignere have developed a compelling argument for policies that redress the sexist pattern of wage discrimination in the United States.[23] Thus far, the literature on comparable worth has focused on market disparities that victimize workers in traditionally female vocations. But because women represent approximately half the work force, the socioeconomic implications of comparable-worth policy are potentially enormous. If it is unacceptable for male executives or physicians to earn ten times more than their female secretaries or nurses, it is also unacceptable that gross economic disparities not related to gender should exist. Here as elsewhere, the policy implications of feminist criticism transcend liberalism. In the case of comparable worth, these implications logically lead to some form of socialist-solidarity wage policy. As Eisenstein and Rosemary Ruether have argued, only an explicitly socialist feminist criticism can fulfill the implicit policy consequences of liberal feminist criticism, as well as resolve the personal contradictions that inevitably accompany feminist reformism in a patriarchal society.

Ruether has further argued that only a decision for socialism can rescue the feminist movement from its historic preoccupation with the personal and professional concerns of middle- and upper-class women. In her landmark work, *Sexism and God-Talk: Toward a Feminist Theology,* she has noted that liberal feminists typically seek to gain for themselves the same rights and opportunities offered to men of their own class. Thus, she recalls, during the later years of the suffrage movement, one faction of the movement promoted female suffrage on racist and classist grounds. Ruether reviews this historical legacy to make the point that while all women are marginalized by their gender, they are otherwise divided among racial and class hierarchies that often command their highest loyalty and sense of identification. While feminist criticism is implicitly radical, she observes, liberal feminism does not necessarily lead to radicalism, because of its position in the class system. Ruether offers a sharp critique of the upscale-capitalist form of feminism, which rationalizes the existence of a large servant class of minimum-wage housekeepers and day-care workers. The "glitter" of this version of feminism, she writes, "as displayed in *Cosmopolitan*

and *Ms.*, both eludes and insults the majority of women who recognize that
its 'promise' is not for them."[24] Like democratic socialism, feminism therefore also needs to overcome the limitations of much of its cultural and
socioeconomic past in order to contribute to the emancipatory vision that
is needed.

Unlike the various authoritarian versions of Christianity and Marxism,
Christian socialism has been characterized through most of its history by a
historical consciousness that assumes the need for continuous reinterpretation and revision. It is further assumed from this perspective that an
adequate vision of religious socialism must include more than the inherited
social wisdom of the Christian past, and that all praxological visions are
limited by the historical and cultural circumstances in which they are conceived. These limitations partly explain the failure of the socialist movement
over much of its history to mount a sustained attack on racial injustice.[25]
The same historical and cultural limitations have prevented the Christian
socialist tradition, through much of its history, from recognizing the importance of feminist criticism. While the theologies of Rauschenbusch, Tillich,
and Moltmann have been at least implicitly feminist in their rejection of
monarchical conceptualities and in their advocacy of democratic egalitarianism, the explicitly feminist implications of these commitments have gone
largely unmentioned in their writings.

The same must be said of most contemporary Latin American liberation
theologians. While some of them have made encouraging statements in
recent years when interviewed on the subject, their major works thus far
have failed to discuss the oppression of women or the implications of feminist criticism for socialist theory.[26] It has often been argued in defense of
this silence that women's liberation in underdeveloped countries must await
the outcome of more fundamental socioeconomic struggles. Like other
arguments of this kind advanced by earlier generations of Christian socialists, this contention is true in one respect while simultaneously undermining
the struggle for social justice. It is unarguably true that the growth of feminism as a political force in the third world is partly dependent upon the
prior fulfillment of fundamental economic needs. What is unacceptable is
that this truism is often taken as a reason to disregard the suffering of
women or the need for a movement that attacks sexism as vigorously as it
opposes racism or economic deprivation.

While it is conventionally assumed that modern Christian socialism has
been discredited by its idealism, my own reading is that this tradition should
be faulted mainly for its *lack* of idealism. The same figures who have found
the courage to face ridicule, isolation, and the "sad smiles of the wise" for
their socialist idealism have historically failed to recognize the importance
of feminism as a dimension of socialist praxis. They have been willing to
face the accusation of idealism on socioeconomic subjects related to feminism, but not explicitly on feminism itself. The unstated assumption in
much of the religious-socialist literature of the past has been that feminist

demands are either secondary in importance or already covered by social-ism. The rebirth of feminist consciousness in our time, however, has rede-fined the ends of liberation. Today the just demands of the feminist movement are as crucial to any socialism worthy of the name as the demands for racial justice, economic democracy, or ecological preservation.

The counterinfluence is equally crucial. As Ruether has argued, the most generative form of religious feminism draws upon the perspective of lib-eration theology. "This perspective does not exclude the invoking of relig-ious symbols from outside the biblical tradition," she explains, "as well as from suppressed traditions that have been condemned as heretical. But it draws in this larger heritage through the liberation theology perspective, rather than from a perspective that opts for one side (maternal, natural, pagan) against the other (paternal, historical, biblical). It seeks to get to the root alienation behind these dualisms, expressed in exploitative social patterns, to create a new humanity and new social relations beyond these divisions."[27] By adopting a liberationist methodological perspective, Ruether argues, religious feminism can offer a communitarian socialist alternative to the present split between the various separatist and liberal versions of feminism.

The core elements of this vision have been outlined in Ruether's major work, *Sexism and God-Talk.* "We seek a society that affirms the values of democratic participation, of the equal value of all persons as the basis for their civil equality and their equal access to the educational and work opportunities of the society," she has written. "But more, we seek a dem-ocratic socialist society that dismantles sexist and class hierarchies, that restores ownership and management of work to the base communities of workers themselves, who then create networks of economic and political relationships. Still more, we seek a society built on organic community, in which the processes of childraising, of education, of work, of culture have been integrated to allow both men and women to share child nurturing and homemaking and also creative activity and decision making in the larger society. Still more, we seek an ecological society in which human and non-human ecological systems have been integrated into harmonious and mutu-ally supportive, rather than antagonistic, relations."[28]

With each "more," of course, Ruether's social vision becomes more explicitly utopian. She therefore acknowledges that the entire vision can only be lived out by communal organizations characterized by high levels of intentionality. Ruether is respectful toward those who have organized alternative communities, but, because of the inherent limitations of these communities and their high rates of failure, she personally opts for a "mosaic" approach that views the various organizations for racial justice, feminism, economic democracy, peace, ecological preservation, and the rest as prefigurative pieces of an unrealized collective vision. The function of the vision is to facilitate some sense of collective purpose among otherwise disparate organizations and individuals working for widely differentiated and often lonely causes.

The dominant Leftist strategies of the past, such as the dream of "One Big Union," have typically emphasized the generative role of mass movements and centralized organizations in the struggle for social change. Given the weakness of North American unionism, however, the question repeatedly arises whether the struggle for democratic empowerment in the United States is realistically worth pursuing. It was Tillich's judgment that such efforts were not worth pursuing (at least not for himself) in a country that lacked an organized proletariat or a political tradition of socialism. In response to this argument, I think it must be acknowledged that the economic goals of democratic socialism are unattainable without a revitalized trade-union movement. The traditional Leftist insistence on this point is irrefutable. I have therefore discussed, in *The Democratic Socialist Vision,* the prospects for a renewal of North American unionism and outlined a union agenda that includes industrial democracy, worker control of pension funds, solidarity wage policies, and decentralized worker ownership. Because social orders are fundamentally shaped by whoever controls the terms, amounts, and direction of credit, the essential economic objective of the Left must be to democratize the process of investment, which is unachievable within large-scale enterprises apart from a renewal of trade unionism. No matter how decentralized, feminist, and communitarian the progressive movement may become, it must deal with the problems of economic power, efficiency, organization, and international competition on the large-scale institutional levels on which these problems exist.

While I concede the point, therefore, that an effective struggle for democratic empowerment would require a transformation in the function and nature of North American trade unionism, I reject the argument advanced by Tillich and others that the only socialist alternative to proletarian socialism is some form of facile moralism. While it is true that religious socialism is ultimately based on a moral commitment, this fact does not necessarily condemn it to moralistic pleading or political irrelevance. The evidence is growing, rather, that the kind of socialism that Tillich wrote off as moralistic has enormous power for social transformation.

The emergence of third-world, black, and feminist theologies of liberation provides the most telling evidence. Liberation theologies have begun to engage the faith and suffering of millions of people unaccounted for in earlier theologies and political movements. The liberationist insistence that theology must begin with the suffering of the poor has created a paradigmatic shift in modern theology in which the previously unknown victims of history have become the interlocutors of religious meaning. Although they are largely overlooked in the classic works of Western socialism, the feminist, black, and third-world theorists of contemporary liberationism have often claimed the socialist tradition for themselves. This is a crucial development, for when such figures as Gutiérrez, Míguez Bonino, West, and

Ruether identify themselves with the socialist tradition they transform this tradition through their commitment and criticism.

Moreover, there are signs that Latin American liberationist theory is beginning to appropriate, in its own contexts, the strategy of communitarian economic democracy that characterizes modern democratic socialism. The shift is marked in such recent works as Jon Sobrino's *The True Church and the Poor* and Leonardo Boff's *Ecclesiogenesis: The Base Communities Reinvent the Church,* where the earlier liberationist dependence on Marxism is eclipsed by an emphasis on developing grassroots democratic counterinstitutions and communitarian forms of socialization. Boff has compellingly argued that liberationist theory needs to reflect more accurately the indigenous, communitarian praxis of the existing base communities. And in the revised edition (1988) of *A Theology of Liberation,* Gutiérrez clearly moves in the same direction, cleansing his text of its earlier Marxist tone and acknowledging that neo-Marxist dependency theory "does not take sufficient account of the internal dynamics of each country or of the vast dimensions of the world of the poor." This shift in emphasis marks a hopeful sign for the future of liberation theology.[29]

Today the major texts of liberation theology are studied in virtually all North American universities and mainline seminaries. Latin American liberationist theologies have exposed a new generation of seminarians to the dynamics of economic dependency and have inspired feelings of solidarity between progressive North American churches and the base communities of Latin America. In recent years, religious organizations in the United States have catalyzed public opposition to U.S. military intervention and established a network of sanctuary churches for Central American refugees fleeing from persecution in their own countries. The conventions and policy agencies of most mainline North American churches have also taken Left-liberal positions on a wide range of economic, social, and foreign-policy issues. Among these statements, the pastoral letters of the U.S. Roman Catholic bishops on nuclear and economic policy have drawn the most attention, but the more telling fact is that nearly all of the mainline churches have issued similar pronouncements on social issues. These statements have aroused intense (and by now, ritualistic) denunciations from the Right, and often a bemused perplexity from the secular media. In both cases, a lack of requisite background and a certain tone deafness to critical religious language have often prevented the interpreters from understanding the shift that has taken place within North American churches.

This shift is not a "squandering of the church's moral authority" or a "substitution of politics for religion," as is repeatedly charged.[30] The church trivializes itself when it restricts itself to pronouncements on personal morality. There are ethical dimensions of public life that the church must address if it takes its own moral commands with any seriousness. Moved by their awareness of the ravages of imperialism, militarism, sexism, racism, and homophobia, the mainline churches of North America have therefore cautiously begun to explore the implications of Christian morality in the face of these complex social evils.

As Frederick Herzog has observed, a new consensus is emerging in the churches in which the priority of a common praxis is assumed, rather than the priority of confessional creeds. The key to this transition is that the process of forming and expressing Christian belief has shifted away from the hierarchical models of the past, in which the identities of confessional communities were definitively decreed by ruling councils, synods, or ecclesiastical leaders. Confessional identity today is more often shaped by the praxis of churches and religious communities at the grass-roots level. This shift has begun to occur even in those denominations in which it is vigorously opposed by ecclesiastical authorities. Herzog notes that the praxological model is based on an ecumenical spirituality of discipleship rather than on doctrine.[31]

The ecumenical movement has been a prototypical example of this shift in ecclesial and spiritual consciousness. Throughout the past century, the spirit of ecumenism has grown within and among the mainstream churches primarily as a result of their cooperative efforts in social ministry. Churches that disagreed on fundamental matters of doctrine have nonetheless reached agreements and worked together on matters of common social concern. As these projects proceeded, the historic barriers to doctrinal dialogue have often begun to be seen in a new light.

Liberation theologies are examples of a similar phenomenon. Modern African-American theologies originated in the struggles of the civil-rights and black-power movements of the 1950s and 1960s. Modern feminist theologies were originally shaped by the political, cultural, and personal struggles of the women's movement of the 1960s and 1970s. Latin American liberation theologies are the products of the political and economic struggles of the base communities. In all of these cases, theopraxis preceded theology. Liberationist theologies only exist, as Gutiérrez has insisted, in order to express the spiritualities of liberationist praxis. Liberation theologies are thus a "secondary act" of reflection that deserve consideration only insofar as they faithfully reflect the concrete struggles of the poor for justice.[32]

The question that remains is whether the shift toward a praxis orientation will continue to grow within the North American churches. Rauschenbusch's works were written in the hopeful expectation that all of the churches would eventually accept the biblical command to build the kingdom. In his classic defense of Christian socialism, *Christianity and the Social Order,* William Temple wrote in 1942 that he hoped *all* Christians would accept his basic arguments for economic democracy.[33]

Today it is difficult to comprehend that such expectations were ever seriously held. In the past decade, the progressive positions taken by the mainline churches on political issues have prompted intense protests from conservative factions within these churches, as well as an enormous backlash of fundamentalist activism. The mainline churches often have difficulty responding to these attacks, in part because these churches are schools of ambiguity, containing nearly the entire range of class interests and ideologies that exist in modern liberal societies. The pervasive ambiguity of middle-class life and the diversity of religious and political viewpoints that exists within mainline congregations often promote a tendency to make tolerance the highest moral value.

That is one way to manage the conflict over social issues. The strengths of this approach are the strengths of skeptical relativism. The problem with this approach is that whenever the churches absolutize the values of tolerance and ambiguity, they implicitly endorse an endless wavering of moral indecision. The notion that one must choose between pluralism and moral coherence is fallacious. The task for the churches in the postmodern era is precisely to appreciate and promote the values of pluralism while, at the same time, finding the basis of their unity within a core of common religious and moral commitments. To shrink from offering a coherent moral vision on account of pluralism is to undermine the social mission of the churches as well as the social value of pluralism. As Sölle has observed, middle-class people often avoid moral questions that are inherently arguable and divisive. Their sensibilities are offended, for reasons that should be respected, by the crudeness of the question, "Which side are you on?" But to avoid the question is to answer it.

An analogous choice faces the various middle-class political organizations within North American progressivism. While it is clear that many of these organizations have made substantial gains in their attempts to create a progressive movement that is more feminist and ecologically conscious than the progressive movements of the past, it is equally clear that they have failed to expand their racial base. Most progressive North American organizations are dominated by middle-class whites. Since these organizations are rightly viewed by people of color as racially and culturally alien, even their most serious attempts to reach out to African American communities usually result in failure. As Cornel West has observed, progressive organizations find themselves caught in a vicious circle. Their economic and cultural remoteness from the lives of most people of color undermines their most serious efforts to improve their racial composition. This failure then desensitizes white organizations to the ongoing importance of the struggle against racism, further widening the cultural gap between people of color and white activists.

The way out of this circle is to take the liberationist option seriously. Strategies based on appealing to white guilt are psychologically and politically paralyzing, while strategies based on making white organizations more attractive to people of color have very limited effectiveness. What is needed within progressive organizations is a commitment of will—the "fundamental option" described by Gutiérrez, Míguez Bonino, and Sölle—to the specific struggles of people of color. As West has explained, what is needed "is more widespread participation by predominantly white democratic socialist organizations in antiracist struggles—whether those struggles be for the political, economic, and cultural empowerment of Latinos, blacks, Asians, and Native Americans or anti-imperialist struggles against U.S. support for oppressive regimes in South Africa, Chile, the Philippines, and the occupied West Bank."[34] The transformation of consciousness that liberation theologians call "conscientization" can only occur, as the liberationists have insisted, through an act of commitment that brings about a new awareness of oppression from the perspective of the oppressed. Only by taking the liberationist option can white activists comprehend or sustain their awareness of the crucial ongoing importance of struggling against racism in all its forms. And as West has observed, only by taking the liberationist option seriously in a common struggle with people of color can progressive activists develop bonds of trust across racial lines. "While engaging in antiracist struggles, democratic socialists can also enter into a dialogue on the power relationships and misconceptions that often emerge in multiracial movements for social justice," West observes. "Honest and trusting coalition work can help socialists unlearn Eurocentrism in a self-critical manner and can also demystify the motivations of white progressives in the movement for social justice."[35]

To take the liberationist option seriously in a North American context is therefore to commit oneself to a social vision that cuts across the cultural boundaries of earlier socialist movements, while retaining the fundamental insistence on collective democratic empowerment that has characterized democratic socialism from the beginning. While it is not the final cure for racism, sexism, militarism, or the other ravages of human depravity, democratic socialism is the social vision most consistent with the struggle to democratize and humanize the social forces that govern us.

Today, conservative and neoconservative justifications of inequality are in the ascendancy. The internationalization of capital is undermining the social gains of the welfare state and striking fear in middle-class people that their jobs will be eliminated or transferred. In this moment, the dominant political culture reinforces our fear of being squeezed out and attempts to reconcile us to an increasingly unjust and maldistributed social order. The retreat from liberalism is marked even in sectors of the mainline churches, where the progressive positions taken by the National Council of Churches are constantly attacked by church members influenced more by the dominant political culture than by the teachings of their own denominations. In this environment, to struggle for a democratized social order is to uphold a long-term vision of the common good while working to achieve attainable gains toward that end. John Kenneth Galbraith has observed that even the most plausible reforms usually look dangerously impractical when they are first presented. "They become commonplace, then banal, then basic human rights, only by discussion," he has written. "It is the business of those who do not expect to hold office to initiate that discussion."[36] That describes the outlook of a prophetic and politically realistic North American praxis.

Notes

Introduction

1. The most egregious examples have been collected in Paul Hollander, *Political Pilgrims: Travels of Western Intellectuals to the Soviet Union, China, and Cuba* (New York: Harper & Row, 1983); and Norman Podhoretz, *Why We Were In Vietnam* (New York: Simon and Schuster, 1982).

2. Cf. Irving Howe, "New Left, New Right, as Long as You Hate Liberals," *Dissent* (Spring 1985): 141; and Bernard Rosenberg, "From *Ramparts* to Reagan," *Dissent* (Summer 1985): 272.

3. Cf. Michael Harrington, "Does the Peace Movement Need the Communists?" (1965); "Harrington Replies" (1965); and "Answering McReynolds: A Question of Philosophy, A Question of Tactics" (1967), originally published in *The Village Voice* and reprinted in Harrington, *Taking Sides: The Education of a Militant Mind* (New York: Holt, Rinehart and Winston, 1985), pp. 106-36; Irving Howe and Michael Walzer, "Were We Wrong About Vietnam?," *The New Republic* (August 18, 1979).

4. Michael Harrington, *The Long Distance Runner: An Autobiography* (New York: Henry Holt and Company, 1988), pp. 160-73.

5. C. B. Macpherson, *The Real World of Democracy* (Toronto: Canadian Broadcasting Corporation, 1965), p. 12.

6. Cf. C. B. Macpherson, *The Life and Times of Liberal Democracy* (Oxford: Oxford University Press, 1977), pp. 1-22; and Robert A. Dahl, *A Preface to Economic Democracy* (Berkeley: University of California Press, 1985), pp. 161-63.

7. Cf. John Stuart Mill, *On Socialism* (Buffalo: Prometheus Books, 1987); Mill, *Principles of Political Economy*, two vols. (New York: D. Appleton and Company, 1884); David Held, *Models of Democracy* (Stanford: Stanford University Press, 1987), pp. 85-104; Amy Gutmann, *Liberal Equality* (Cambridge: Cambridge University Press, 1980), pp. 48-68.

8. Samuel Bowles and Herbert Gintis, *Democracy and Capitalism: Property, Community, and the Contradictions of Modern Social Thought* (New York: Basic Books, 1986). For two excellent discussions of the relationship between liberalism and democratic socialism, see Perry Anderson, "The Affinities of Norberto Bobbio," *New Left Review* no. 170 (July/August 1988): 3-36; and Irving Howe, "Socialism and Liberalism: Articles of Conciliation?," *Dissent* (Winter 1977): 22-35; reprinted in Howe, *Socialism and America* (New York: Harcourt, Brace, Jovanovich, 1985), pp. 147-75.

9. Bowles and Gintis, *Democracy and Capitalism*, p. 177.

10. "The Frankfurt Declaration," in *Aims and Tasks of Democratic Socialism* (London: The Socialist International, 1951), pp. 1-8; reprinted in *The New International Review* no. 1 (Winter 1977): 5-10.

11. Cf. Gary Dorrien, *The Democratic Socialist Vision* (Totowa: Rowman & Littlefield, 1986); Alec Nove, *The Economics of Feasible Socialism* (London: Allen & Unwin, 1983); Radoslav Selucky, *Marxism, Socialism and Freedom* (London: Macmillan, 1979).

12. For arguments similar to my own, see Robert Bellah and William Sullivan, "The Common Good," *Tikkun* (July/August 1988); Sullivan, *Reconstructing Public Philosophy* (Berkeley: University of California Press, 1986); and Marcus G. Raskin, *The Common Good: Its Politics, Policies and Philosophy* (New York: Routledge & Kegan Paul, 1986). For an interesting collection of articles on the subject, see Oliver F. Williams and John W. Houck, eds., *The Common Good and U.S. Capitalism* (Lanham, MD: University Press of America, 1987).

13. Chantal Mouffe, "Towards a Radical Democratic Citizenship," *Democratic Left* (March/April 1989): 7.

14. Harvey Cox, *Religion in the Secular City: Toward a Postmodern Theology* (New York: Simon and Schuster, 1984), p. 183.

1. Theology and the Democratic Faith

1. Friedrich Nietzsche, *The Antichrist*, reprinted in *The Portable Nietzsche*, Walter Kaufmann, ed. (New York: Viking, 1968), pp. 570, 619, 647.

2. Cf. Richard John Neuhaus, "A Death Much Exaggerated," *National Review* (August 28, 1987): 44; Neuhaus, "The World Council of Churches and Radical Chic,"(Georgetown University: Ethics and Public Policy Center Reprint #2, 1977); Edward Norman, *Christianity and the World Order* (Oxford: Oxford University Press, 1979).

3. Paul Johnson, *Modern Times: The World From the Twenties to the Eighties* (New York: Harper & Row, 1983), pp. 165-66.

4. William Temple, *Christianity and the Social Order* (Middlesex: Penguin Books, 1942), p. 14.

5. Harvey Cox, *Religion in the Secular City: Toward a Postmodern Theology* (New York: Simon & Schuster, 1984), p. 95.

6. *Religion in the Secular City*, p. 96.

7. Cf. C. B. Macpherson, *Democratic Theory: Essays in Retrieval* (London: Oxford University Press, 1973); Macpherson, *The Life and Times of Liberal Democracy* (New York: Oxford University Press, 1977); Macpherson, *The Rise and Fall of Economic Justice* (New York: Oxford University Press, 1987); Amy Gutmann, *Liberal Equality* (Cambridge: Cambridge University Press, 1980); David Held, *Models of Democracy* (Stanford: Stanford University Press, 1987); Frank Cunningham, *Democratic Theory and Socialism* (Cambridge: Cambridge University Press, 1987).

8. For informative and insightful interpretations of the liberationist critique of modernity, see Rebecca Chopp, *The Praxis of Suffering: An Interpretation of Liberation and Political Theologies* (Maryknoll, NY: Orbis Books, 1986), and Cox's *Religion in the Secular City*. For discussions of postmodernism, see Stanley Aronowitz, "Postmodernism and Politics," *Social Text: Theory/Culture/Ideology*, no. 18 (Winter 1987/88): 99-115; Jean-François Lyotard, *La Condition Postmodern Rapport Sur le Savoir* (Paris: Les Editions de Minuit, 1979); Fred Dallmayr, *Twilight of Subjectivity: Contributions to a Post-Individualist Theory of Politics* (Amherst: University of Massachusetts Press, 1981).

9. Robert McAfee Brown, *Theology in a New Key: Responding to Liberation*

Themes (Philadelphia: Westminster Press, 1978), pp. 140-43; Brown, *Gustavo Gutiérrez* (Atlanta: John Knox Press, 1980), pp. 75-76; Brown, "A Preface and a Conclusion," in *Theology in the Americas*, Sergio Torres and John Eagleson, eds. (Maryknoll, NY: Orbis Books, 1976), pp. xxii-xxiii.

10. Cf. Eugene V. Debs, *Writings and Speeches of Eugene V. Debs*, ed. Joseph M. Bernstein (New York: Hermitage Press, 1948); Nick Salvatore, *Eugene V. Debs: Citizen and Socialist* (Urbana: University of Illinois Press, 1982); G. Bernard Shaw, ed., *Fabian Essays in Socialism* (Gloucester, MA: Peter Smith, 1967, c1889); Henry M. Hyndman, *Economics of Socialism* (London: Twentieth Century Press, 1896).

11. On pre-Marxist Anglican socialism, see Maurice B. Reckitt, *Maurice to Temple: A Century of the Social Movement in the Church of England* (London: Faber and Faber, 1946); Gilbert C. Binyon, *The Christian Socialist Movement in England* (New York: Macmillan, 1931); Peter d'A. Jones, *The Christian Socialist Revival 1877-1914* (Princeton: Princeton University Press, 1968).

12. Cf. Gary Dorrien, *The Democratic Socialist Vision* (Totowa, NJ: Rowman & Littlefield, 1986), pp. 160-66.

13. For neoconservative interpretations of Niebuhr, see Michael Novak, "Needing Niebuhr Again," *Commentary* (September 1972); Novak, "Reinhold Niebuhr: Model for Neoconservatives," *The Christian Century* (January 22, 1986): 69-71; and Richard John Neuhaus, "Theologian and Activist," *Commentary* (March 1986): 58-64. For a variety of alternative readings of Niebuhr, see the Forty-fifth Anniversary Edition of *Christianity & Crisis*, "Remembering Reinhold Niebuhr," (February 3, 1986); Bill Kellermann, "Apologist of Power: The Long Shadow of Reinhold Niebuhr's Christian Realism," *Sojourners* (March 1987): 14-20; and Robert McAfee Brown, "Reinhold Niebuhr: His Theology in the 1980s," *The Christian Century* (January 22, 1986): 66-68.

14. Reinhold Niebuhr, *The Children of Light and the Children of Darkness: A Vindication of Democracy and a Critique of Its Traditional Defence* (New York: Scribner's, 1944), pp. x-xiii.

15. Cf. Gregory Fossedal, "Corporate Welfare Out of Control," *New Republic* (February 25, 1985): 17-20; Michael Harrington, "Is Capitalism Still Viable?," *Journal of Business Ethics* 1 (Dordrecht and Boston: D. Reidel, 1982); Harrington, "Corporate Collectivism: A System of Social Injustice" in *Contemporary Readings in Social and Political Ethics*, Garry Brodsky, John Troyer, David Vance, eds. (Buffalo: Prometheus Books, 1984).

16. The concept of the "broker state" is used by Gar Alperovitz and Jeff Faux in *Rebuilding America: A Blueprint for the New Economy* (New York: Pantheon Books, 1984). See also Michael Harrington, *Decade of Decision: The Crisis of the American System* (New York: Simon and Schuster, 1980); and James O'Connor, *The Fiscal Crisis of the State* (New York: St. Martin's Press, 1973).

17. Cf. David Stockman, *The Triumph of Politics* (New York: Harper & Row, 1986).

18. My argument on the inevitability of economic planning is developed in greater detail in *The Democratic Socialist Vision*.

19. Cf. Graham Wooton, *Workers, Unions and the State* (London: Routledge & Kegan Paul, 1986); C. George Benello and Dimitrios Roussopoulos, eds., *The Case for Participatory Democracy* (New York: Grossman Publishers, 1971); Carole Pateman, *Participation and Democratic Theory* (Cambridge: Cambridge University Press, 1970).

20. Cf. Held, *Models of Democracy*, pp. 280-83; Peter Clecak, *Crooked Paths: Reflections on Socialism, Conservatism, and the Welfare State* (New York: Harper & Row, 1977), pp. 112-20.

21. Cf. Frank Lindenfelt and Joyce Rothschild-Whitt, *Workplace Democracy and Social Change* (Boston: Porter Sargent, 1982), pp. 87-124; John F. Witte, *Democracy, Authority, and Alienation in Work* (Chicago: University of Chicago Press, 1989), pp. 130-50; J. Maxwell Elden, "Political Efficacy at Work," *American Political Science Review* 75 (March 1981):43-58; Eric C. Einhorn and John Logue, eds., *Democracy on the Shop Floor?* (Kent, OH: Kent Popular Press, 1982), pp. 9-78; Martin Carnoy and Derek Shearer, *Economic Democracy: The Challenge of the 1980s* (Armonk, NY: M.E. Sharpe, 1980), pp. 125-94.

22. Robert Dahl, *A Preface to Economic Democracy* (Berkeley: University of California Press, 1985), p. 98.

23. For discussions of the economic vision of modern democratic socialism, see Alec Nove, *The Economics of Feasible Socialism* (London: George Allen & Unwin, 1983); Branko Horvat, *The Political Economy of Socialism: A Marxist Social Theory* (Armonk: M.E. Sharpe, 1982); David Schweickart, *Capitalism or Worker Control?: An Ethical and Economic Appraisal* (New York: Praeger, 1980); Radoslav Selucky, *Marxism, Socialism, and Freedom* (London: Macmillan, 1979).

2. Walter Rauschenbusch and the Legacy of the Social Gospel

1. John C. Bennett, "The Social Interpretation of Christianity," *The Church Through Half a Century: Essays in Honor of William Adams Brown*, Samuel Cavert and Henry Van Dusen, eds. (New York: Scribner's, 1936), p. 113; Reinhold Niebuhr, "Walter Rauschenbusch in Historical Perspective," *Religion in Life*, XXVII, 1958; W. A. Visser't Hooft, *The Background of the Social Gospel in America*, (Haarlem: Tjeenk Willink and Zoon, 1928).

2. John C. Bennett, "The Social Gospel Today," *The Social Gospel: Religion and Reform in Changing America*, Ronald C. White, Jr. and C. Howard Hopkins, eds. (Philadelphia: Temple University Press, 1976), pp. 285-86.

3. Bennett, "The Social Interpretation of Christianity," pp. 120-21.

4. John C. Bennett, "After Liberalism—What?" *The Christian Century*, 50 (1933): 1403; Reinhold Niebuhr, "Intellectual Autobiography," *Reinhold Niebuhr: His Religious, Social and Political Thought*, Charles Kegley and Robert Bretall, eds. (New York: Macmillan, 1956), p. 13.

5. Cf. Paul M. Minus, *Walter Rauschenbusch: American Reformer* (New York: Macmillan, 1988), pp. 10-16.

6. Quoted in Dores Robinson Sharpe, *Walter Rauschenbusch* (New York: Macmillan, 1942), p, 43; and Minus, *Walter Rauschenbusch: American Reformer*, p. 17.

7. Sharpe, *Walter Rauschenbusch*, p. 43.

8. Ibid., p. 53.

9. Cf. Ibid., pp. 55-58; Minus, *Walter Rauschenbusch: An American Reformer*, pp. 51-52; and Rauschenbusch, *Walter Rauschenbusch: Selected Writings*, Winthrop Hudson, ed. (New York: Paulist Press, 1984), p. 7. Based on a report by Rauschenbusch's friend, F. W. C. Meyer, Winthrop Hudson argues that Rauschenbusch gave up his plan to enter the mission field largely on account of his hearing defect.

10. Cf. C. Howard Hopkins, *The Rise of the Social Gospel in American Protestantism, 1865-1915* (New Haven: Yale University Press, 1940); Henry May, *Protestant*

Churches and Industrial America (New York: Harper & Row, 1949); Winthrop Hudson, *Religion in America: An Historical Account of the Development of American Religious Life* (New York: Scribner's, 1973); Martin E. Marty, *Righteous Empire: The Protestant Experience in America* (New York: Dial Press, 1970); James Dombrowski, *The Early Days of Christian Socialism in America* (New York: Columbia University Press, 1936).

11. Robert T. Handy, ed., *The Social Gospel In America* (New York: Oxford University Press, 1966), p. 255.

12. Cf. Henry George, *Progress and Poverty* (New York: Robert Schalkenbach Foundation, 1955, c1879).

13. Walter Rauschenbusch, *Christianizing the Social Order* (New York: Macmillan, 1919, c1912), p. 394.

14. Rauschenbusch, *Selected Writings*, p. 13.

15. Ibid., pp. 38-39.

16. Cf. Walter Rauschenbusch, *For God and the People: Prayers of the Social Awakening* (Boston: Pilgrim Press, 1910).

17. Quoted in Sharpe, *Walter Rauschenbusch*, pp. 81-82.

18. Walter Rauschenbusch, "The Kingdom of God," *Cleveland's Young Men* 27(January 9, 1913), quoted in Vernon P. Bodein, *The Social Gospel of Walter Rauschenbusch and Its Relation to Religious Education* (New Haven: Yale University Press, 1944), pp. 7-8, reprinted in *The Social Gospel in America*, pp. 264-67.

19. Rauschenbusch, *Christianizing the Social Order*, pp. 93-94.

20. Ibid., p. 49.

21. Quoted by C. Howard Hopkins, biographical preface in *A Gospel for the Social Awakening: Selections from the Writings of Walter Rauschenbusch*, ed. Benjamin E. Mays (New York: Association Press, 1950), p. 13.

22. Cf. Rauschenbusch, *Selected Writings*, pp. 23-26; *The Social Gospel in America*, p. 27.

23. Arguing at the outset that "Christianity is in its nature revolutionary," Rauschenbusch's proposed title for this book was *Revolutionary Christianity*. He later recalled, however, that despite his numerous attempts to complete the manuscript, he repeatedly found that he had "outgrown" the book's arguments, and therefore eventually abandoned the idea of publishing it. Many years after his death, the texts were deposited and misfiled in the American Baptist Historical Archives in Rochester where they remained until their rediscovery in the 1960s by Max Stackhouse, who edited and published the book under the title, *The Righteousness of the Kingdom*. For Stackhouse's account of the history of the text, see *The Righteousness of the Kingdom* (Nashville: Abingdon Press, 1968), pp. 14-18. Additional information on the first draft of this manuscript can be found in Minus's biography, *Walter Rauschenbusch: American Reformer*, pp. 77-81.

24. Walter Rauschenbusch, "A Conquering Idea," *Selected Writings*, pp. 71-74.

25. Walter Rauschenbusch, "The Kingdom of God," *Selected Writings*, pp. 76-79.

26. Quoted in Sharpe, *Walter Rauschenbusch*, p. 134.

27. Cf. Walter Rauschenbusch, *Das Leben Jesu: Ein systematischer Studiengang für Jugendvereine und Bibelklassen* (Cleveland: P. Ritter, 1895); Walter Rauschenbusch, with Ira D. Sankey, *Evangeliums-Lieder 1 und 2* (New York: Biglow & Main, 1897); Walter Rauschenbusch with Ira D. Sankey, *Evangeliums-Sanger 3: 150 Neuere*

Lieder für Abendgottesdienste und besondere Versammelungen (Kassel: J.G. Oncken, 1907).

28. Walter Rauschenbusch, *Christianity and the Social Crisis* (New York: Hodder & Stoughton/Macmillan, 1907), p. xiii.

29. For a structuralist interpretation emphasizing the polemical intent of the parables, see John Dominac Crossan, *The Dark Interval: Towards a Theology of Story* (Niles, IL: Argus Communications, 1975).

30. Rauschenbusch, *Christianity and the Social Crisis*, p. 63.

31. Cf. Albert Schweitzer, *The Quest of the Historical Jesus* (New York: Macmillan, 1960, c1906).

32. Rauschenbusch, *Christianity and the Social Crisis*, p. 160.

33. Quoted in Sharpe, *Walter Rauschenbusch*, p. 214.

34. Rauschenbusch, *Christianity and the Social Crisis*, p. 400.

35. Ibid., p. 325.

36. Ibid., p. 401.

37. Ibid., p. 401.

38. Ibid., p. 409.

39. Ibid., pp. 400-22.

40. Walter Rauschenbusch, "Our Attitude Toward Millenarianism," *Selected Writings*, p. 90.

41. Cf. Carl N. Degler, *Out of Our Past: The Forces That Shaped Modern America* (New York: Harper & Brothers, 1959), pp. 346-48; Marty, *Righteous Empire*, pp. 206-9; Sidney E. Mead, *The Lively Experiment: The Shaping of Christianity in America* (New York. Harper & Row, 1963), pp. 177-83.

42. Rauschenbusch, *Christianizing the Social Order*, pp. 71-90.

43. Ibid., p. 90.

44. Ibid., p. 125.

45. Ibid., pp. 136-53.

46. Ibid., pp. 313, 317.

47. Ibid., p. 288

48. Ibid., pp. 227-34.

49. Ibid., p. 313.

50. Ibid., p. 343.

51. Ibid., pp. 349, 353.

52. Ibid., p. 361.

53. John Stuart Mill, *Principles of Political Economy*, Vol. II, (New York: Appleton & Company, 1884), pp. 357-59; Rauschenbusch, *Christianizing the Social Order*, p. 357. For liberal socialist interpretations of Mill's political theory, see C. B. Macpherson, *The Life and Times of Liberal Democracy* (Oxford: Oxford University Press, 1977), pp. 44-69; Amy Gutmann, *Liberal Equality* (Cambridge: Cambridge University Press, 1980), pp. 48-68; and David Held, *Models of Democracy* (Stanford: Stanford University Press, 1987), pp. 85-104.

54. John C. Cort, *Christian Socialism: An Informal History* (Maryknoll, NY: Orbis Books, 1987), p. 254.

55. Rauschenbusch, *Christianizing the Social Order*, pp. 419-29.

56. Ibid., pp. 430-47.

57. Ibid., p. 458.

58. Rauschenbusch, *For God and the People*, p. 126.

59. Walter Rauschenbusch, *Unto Me* (Boston: Pilgrim Press, 1912).

60. Walter Rauschenbusch, *The Social Principles of Jesus* (New York: Grosset & Dunlap, 1916), p. iii.

61. *The Social Principles of Jesus*, p. 197.

62. Walter Rauschenbusch, *A Theology for the Social Gospel* (New York: Macmillan, 1917), p. 4. Though this work was less imaginative and vigorous in style than Rauschenbusch's earlier works, it has nonetheless been generally regarded as the classic *theological* statement of the Social Gospel position. See Clifton E. Olmsted, *Religion in America: Past and Present*, pp. 128-30; and Claude Welch, *Protestant Thought in the Nineteenth Century*, Vol. 2, 1870-1914 (New Haven: Yale University Press, 1985), pp. 263-65.

63. Rauschenbusch, *Christianizing the Social Order*, p. 121.

64. Cf. Rauschenbusch, *A Theology for the Social Gospel*, pp. 77-94.

65. Ibid., pp. 59, 79.

66. For an excellent discussion of Rauschenbusch's historicism, see Ronald Massanari, "The Sacred Workshop of God: Reflections on the Historical Perspective of Walter Rauschenbusch," *Religion in Life* XL, 2, (Summer, 1971): 257-66.

67. Rauschenbusch, *A Theology for the Social Gospel*, p. 279.

68. Sharpe, *Walter Rauschenbusch*, p. 448.

69. Rauschenbusch, *Selected Writings*, pp. 45-46.

70. Ibid., pp. 46-47; also reprinted in Sharpe, *Walter Rauschenbusch*, pp. 451-52.

71. Cf. Sharpe, *Walter Rauschenbusch*, p. 453; Rauschenbusch, *A Theology for the Social Gospel*, p. 141.

72. Martin Luther King, Jr., *Stride Toward Freedom: The Montgomery Story* (New York: Harper, 1958), p. 91; and King, "Pilgrimage to Nonviolence," *The Christian Century*, LXXVII, (April 13, 1960): 439.

73. Rauschenbusch, *Christianizing the Social Order*, p. 326.

74. The paucity of direct evidence on this point has permitted opposite conclusions by Rauschenbusch's interpreters. For example, Bennett has claimed that Rauschenbusch definitely supported the suffrage movement, while Martin Marty has argued that he opposed it. The weight of evidence favors Marty's side of the argument, since Rauschenbusch always emphasized the importance of maternal nurture and because he expressed his lack of support, in 1912, for the suffrage plank in the Democratic Party platform. It seems most accurate to conclude, however, that Rauschenbusch was torn between his conservative and socialist convictions on this issue, and never resolved the conflict that the suffrage issue raised for him. Cf. Bennett, "The Social Gospel Today," p. 288; Martin E. Marty, *Modern American Religion*, Vol. 1: *The Irony of It All, 1893-1919* (Chicago: University of Chicago Press, 1986), p. 292.

75. Cf. John R. Aiken, "Walter Rauschenbusch and Education for Reform," *Church History* 36 (December 1967): 459-460; Sharpe, *Walter Rauschenbusch*, p. 367; *Modern American Religion*, Volume 1, p. 294; and Minus, *Walter Rauschenbusch: American Reformer*, p. 105. I am grateful to Max Stackhouse for his personal correspondence on this point.

76. Cf. Rauschenbusch, *Christianity and the Social Crisis*, pp. 143-210.

77. Robert D Cross, Introduction to the Harper Torchbooks edition of Rauschenbusch, *Christianity and the Social Crisis*, (New York: Harper Torchbooks, 1964), p. xiv.

78. Marty, *Modern American Religion*, Vol. 1, pp. 286-97.

79. Rauschenbusch, *Christianity and the Social Crisis*, pp. 400-401.

80. Ibid., p. 400; Rauschenbusch, *A Theology for the Social Gospel*, p. 19.

81. Rauschenbusch, *Christianizing the Social Order*, pp. 222-34, 311-23, 332-40, 357.

82. Ibid., pp. 346-48.

83. Cf. Bennett, "The Social Gospel Today," pp. 285-88; Reinhold Neibuhr, "Walter Rauschenbusch in Historical Perspective," pp. 528-31.

84. Cf. Michael Novak, *The Spirit of Democratic Capitalism* (New York: American Enterprise Institute/Simon & Schuster, 1982); Irving Kristol, *Two Cheers for Capitalism* (New York: Basic Books, 1978); George Gilder, *Wealth and Poverty* (New York: Basic Books, 1981); Peter Berger, *The Capitalist Revolution: Fifty Propositions About Prosperity, Equality, and Liberty* (New York: Basic Books, 1986).

85. Rauschenbusch, *Christianizing the Social Order*, pp. 325-26.

86. Rauschenbusch, *Christianity and the Social Crisis*, pp. 420-21.

3. Paul Tillich and the Theology of Religious Socialism

1. Paul Tillich, *On the Boundary: An Autobiographical Sketch* (New York: Scribner's, 1966), pp. 21-22.

2. Paul Tillich, *The New Being* (New York: Scribner's, 1955), p. 52; Wilhelm and Marion Pauck, *Paul Tillich: His Life and Thought* (New York: Harper & Row, 1976), pp. 40-41.

3. Paul Tillich, "Autobiographical Reflections," in *The Theology of Paul Tillich*, Charles W. Kegley and Robert W. Bretall, eds. (New York: Macmillan, 1952), p. 12.

4. Pauck and Pauck, *Paul Tillich*, p. 51.

5. Tillich, *On the Boundary*, p. 52.

6. Pauck and Pauck, *Paul Tillich*, p. 70.

7. Cf. Eduard Heimann, "Tillich's Doctrine of Religious Socialism," in Kegley and Bretall, eds., *The Theology of Paul Tillich*, pp. 312-25.

8. Paul Tillich, "Kairos," reprinted in *The Protestant Era*, ed. James Luther Adams (London: Nisbet, 1951), p. 53.

9. Tillich, *On the Boundary*, pp. 78, 81.

10. Paul Tillich, *Systematic Theology*, Vol. 3 (Chicago: University of Chicago Press, 1967, c1963), pp. 370-71.

11. Cf. Alice Gallin, *Midwives to Nazism: University Professors in Weimar Germany, 1925-1933* (Macon, GA: Mercer University Press, 1986).

12. Paul Tillich, "Basic Principles of Religious Socialism," reprinted in *Political Expectation*, James Luther Adams, Victor Nuovo, and Hannah Tillich, eds. (New York: Harper & Row, 1971), p. 60.

13. Ibid., p. 61.

14. See the essays on this subject by Tillich, Karl Barth, Adolf von Harnack, Friedrich Gogarten, Ernst Troeltsch, Rudolf Bultmann and others in *The Beginnings of Dialectic Theology*, Vol. 1, ed. James M. Robinson (Richmond, VA: John Knox Press, 1968); and Hugh Ross Mackintosh, *Types of Modern Theology: Schleiermacher to Barth* (New York: Scribner's, 1937).

15. Albert Schweitzer, *The Quest of the Historical Jesus* (New York: Macmillan, 1960, c1906).

16. Tillich, "Basic Principles of Religious Socialism," p. 64.

17. Ibid., p. 66.

18. Ibid. p. 69.

19. Ibid., pp. 66-73.

20. Ibid., p. 74.

21. Ibid., p. 75.

22. Ibid., pp. 78-79.

23. Ibid., p. 82.

24. Ibid., p. 85.

25. Ibid., pp. 81-88.

26. Hannah Tillich, *From Time to Time* (New York: Stein and Day, 1973); Rollo May, *Paulus: Reminiscences of a Friendship* (New York: Harper & Row, 1973).

27. Pauck and Pauck, *Paul Tillich*, pp. 94-98; Hannah Tillich, *From Time to Time*, p. 115.

28. Cf. Max Weber, *The Protestant Ethic and the Spirit of Capitalism*, (New York: Scribner's, 1930).

29. Paul Tillich, *The Religious Situation* (Cleveland: Meridian Books/World Publishing, 1956, c1932), pp. 47-48.

30. Ibid., p. 48.

31. Cf. Paul Tillich, "Realism and Faith," in *The Protestant Era*, pp. 74-92.

32. Tillich, *The Religious Situation*, p. 216.

33. Rudolf Otto, *The Idea of the Holy* (London: Oxford University Press, 1977, c1923).

34. Tillich, "Realism and Faith," in *The Protestant Era*, ed. James Luther Adams, p. 91.

35. Cf. Tillich, "Christianity and Modern Society," in Tillich, *Political Expectation*, pp. 1-9; and Tillich, "The Protestant Message and the Man of Today," in *The Protestant Era*, ed. James Luther Adams, pp. 189-204.

36. Paul Tillich, "The Protestant Principle and the Proletarian Situation," in *The Protestant Era*, ed. James Luther Adams, p. 239.

37. Ibid., p. 240.

38. Ibid., p. 246.

39. Ibid., p. 252.

40. Tillich, *On the Boundary*, p. 62.

41. Pauck and Pauck, *Paul Tillich: His Life and Thought*, p. 125.

42. Paul Tillich, *The Socialist Decision* (New York: Harper & Row, 1977, c1933), p. xxxiv.

43. Cf. Karl Marx, *Economic and Philosophic Manuscripts of 1844* (New York: International Publications, 1974).

44. Tillich, *The Socialist Decision*, p. 163.

45. Cf. Marquis Childs, *Sweden: The Middle Way* (New Haven: Yale University Press, 1961, c1936).

46. Tillich, *On the Boundary*, p. 46.

47. Tillich, *The Socialist Decision*, pp. 160-62.

48. Ibid., p. 4.

49. Ibid., pp. 27-44.

50. Ibid., pp. 47-65.

51. Ibid., p. 79.

52. Ibid., p. 80.

53. Ibid., pp. 176, 145.

54. Ibid., p. 162.

55. Ibid., p. 160.

56. Quoted in Pauck and Pauck, *Paul Tillich*, p. 132.

57. Tillich, "Autobiographical Reflections," in Kegley and Bretall, eds., *The Theology of Paul Tillich*, p. 12.

58. Ibid., p. 13.

59. Cf. Herbert Marcuse, *Eros and Civilization: A Philosophical Inquiry into Freud* (Boston: Beacon Press, 1955), p. xi.

60. Paul Tillich, *Love, Power, and Justice: Ontological Analyses and Ethical Applications* (New York: Oxford University Press, 1954), p. 56.

61. Tillich, *Systematic Theology*, Vol. 3, pp. 356-93.

62. Ronald H. Stone, *Paul Tillich's Radical Social Thought* (Atlanta: John Knox Press, 1980), p. 153.

63. Pauck and Pauck, *Paul Tillich: His Life and Thought*, p. 275; Hannah Tillich, *From Time to Time*, p. 242.

64. Pauck and Pauck, *Paul Tillich: His Life and Thought*, p. 274.

65. Paul Tillich, "Open Letter to Emanuel Hirsch," reprinted in *The Thought of Paul Tillich*, ed. James Luther Adams, Wilhelm Pauck, and Roger Lincoln Shinn, (San Francisco: Harper & Row, 1985), p. 363.

66. Ibid., pp. 364-66.

67. Ibid., p. 385.

68. Richard John Neuhaus, "The Obligations and Limits of Political Commitment," *This World* (Spring/Summer 1986): No. 14, p. 64.

69. Tillich, "Open Letter to Emanuel Hirsch," in *The Thought of Paul Tillich*, p. 386.

70. Tillich, *On the Boundary*, p. 79.

4. Jürgen Moltmann and the Dialectics of Hope

1. José Míguez Bonino, *Doing Theology in a Revolutionary Situation* (Philadelphia: Fortress, 1975), p. 144.

2. Much of the information in this chapter on Moltmann's personal background is based upon interviews that I conducted with him on October 5, 6, and 7, 1988, at Kalamazoo College. I have also drawn upon interviews conducted by Teofilo Cabestrero and Craig A. Thomas. See Cabestrero, ed., *Faith: Conversations with Contemporary Theologians* (Maryknoll, NY: Orbis Books, 1980), p. 122; and Thomas, "Theologian Sees Joy in Existence, Hope in Suffering," *Kalamazoo Gazette* (October 10, 1988): B1, 2.

3. Jürgen Moltmann, *Experiences of God* (Philadelphia: Fortress Press, 1980), pp. 7-8.

4. Ibid., p. 6.

5. For an account of Moltmann's intellectual formation during the 1950s, see M. Douglas Meeks, *Origins of the Theology of Hope* (Philadelphia: Fortress Press, 1974).

6. Cabestrero, ed., *Faith*, p. 123.

7. Ernst Bloch, *Avicenna und die Aristotelische Linke* (Frankfurt: Surkamp Verlag, 1963).

8. Ernst Bloch, *Das Prinzip Hoffnung* (Frankfurt: Surkamp Verlag, 1959).

9. Cabestrero, *Faith*, p. 123.

10. Jürgen Moltmann, *Theology of Hope: On the Ground and the Implications of*

a Christian Eschatology (London: SCM Press, 1967), p. 16.

11. Jürgen Moltmann, "Theology as Eschatology," in *The Future of Hope*, Frederick Herzog, ed. (New York: Herder & Herder, 1970), pp. 10-11; cf. Jürgen Moltmann, *Religion, Revolution, and the Future* (New York: Scribner's, 1969), pp. 177-99.

12. Cf. Christopher Morse, *The Logic of Promise in Moltmann's Theology* (Philadelphia: Fortress Press, 1975); Lonnie Kliever, *The Shattered Spectrum: A Survey of Contemporary Theology* (Atlanta: John Knox, 1981).

13. Moltmann, *Theology of Hope*, p. 16; cf. Morse, *The Logic of Promise in Moltmann's Theology*, pp. 49-81.

14. Rudolf Bultmann, "Religion and Culture," in *The Beginnings of Dialectic Theology*, James M. Robinson, ed. (Atlanta: John Knox Press, 1968), p. 211; cf. Bultmann, *New Testament and Mythology*, Schubert M. Ogden, ed. (Philadelphia: Fortress Press, 1984) and Bultmann, *Jesus Christ and Mythology* (New York: Scribner's, 1958).

15. Moltmann, *Theology of Hope*, p. 316; Moltmann, *Religion, Revolution, and the Future*, pp. 83-107.

16. Moltmann, *Theology of Hope*, p. 30.

17. Ibid., p. 16.

18. Ibid., p. 21.

19. Ibid., p. 334.

20. Jürgen Moltmann, *The Crucified God: The Cross of Christ as the Foundation and Criticism of Christian Theology* (New York: Harper & Row, 1974), p. 62.

21. Quoted in Moltmann, *The Crucified God*, p. 148.

22. Moltmann, *The Crucified God*, pp. 202-207.

23. Moltmann, *Theology of Hope*, p. 337.

24. Moltmann, *The Crucified God*, p. 7.

25. Jürgen Moltmann, *The Experiment Hope* (Philadelphia: Fortress Press, 1975), pp. 50-51.

26. Moltmann, *The Crucified God*, p. 2.

27. Ibid., pp. 325-29.

28. Ibid., p. 149.

29. Cf. Rubem Alves, *A Theology of Human Hope* (Washington DC: Corpus, 1969), pp. 55-68; Gustavo Gutiérrez, *A Theology of Liberation* (Maryknoll, NY: Orbis Books, 1973), pp. 216-18; Langdon Gilkey, *Naming the Whirlwind: The Renewal of God Language* (New York: Bobbs-Merrill, 1969), pp. 339, 346, 397.

30. Cf. Rebecca Chopp, *The Praxis of Suffering: An Interpretation of Liberation and Political Theologies* (Maryknoll, NY: Orbis Books, 1986), p. 107.

31. Moltmann, *The Crucified God*, pp. 329-35.

32. Míguez Bonino, *Doing Theology in a Revolutionary Situation*, pp. 147-50.

33. Cabestrero, ed., *Faith: Conversations with Contemporary Theologians*, p. 127.

34. Jürgen Moltmann, "On Latin American Liberation Theology: An Open Letter to José Míguez Bonino," *Christianity & Crisis* (March 29, 1976): 62.

35. Jürgen Moltmann, *On Human Dignity: Political Theology and Ethics* (Philadelphia: Fortress Press, 1984), p. 174.

36. Moltmann, "On Latin American Liberation Theology," p. 62.

37. Moltmann, *The Crucified God*, p. 55.

38. Moltmann, *The Experiment Hope*, pp. 136-37.

39. Cabestrero, ed., *Faith*, p. 136.

40. Ibid., pp. 137, 142-43.

41. George Hunsinger, "The Crucified God and the Political Theology of Violence: A Critical Survey of Jürgen Moltmann's Recent Thought," *The Heythrop Journal* 14, nos. 1, 2; (1973): 379-95. For the same criticism, see Jon P. Gunnemann, *The Moral Meaning of Revolution* (New Haven: Yale University Press, 1979), pp. 206-11.

42. John Howard Yoder, *The Original Revolution* (Scottdale, PA: Herald Press, 1971), p. 58.

43. Moltmann, *On Human Dignity*, pp. 116-20; cf. *The Book of Concord: The Confessions of the Evangelical Lutheran Church* (Philadelphia: Fortress Press, 1959); George H. Williams, *The Radical Reformation* (Philadelphia: Westminster Press, 1962); John Howard Yoder, *The Varieties of Religious Pacifism* (Scottdale, PA: Herald Press, 1971).

44. Moltmann, *On Human Dignity*, pp. 124-26.

45. Cf. Dietrich Bonhoeffer, *Letters and Papers from Prison* (New York: Macmillan, 1971, c1953), pp. 360-61; Cabestrero, ed., *Faith*, p. 124.

46. *On Human Dignity*, pp. 127-31.

47. On the just-war tradition, see Paul Ramsey, *War and the Christian Conscience: How Shall Modern War Be Conducted Justly* (Durham: Duke University Press, 1961); Ramsey, *The Just War: Force and Political Responsibility* (New York: Scribners, 1968); Edward L. Long, *War and Conscience in America* (Philadelphia: Westminster Press, 1968); James T. Johnson, *The Just War Tradition and the Restraint of War: A Moral and Historical Inquiry* (Princeton: Princeton University Press, 1981); and Michael Walzer, *Just and Unjust Wars: A Moral Argument with Historical Illustrations* (New York: Basic Books, 1977).

48. Cf. Langdon Gilkey, "The Universal and Immediate Presence of God," and John Macquarrie, "Eschatology and Time," in Herzog, ed., *The Future of Hope*, pp. 81-109, 110-25.

49. Jürgen Moltmann, *The Trinity and the Kingdom of God: The Doctrine of God* (New York: Harper & Row, 1981), pp. 191-92.

50. Ibid., pp. 21, 56.

51. Jürgen Moltmann, *God in Creation: A New Theology of Creation and the Spirit of God* (San Francisco: Harper & Row, 1985), pp. 1-2.

52. Ibid., p. 99.

53. Cf. Karl Heim, *The Transformation of the Scientific World View* (New York: Harper & Brothers, 1953); and Heim, *Christian Faith and Natural Science* (New York: Harper & Brothers, 1953); Moltmann, *God in Creation*, p. 17.

54. Cf. Cabestrero, ed., *Faith*, p. 126.

55. Jürgen Moltmann, *The Church in the Power of the Spirit: A Contribution to Messianic Ecclesiology* (New York: Harper & Row, 1977), p. 19.

56. Jürgen Moltmann, *The Future of Creation: Collected Essays* (Philadelphia: Fortress Press, 1979), pp. 97-98.

57. Chopp, *The Praxis of Suffering*, p. 102.

58. The limitations of Moltmann's neo-orthodox method have also been noted, for reasons different from my own, in David Tracy, *Blessed Rage for Order: The New Pluralism in Theology* (New York: Seabury Press, 1975), pp. 240-50.

59. Chopp, *The Praxis of Suffering*, p. 116.

60. Cf. Jürgen Moltmann, "The Ecological Crisis: Peace with Nature?," *The Scottish Journal of Religious Studies*, 9, no. 1 (Spring, 1988): 5-18; Moltmann, *Creating*

a Just Future (Philadelphia: Trinity Press International, 1989).

61. Jürgen Moltmann, et al., *Diskussion üeber die "Theologie der Hoffnung"* (Munich: Kaiser Verlag, 1967), pp. 210-11.

5. Gustavo Gutiérrez and the Theologies of Liberation

1. I was a student in this seminar.

2. For information on Gutiérrez's early career, cf. Robert McAfee Brown, *Gustavo Gutiérrez: An Introduction to Liberation Theology* (Maryknoll, NY: Orbis Books, 1990); Curt Cadorette, *From the Heart of the People: The Theology of Gustavo Gutiérrez* (Oak Park, IL: Meyer-Stone Books, 1988); and Deane William Ferm, *Third World Liberation Theologies: An Introductory Survey* (Maryknoll, NY: Orbis Books, 1986).

3. Quoted in Robert McAfee Brown, *Theology in a New Key*, (Philadelphia: Westminster Press, 1978), p. 93; cf. John Gerassi, ed., *Revolutionary Priest: The Complete Writings and Messages of Camilo Torres* (New York: Vintage Books, 1971).

4. Cf. Gustavo Gutiérrez, "Freedom and Salvation: A Political Problem," in *Liberation and Change*, Ronald H. Stone, ed. (Atlanta: John Knox Press, 1977), pp. 60-69; Gustavo Gutiérrez, *The Power of the Poor in History* (Maryknoll, NY: Orbis Books, 1983), pp. 194-97.

5. Quoted in Cadorette, *From the Heart of the People*, p. 79; cf. Miguel Monsignori, *Teología y salvacíon en la obra de Gustavo Gutiérrez* (Bilbao: University of Deusto, 1978), p. 131.

6. Segunda Conferencia General del Episcopado Latinoamericano, *Conclusiones: Presencia de la Iglesia en la actual transformacion de America latina* (Bogotá: General Secretariat of CELAM, 1971), no. 16. English edition: *The Church in the Present-Day Transformation of Latin America in the Light of the Council: Conclusions* (Bogotá: General Secretariat of CELAM, 1970).

7. Ibid., no. 8.

8. Gustavo Gutiérrez, *A Theology of Liberation: History, Politics, and Salvation* (Maryknoll, NY: Orbis Books, 1973), p. ix.

9. Ibid., p. 11; cf. Gutiérrez, *The Power of the Poor in History*, p. 37.

10. Cf. Lonnie D. Kliever, *The Shattered Spectrum: A Survey of Contemporary Theology* (Atlanta: John Knox Press, 1981), p. 86; Jürgen Moltmann, "On Latin American Liberation Theology: An Open Letter to José Migúez Bonino," in *Christianity & Crisis* (March 29, 1976), 57-59, also in Alfred T. Hennelly, ed., *Liberation Theology: A Documentary History* (Maryknoll, NY: Orbis Books, 1990).

11. Cf. Alfredo Fierro, *The Militant Gospel: A Critical Introduction to Political Theologies* (Maryknoll, NY: Orbis Books, 1977), pp. 323-29, 339-48; Dennis P. McCann, *Christian Realism and Liberation Theology: Practical Theologies in Creative Conflict* (Maryknoll, NY: Orbis Books, 1981), pp. 182-207.

12. Cf. *A Theology of Liberation*, pp. 154-65, 213-50.

13. Gutiérrez, *The Power of the Poor*, p. 91.

14. Cf. Peruvian Bishops' Commission for Social Action, *Between Honesty and Hope: Documents from and about the Church in Latin America* (Maryknoll, NY: Maryknoll Publications, 1970); *Iglesia latinoamericana: Protesta o profecia?* (Avellaneda, Argentina: Busqueda, 1969).

15. Gutiérrez, *A Theology of Liberation*, p. 112.

16. Gustavo Gutiérrez, "Liberation Praxis and Christian Faith," in *Frontiers of*

Theology in Latin America, Rosino Gibellini, ed. (Maryknoll, NY: Orbis Books, 1979), p. 1.

17. Gustavo Gutiérrez, "Two Theological Perspectives: Liberation Theology and Progressivist Theology," in *The Emergent Gospel: Theology from the Developing World*, Sergio Torres and Virginia Fabella, eds., (Maryknoll, NY: Orbis Books, 1978), pp. 240-41; Gutiérrez, *The Power of the Poor*, pp. 44-45.

18. Cf. Friedrich Schleiermacher, *On Religion: Addresses in Response to its Cultured Critics* (Richmond, VA: John Knox Press, 1969); Richard R. Niebuhr, *Schleiermacher on Christ and Religion* (New York: Harper & Row, 1964).

19. Gutiérrez, "Two Theological Perspectives: Liberation Theology and Progressivist Theology," in *The Emergent Gospel*, Torres and Fabella, eds., p. 241.

20. Cf. Gutiérrez, *The Power of the Poor*, pp. 45, 191-93; "Two Theological Perspectives," pp . 236-37 .

21. Cf. Gustavo Gutiérrez, "Terrorism, Liberation, and Sexuality," in *The Witness* (April 1977): 10.

22. Cf. Raymond Bonner, "Peru's War," in *The New Yorker* (January 4, 1988): 31-58; "Garcia Plays with Fire," in *The Economist* (August 8, 1987): 13; The Debt Crisis Network, *From Debt to Development: Alternatives to the International Debt Crisis* (Washington, D.C.: Institute for Policy Studies, 1985).

23. Gutiérrez, *The Power of the Poor*, p. 117.

24. Gutiérrez, "Terrorism, Liberation, and Sexuality," p. 10; Gutiérrez, *The Power of the Poor*, pp. 27-29.

25. Gutiérrez, "Two Theological Perspectives," p. 237.

26. Ibid., p. 252.

27. Gutiérrez, *The Power of the Poor*, pp. 186, 191.

28. Gutiérrez, "Freedom and Salvation: A Political Problem," p. 77.

29. Fernando Henrique Cardoso and Enzo Falleto, *Dependencia y Desarrollo en América Latina: ensayo de interpretacíon sociológica* (Mexico City: Siglo Veintiuno, 1969), p. 24.

30. Gutiérrez, *The Power of the Poor*, p. 117; Juan Luis Segundo, *Jesus of Nazareth Yesterday and Today*, Vol. 1, *Faith and Ideologies* (Maryknoll, NY: Orbis Books, 1984), p. 291.

31. Gutiérrez, *The Power of the Poor*, pp. 37, 46; Gutiérrez, "Freedom and Salvation: A Political Problem," pp. 76-77.

32. Gutiérrez, "Freedom and Salvation: A Political Problem," p. 83.

33. Juan Luis Segundo, "Capitalism versus Socialism: Crux Theologica," in Rosino Gibellini, ed., *Frontiers of Theology in Latin America*, p. 249.

34. Ibid., pp. 249-50.

35. On the theory of modern democratic socialism, cf. Alec Nove, *The Economics of Feasible Socialism* (London: Allen & Unwin, 1983); Michael Harrington, *Socialism* (New York: Saturday Review Press, 1972); David Schweickart, *Capitalism or Worker Control? An Ethical and Economic Appraisal* (New York: Praeger, 1980).

36. Juan Luis Segundo, *The Liberation of Theology* (Maryknoll, NY: Orbis Books, 1976), p. 8.

37. Ibid., p. 17.

38. Cf. Ibid., pp. 13-19.

39. Segundo bases this discussion upon James Cone, *A Black Theology of Liberation* (Philadelphia; Lippincott Co., 1970/Maryknoll, NY: Orbis Books, 1986). Although Cone's position has not substantially changed since the publication of *A*

Black Theology of Liberation, he has been moved by feminist and third world liberationist criticism to develop a more inclusive version of his position. Cf. James Cone, *God of the Oppressed* (New York: Seabury Press, 1975); James Cone, "Black Theology and the Black Church: Where Do We Go From Here?," in Gerald H. Anderson and Thomas F. Stransky, eds., *Mission Trends No. 4: Liberation Theologies in North America and Europe* (New York: Paulist Press, 1979); and "Christian Faith and Political Praxis," in Brian Mahan and L. Dale Richesin, eds. *The Challenge of Liberation Theology: A First World Response* (Maryknoll, NY: Orbis Books, 1981).

40. Segundo, *The Liberation of Theology*, p. 26.

41. Cone, *A Black Theology of Liberation*, p. 33.

42. Ibid., pp. 156, 108; cf. Segundo, *The Liberation of Theology*, pp. 31-34.

43. Segundo, *The Liberation of Theology*, p. 33.

44. Ibid., pp. 102, 155.

45. Hugo Assmann, *Opresión-Liberación: Desafío a los cristianos* (Montevideo: Tierra Nueva, 1971), p. 20.

46. Juan Luis Segundo, *Masas y minorías en la dialéctica divina de la liberación* (Buenos Aires: La Aurora, 1973), pp. 74-90. In recent years, Hugo Assmann has considerably toned down what he calls the "aggressive style" of his early works. See his paper "The Improvement of Democracy in Latin America and the Debt Crisis" and the subsequent conference discussion reprinted in Michael Novak, ed., *Liberation Theology and the Liberal Society* (Washington, DC: American Enterprise Institute, 1987), pp. 37-62.

47. Juan Luis Segundo, *Theology and the Church: A Response to Cardinal Ratzinger and a Warning to the Whole Church* (Minneapolis: Winston Press, 1985).

48. Cf. McCann, *Christian Realism and Liberation Theology*, p. 221.

49. Segundo, *Jesus of Nazareth Yesterday and Today*. Vol. 1, *Faith and Ideologies*, p. 286. See also Segundo, *Theology and the Church*, p. 130, where he argues that the effects of a prolonged guerrilla war are "perhaps more destructive of the social ecology than a war between countries."

50. Segundo, *The Liberation of Theology*, p. 120.

51. Ibid., p. 109.

52. Ibid., p. 108.

53. Ibid., p. 121.

54. Ibid., pp. 120-22.

55. Ibid., pp. 43, 116.

56. Ibid., pp. 145-48.

57. Ibid., pp. 185-92.

58. Ibid., pp. 196, 112.

59. Juan Luis Segundo, *A Theology for Artisans of a New Humanity*. Vol. 3, *Our Idea of God* (Maryknoll, NY: Orbis Books, 1974), p. 36.

60. Juan Luis Segundo, "Las 'elites' latinamericanas: problematica humana y cristiana ante el cambio social," in *Fe cristiana y cambio social en America latina* (Salamanca: Sigueme, 1973), p. 204.

61. Cf. Richard Shaull, "Christian Faith as Scandal in a Technocratic World," in Martin E. Marty and Dean G. Peerman, eds., *New Theology no. 6* (New York: Macmillan, 1969), pp. 123-34; Segundo, *The Liberation of Theology*, p. 202.

62. Rubem Alves, *A Theology of Human Hope* (Washington, DC: Corpus Books, 1969), p. 155; cf. Segundo, *The Liberation of Theology*, pp. 145-46.

63. Cf. Rubem Alves, *What Is Religion?* (Maryknoll, NY: Orbis Books, 1984);

and Alves, "From Paradise to the Desert: Autobiographical Musings," in Gibellini, ed., *Frontiers of Theology in Latin America*, pp. 284-303.

64. Segundo, "Capitalism Versus Socialism: Crux Theologica," p. 247.

65. Ibid., pp. 257-58; cf. Segundo, *The Liberation of Theology*, pp. 147-48.

66. Gutiérrez, "Liberation Praxis and Christian Faith," p. 7; *The Power of the Poor*, p. 44.

67. Gutiérrez, *A Theology of Liberation*, p. 171.

68. Gutiérrez, *The Power of the Poor*, pp. 91, 22; cf. Segundo, *Theology and the Church*, pp. 148-50, 168, and *The Liberation of Theology*, pp. 216-21. For an interesting discussion of Segundo's denigration of popular Latin American religion, cf. Harvey Cox, *Religion in the Secular City: Toward a Postmodern Theology* (New York: Simon & Schuster, 1984), pp. 240-47. For Míguez Bonino's attitude toward popular religion, see his essay "Popular Piety in Latin America," in *Cristianismo Sociedad*, Vol. I, no. 1 (1976): 31-38. Míguez Bonino asserts, "From a theological as well as a political perspective the popular piety that used to exist and that still predominates in Latin America can only be considered as a profoundly alienated and alienating piety, a manifestation of an enslaved consciousness and, at the same time, a ready instrument for the continuation and consolidation of oppression." Gutiérrez's writings contain numerous indirect criticisms of this attitude, especially in his essay "Theology from the Underside of History," reprinted in *The Power of the Poor*, and in "Freedom and Salvation: A Political Problem."

69. Quoted in Brown, *Gustavo Gutiérrez*, p. 20.

70. From the foreword to Gustavo Gutiérrez, *We Drink From Our Own Wells: The Spiritual Journey of a People* (Maryknoll, NY: Orbis Books, 1984), p. xviii.

71. Quoted in ibid., p. 108.

72. Ibid., p. 29.

73. Cf. Dietrich Bonhoeffer, *Letters and Papers from Prison* (New York: Macmillan, 1971, c1953), pp. 382-83.

74. Cf. Richard J. Neuhaus, "Liberation Theology and the Captivities of Jesus," in *Worldview* (June 1973), reprinted in *Mission Trends no. 3: Third World Theologies*, Gerald E. Anderson and Thomas F. Stransky, C.S.P., eds. (New York: Paulist Press, 1976), pp. 41-61; James V. Schall, S.J., "Liberation Theology in Latin America," in *Liberation Theology*, Ronald Nash, ed., (Milford, MI: Mott Media, 1984), pp. 73-97; François Hubert Lepargneur, "The Theologies of Liberation and Theology," in *Liberation Theology in Latin America*, James V. Schall, S.J., ed., (San Francisco: Ignatius Press, 1982), pp. 208-25; Michael Novak, *Will It Liberate? Questions About Liberation Theology* (New York: Paulist Press, 1986).

75. Gutiérrez, *A Theology of Liberation*, p. 266.

76. Ibid., p. 267.

77. Quoted in "Statement by José Míguez Bonino," in *Theology in the Americas*, Sergio Torres and John Eagleson, eds., (Maryknoll, NY: Orbis Books, 1976), p. 278.

78. Cf. José María Arguedas, *Deep Rivers* (Austin: University of Texas Press, 1978).

79. Quoted in Cadorette, *From the Heart of the People*, p. 72.

80. Quoted in ibid., p. 73; cf. Gutiérrez, *We Drink From Our Own Wells*, p. 152.

81. Gutiérrez, *The Power of the Poor*, p. 101.

82. Cf. Novak, *Will It Liberate?*, pp. 243-44.

83. Gutiérrez, "Freedom and Salvation," p. 92.

84. Cf. Gustavo Gutiérrez, "Reflections from a Latin American Perspective: Finding Our Way to Talk about God," in *Irruption of the Third World: Challenge to Theology*, Virginia Fabella and Sergio Torres, eds. (Maryknoll, NY: Orbis Books, 1983), pp. 232-34; Gustavo Gutiérrez, *On Job: God-Talk and the Suffering of the Innocent* (Maryknoll, NY: Orbis Books, 1987), p . xiii.

6. José Míguez Bonino and the Underside of Modernity

1. Cf. José Míguez Bonino, *Christians and Marxists: The Mutual Challenge to Revolution* (Grand Rapids: Eerdmans, 1976), pp. 15-28.

2. "Democratic Argentina: An Interview with José Míguez Bonino," *Christianity & Crisis* (May 5, 1986): 149-51.

3. Ibid., p. 151.

4. José Míguez Bonino, *Toward a Christian Political Ethics* (Philadelphia: Fortress Press, 1983), p. 7.

5. Ibid., pp. 7-9.

6. José Míguez Bonino, "For Life and against Death: A Theology That Takes Sides," in *Theologians in Transition*, James M. Wall, ed. (New York: Crossroad, 1981), p. 169.

7. Míguez Bonino, *Christians and Marxists*, p. 7.

8. José Míguez Bonino, *Doing Theology in a Revolutionary Situation* (Philadelphia: Fortress Press, 1975), p. 101.

9. Míguez Bonino, "For Life and against Death," p. 173.

10. Míguez Bonino, *Doing Theology*, pp. xix, xx.

11. Ibid., p. 7.

12. Ibid., p. 9; cf. Leopoldo Zea, *The Latin American Mind*, (Norman, OK: University of Oklahoma Press, 1963).

13. Míguez Bonino, *Doing Theology*, p. 14.

14. Peruvian Bishops' Conference, "La Justicia en el Mundo," 1969, cited in *Development-Dependency: The Role of Multinational Corporations* (Washington, DC: U.S. Catholic Conference, 1974), pp. 7-8, n. 16.

15. Míguez Bonino, *Doing Theology*, p. 14.

16. Cf. Stephen Schlesinger and Stephen Kinzer, *Bitter Fruit: The Untold Story of the American Coup in Guatemala* (New York: Doubleday, 1982); Walter LaFeber, *Inevitable Revolutions: The United States in Central America* (New York: W.W. Norton, 1983); Lars Schoultz, *Human Rights and U.S. Policy Towards Latin America* (Princeton: Princeton University Press, 1981).

17. Míguez Bonino, *Doing Theology*, pp. 16, 26.

18. Cited in *Development-Dependency*, p. ii.

19. Fernando Fajnzylber, *Estrategia Industrial y Empresas Internacionales Posicion relativa de America y Brasil* (Rio de Janeiro: United Nations, CEPAL, November 1970): 65; Richard J. Barnet and Ronald E. Muller, *Global Reach: The Power of the Multinational Corporations* (New York: Simon & Schuster, 1974), pp. 152-53.

20. Cited in Barnet and Muller, *Global Reach*, p. 153; cf. Aldo Ferrer, "Towards a Theory of Independence," in *Latin America in the World Economy*, ed. Diana Tussie (New York: St. Martin's Press, 1983), pp. 89-108.

21. Gary Dorrien, *The Democratic Socialist Vision* (Totowa, NJ: Rowman & Littlefield, 1986), p. 93.

22. Cf. C. Abel and C. Lewis, *Economic Imperialism in Latin America* (London:

London University Press, 1983); Fernando Cardoso and E. Faletto, *Dependencia y Desarrollo en América Latina* (Mexico City: Siglo Veintiuno, 1969); Andre Gunder Frank, *Dependent Accumulation and Underdevelopment* (New York: Monthly Review Press, 1979) and *Capitalism and Underdevelopment in Latin America* (New York: Monthly Review Press, 1967); Raul Prebisch, *The Economic Development of Latin America and its Principal Problems* (New York: United Nations, 1950). For an excellent overview of the differing forms of dependency theory, see Arthur F. McGovern, "Latin America and Dependency Theory," *This World*, 14 (Spring/Summer 1986): 104-23.

23. Cf. U.S. Bureau of the Census, *Statistical History of the United States* (New York: Basic Books, 1978), tables U-318-23, U-43-45; Michael Novak, *The Spirit of Democratic Capitalism* (New York: Simon & Schuster, 1982), pp. 301-302; Joseph Ramos, "Dependency and Development: An Attempt to Clarify the Issues," *Liberation South, Liberation North*, Michael Novak, ed. (Washington, DC: American Enterprise Institute, 1981), pp. 61-67.

24. Jürgen Moltmann, "On Latin American Liberation Theology: An Open Letter to José Míguez Bonino," *Christianity & Crisis* (March 29, 1976): 62.

25. Cf. *Taller de Teologia*, 1, no. 1, (Mexico City: Communidad Teologica de Mexico, 1976), esp. Gustavo Gutiérrez, "Teologia Desde el Reverso de la Historia."

26. Míguez Bonino, *Doing Theology*, p. 25.

27. Míguez Bonino, *Toward a Christian Political Ethics*, pp. 28, 68.

28. Míguez Bonino, *Doing Theology*, p. 28.

29. Míguez Bonino, *Toward a Christian Political Ethics*, p. 70.

30. Míguez Bonino, *Doing Theology*, p. 29.

31. Interview with Octavio Paz, "After the Cultural Delirium," *Encounter* (July/August 1986): 66.

32. Cf. Míguez Bonino, *Doing Theology*, pp. 39-40.

33. Míguez Bonino, "For Life and against Death," pp. 175-76.

34. Ibid., p. 176.

35. Míguez Bonino, *Christians and Marxists*, p. 87.

36. Ibid., p. 89.

37. Ibid., pp. 89-91, 96.

38. Míguez Bonino, *Doing Theology*, pp. 90-91.

39. Ibid., p. 93.

40. Ibid., p. 93.

41. Cf. Rebecca S. Chopp, *The Praxis of Suffering: An Interpretation of Liberation and Political Theologies* (Maryknoll, NY: Orbis Books, 1986) p. 88.

42. Míguez Bonino, *Toward a Christian Political Ethics*, p. 25.

43. Ibid., p. 24.

44. José Míguez Bonino, "Historical Praxis and Christian Identity," in *Frontiers of Theology in Latin America*, Rosino Gibellini, ed. (Maryknoll, NY: Orbis Books, 1979), p. 271.

45. Ibid., p. 269.

46. Cf. Gustavo Gutiérrez, *A Theology of Liberation* (Maryknoll, NY: Orbis Books, 1973).

47. Míguez Bonino, "Historical Praxis and Christian Identity," p. 273.

48. Jürgen Moltmann, *The Crucified God: The Cross of Christ as the Foundation and Criticism of Christian Theology* (New York: Harper & Row, 1974), p. 305.

49. Míguez Bonino, *Doing Theology*, p. 148.

50. Ibid., pp. 149-50.

51. Míguez Bonino, *Toward a Christian Political Ethics*, p. 26.

52. Ibid., p. 27.

53. José Míguez Bonino, "Violence: A Theological Reflection," in *Mission Trends No. 3: Third World Theologies*, Gerald H. Anderson and Thomas F. Stransky, eds. (New York: Paulist Press, 1976), p. 119.

54. Karl Marx, "On James Mill," in *The Early Texts*, ed. D. McLellan (New York: Barnes & Noble, 1971), p. 192. Cited in Míguez Bonino, *Toward a Christian Political Ethics*, p. 27.

55. Karl Marx, "The Communism of the *Rheinischer Beobachter*," *Werke*, vol. 4 (Berlin: Kietz Verlag, 1959-1971), p. 200. Cited in Míguez Bonino, *Toward a Christian Political Ethics*, p. 27.

56. Míguez Bonino, *Doing Theology*, p. 119.

57. Míguez Bonino, *Christians and Marxists*, pp. 134-36.

58. Ibid., p. 134.

59. Míguez Bonino, *Toward a Christian Political Ethics*, pp. 22-36.

60. Míguez Bonino, *Christians and Marxists*, p. 131.

61. Ibid., p. 130.

62. Míguez Bonino, *Toward a Christian Political Ethics*, pp. 29-31.

63. Ibid., pp. 107-8.

64. Ibid., pp. 65-75.

65. Míguez Bonino, "For Life and Against Death," p. 176.

66. Cf. ibid., p. 176; Míguez Bonino, *Toward a Christian Political Ethics*, p. 77.

67. Gustavo Gutiérrez, *The Power of the Poor in History* (Maryknoll, NY: Orbis Books, 1983), pp. 37-38.

68. Míguez Bonino, *Doing Theology*, p. 99.

69. Ibid., p. 149.

7. Toward a Theopraxis of the Common Good

1. Cf. Ray Ginger, *The Bending Cross: A Biography of Eugene Victor Debs* (New Brunswick: Rutgers University Press, 1949), pp. 259-61; Nick Salvatore, *Eugene V. Debs: Citizen and Socialist* (Urbana: University of Illinois Press, 1982), pp. 225-30; Michael Harrington, "Response to James Cone," in James H. Cone, "The Black Church and Marxism: What Do They Have To Say To Each Other?" (New York: Institute for Democratic Socialism, 1980), pp. i–iv.

2. Jürgen Moltmann, "On Latin American Liberation Theology: An Open Letter to José Míguez Bonino," *Christianity & Crisis* (March 29, 1976): 61–63.

3. Sharon D. Welch, *Communities of Resistance and Solidarity: A Feminist Theology of Liberation* (Maryknoll, NY: Orbis Books, 1985), pp. 74–92. Cf. Michel Foucault, *Power/Knowledge: Selected Interviews and Other Writings* (New York: Pantheon Books, 1980).

4. For example, see William Sullivan, *Reconstructing Public Philosophy* (Berkeley: University of California Press, 1982); Michael Walzer, *Spheres of Justice: A Defense of Pluralism and Equality* (New York: Basic Books, 1983); Robert Bellah, et al., *Habits of the Heart: Individualism and Commitment in American Life* (Berkeley: University of California Press, 1985); and Letty M. Russell, *Human Liberation in a Feminist Perspective—A Theology* (Philadelphia: Westminster Press, 1974).

5. Cornel West, "Harrington's Socialist Vision," *Christianity & Crisis* (December

12, 1983): 484; reprinted in West, *Prophetic Fragments* (Grand Rapids: Eerdmans Publishing Company, 1988), pp. 25–29.

6. Cornel West, *Prophesy Deliverance! An Afro-American Revolutionary Christianity* (Philadelphia: Westminster Press, 1982), pp. 134–37; Cf. Cornel West, "Black Theology and Marxist Thought," in *Black Theology: A Documentary History*, ed. G. S. Wilmore and James Cone (Maryknoll, NY: Orbis Books, 1979), pp. 552–67.

7. West, *Prophesy Deliverance!* p. 137. On Councilism, see Serge Bricianer, *Pannekoek and the Workers' Councils* (St. Louis: Telos Press, 1978); Stanley Aronowitz, *The Crisis in Historical Materialism: Class, Politics and Culture in Marxist Theory* (New York: Praeger Publishers, 1981); and Rosa Luxemburg, *Selected Political Writings of Rosa Luxemburg*, Dick Howard, ed. (New York: Monthly Review Press, 1971). On Bernsteinian democratic socialism, see Eduard Bernstein, *Evolutionary Socialism* (New York: Schocken Books, 1963, c1899); Peter Gay, *The Dilemma of Democratic Socialism: Eduard Bernstein's Challenge to Marx* (New York: Columbia University Press, 1952); and Harry W. Laidler, *A History of Socialist Thought* (New York: Thomas Y. Crowell, 1933), pp. 295–320.

8. Cf. Michael Harrington, *Fragments of the Century* (New York: Saturday Review Press/E. P. Dutton, 1973), pp. 91–93.

9. Cf. G. D. H. Cole, *Guild Socialism Restated* (New Brunswick, NJ: Transaction Books, 1980, c1920); and G. D. H. Cole, *Self Government in Industry* (London: Bell, 1920).

10. Cf. Cornel West, "Critical Theory and Christian Faith" (1986), "Alasdair MacIntyre, Liberalism, and Socialism: A Christian Perspective," (1985); and "Left Strategies Today" (1986), reprinted consecutively in West, *Prophetic Fragments*, pp. 112–43.

11. Cf. Alec Nove, *The Economics of Feasible Socialism* (London: George Allen & Unwin, 1983); and Wlodzimierz Brus, *The Economics and Politics of Socialism* (London: Routledge & Kegan Paul, 1973). West has also acknowledged the influence of Branko Horvat and John Kenneth Galbraith upon his recent thought, especially in Horvat, *The Political Economy of Socialism: A Marxist Social Theory*, (Armonk, NY: M. E. Sharpe, 1982); and in Galbraith, *Economics and the Public Purpose* (Boston: Houghton Mifflin, 1973).

12. Cf. Oskar Lange and F. M. Taylor, *On the Economic Theory of Socialism* (New York: McGraw-Hill, 1964, c1931); C. A. R. Crosland, *The Future of Socialism* (New York: Macmillan, 1957), p. 496.

13. "The Frankfurt Declaration," (adopted at the Founding Congress of the Socialist International at Frankfurt, West Germany, July 1951). Published in *Aims and Tasks of Democratic Socialism* (London: The Socialist International, 1951), pp. 1–8. Reprinted in *New International Review* 1, no. 1 (Winter 1977): 5–10.

14. Cf. Rudolf Meidner, *Employee Investment Funds: An Approach to Collective Capital Formation* (London: George Allen & Unwin, 1978); Meidner, "A Swedish Union Proposal for Collective Capital Sharing," in *Eurosocialism and America: Political Economy for the 1980s*, Nancy Lieber, ed. (Philadelphia: Temple University Press, 1982); and Robert Kuttner, *The Economic Illusion: False Choices Between Prosperity and Social Justice* (Boston: Houghton Mifflin, 1984).

15. West, *Prophetic Fragments*, p. 122.

16. Cf. Robert Dahl, *Dilemmas of Pluralist Democracy: Autonomy vs. Control* (New Haven: Yale University Press, 1982), p. 162.

17. Cf. Søren Kierkegaard, *Either/Or: A Fragment of Life*, 2 volumes (Princeton:

Princeton University Press, 1944, cl843); Søren Kierkegaard, *Concluding Unscientific Postscript* (Princeton, NJ: Princeton University Press, 1941, cl846).

18. Dorothee Sölle, *Beyond Mere Dialogue: On Being Christian and Socialist* (Detroit: Christians for Socialism in the United States, 1978), pp. 16–30.

19. The phrase is Hugo Assmann's. Cf. Assmann, *Theology for a Nomad Church* (Maryknoll, NY: Orbis Books, 1976).

20. Quoted in West, *Prophesy Deliverance!* p. 171.

21. Cf. Zillah R. Eisenstein, *The Radical Future of Liberal Feminism* (New York: Longman, 1981).

22. Cf. Rosemary Radford Ruether, *Sexism and God-Talk: Toward a Feminist Theology* (Boston: Beacon Press, 1983); Michael Levin, "Comparable Worth: The Feminist Road to Socialism," *Commentary* (September 1984); Michael Levin, *Feminism and Freedom* (New Brunswick: Transaction Books, 1987); George Gilder, *Sexual Suicide* (New York: Quadrangle/New York Times Book Company, 1973).

23. Cf. Ronnie Steinberg, "The Debate on Comparable Worth," *New Politics* 1, no. 1 (Summer 1986): 108–26; Ronnie Steinberg and Lois Haignere, "Separate but Equivalent: Equal Pay for Work of Comparable Worth," in *Gender at Work: Perspectives on Occupational Segregation and Comparable Worth* (Washington, D.C.: Women's Research and Education Institute), 1984.

24. Ruether, *Sexism and God-Talk*, p. 222.

25. Cf. Philip S. Foner, *American Socialism and Black Americans: From the Age of Jackson to World War II* (Westport, CT: Greenwood Press, 1977); James H. Cone, "The Black Church and Marxism: What Do They Have To Say To Each Other?", pp. 1–10.

26. For a collection of interviews that reveals a growing feminist consciousness among Latin American liberationist theologians, see Elsa Tamez, *Against Machismo* (Oak Park, IL: Meyer Stone Books, 1987).

27. Rosemary Radford Ruether, "Feminist Theology and Spirituality," in *Christian Feminism: Visions of a New Humanity*, Judith L. Weidman, ed. (New York: Harper & Row, 1984), pp. 15–16.

28. Ruether, *Sexism and God-Talk*, pp. 232–33.

29. Cf. Jon Sobrino, *The True Church and the Poor* (Maryknoll, NY: Orbis Books, 1984); Leonardo Boff, *Ecclesiogenesis: The Base Communities Reinvent the Church* (Maryknoll, NY: Orbis Books, 1986). For a similar perspective, see Richard Shaull, *Heralds of a New Reformation: The Poor of South and North America* (Maryknoll, NY: Orbis Books, 1984); Gustavo Gutiérrez, *A Theology of Liberation*, rev. ed. (Maryknoll, NY: Orbis Books, 1988), p. xxiv.

30. For conservative critiques of the shift toward a praxis orientation in the churches, see Stanley Atkins and Theodore McConnell, eds., *Churches on the Wrong Road* (Chicago: Regnery Gateway, 1986); and Edward Norman, *Christianity and the World Order* (Oxford: Oxford University Press, 1979). For similar criticisms that focus on liberation theology, see Ronald Nash, ed., *Liberation Theology* (Milford, MI: Mott Media, 1984); and James V. Schall, S.J., ed., *Liberation Theology in Latin America* (San Francisco: Ignatius Press, 1982).

31. Frederick Herzog, "A New Spirituality: Shaping Doctrine at the Grass Roots," in *The Christian Century* (July 30–August 6, 1986): 680–81. For two examples of praxis-oriented North American theological literature, see William K. Tabb, ed., *Churches in Struggle: Liberation Theologies and Social Change in North America* (New

York: Monthly Review Press, 1986); and Susan Thistlethwaite, ed., *A Just Peace Church* (New York: United Church Press, 1986).

32. Cf. Gustavo Gutiérrez, *The Power of the Poor in History* (Maryknoll, NY: Orbis Books, 1983), pp. 36–74.

33. William Temple, *Christianity and the Social Order* (Baltimore: Penguin Books, 1956, c1942), p. 101.

34. Cornel West, "Toward a Socialist Theory of Racism," (New York: The Institute for Democratic Socialism, 1986), p. 6; reprinted in West, *Prophetic Fragments,* pp. 97–108, quotation on p. 108.

35. West, *Prophetic Fragments,* p. 108.

36. John Kenneth Galbraith, *The American Left and Some British Comparisons* Fabian Tract No. 405, (London: The Fabian Society, 1971), p. 36.

Bibliography

Aiken, John R. "Walter Rauschenbusch and Education for Reform." *Church History* 36 (December 1967).

Alperovitz, Gar, and Jeff Faux. *Rebuilding America: A Blueprint for the New Economy*. New York: Pantheon Books, 1984.

Alves, Rubem. "From Paradise to the Desert: Autobiographical Musings." In *Frontiers of Theology in Latin America*, edited by Rosino Gibellini. Maryknoll, NY: Orbis Books, 1979.

———. *A Theology of Human Hope*. New York: Corpus Books, 1969.

———. *What Is Religion?* Maryknoll, NY: Orbis Books, 1984.

Amin, S. *Imperialism and Unequal Development*. New York: Monthly Review Press, 1977.

Anderson, Gerald H., and Thomas F. Stransky, eds. *Mission Trends No. 3: Third World Theologies*. New York: Paulist Press, 1976.

———. *Mission Trends No. 4: Liberation Theologies in North America and Europe*. New York: Paulist Press, 1979.

Anderson, Perry. "The Affinities of Norberto Bobbio." *New Left Review* 170 (July/August 1988).

———. *Lineages of the Absolutist State*. London: Verso, 1979.

Arguedas, José María. *Deep Rivers*. Austin: University of Texas Press, 1978.

Aronowitz, Stanley. *The Crisis in Historical Materialism: Class, Politics, and Culture in Marxist Theory*. New York: Praeger, 1981.

———. "Postmodernism and Politics." *Social Text: Theory/Culture/Ideology* (Winter 1987/88).

Assmann, Hugo. "Democracy and the Debt Crisis." *This World* 14 (Spring/Summer 1986).

———. *Opresión-Liberación: Desafío a los cristianos*. Montevideo: Tierra Nueva, 1971.

———. *Theology for a Nomad Church*. Maryknoll, NY: Orbis Books, 1976.

Atkins, Stanley, and Theodore McConnell, eds. *Churches on the Wrong Road*. Chicago: Regnery Gateway, 1986.

Barnet, Richard, and Ronald E. Muller. *Global Reach: The Power of the Multinational Corporations*. New York: Simon & Schuster, 1974.

Barth, Karl. *Church Dogmatics: The Doctrine of the Word of God*. Vol. 1, Part 1. Edinburgh: T.&T. Clark, 1936.

Baum, Gregory. *Religion and Alienation: A Theological Reading of Sociology*. New York: Paulist Press, 1975.

Bell, Daniel. *The Cultural Contradictions of Capitalism*. New York: Basic Books, 1978.

———. *Marxian Socialism in the United States*. Princeton: Princeton University Press, 1967.

Bellah, Robert, et al. *Habits of the Heart: Individualism and Commitment in American Life*. Berkeley: University of California Press, 1985.

Bellah, Robert, and William Sullivan. "The Common Good." *Tikkun* (July/August 1988).

Benello, C. George, and Dimitrios Roussopoulos, eds. *The Case for Participatory Democracy*. New York: Grossman, 1971.

Bennett, John C. "After Liberalism—What?" *The Christian Century* 50 (1933).

———. "Liberation Theology and Christian Realism." *Christianity and Crisis* 33 (1973).

———. *The Radical Imperative: From Theology to Social Ethics*. Philadelphia: Westminster Press, 1975.

———. "Reinhold Niebuhr's Social Ethics." In *Reinhold Niebuhr: His Religious, Social, and Political Thought*, edited by Charles W. Kegley and Robert W. Bretall. New York: Macmillan, 1956.

———. "The Social Gospel Today." In *The Social Gospel: Religion and Reform in Changing America*, edited by Ronald C. White Jr. and C. Howard Hopkins. Philadelphia: Temple University Press, 1976.

———. "The Social Interpretation of Christianity." In *The Church through Half a Century: Essays in Honor of William Adams Brown*, edited by Samuel Cavert and Henry Van Dusen. New York: Scribner's, 1936.

———. *Social Salvation: A Religious Approach to the Problems of Social Change*. New York: Scribner's, 1935.

Berger, Peter. *The Capitalist Revolution: Fifty Propositions about Prosperity, Equality, and Liberty*. New York: Basic Books, 1986.

———. *Facing Up to Modernity: Excursions in Society, Politics, and Religion*. New York: Basic Books, 1977.

———. *Pyramids of Sacrifice: Political Ethics and Social Change*. New York: Basic Books, 1974.

Bernstein, Eduard. *Evolutionary Socialism*. New York: Schocken Books, 1961, c1899.

Bernstein, Richard J. *The Restructuring of Social and Political Theory*. New York: Harcourt Brace Jovanovich, 1976.

Berryman, Phillip. *Liberation Theology*. New York: Pantheon Books, 1987.

———. *The Religious Roots of Rebellion: Christians in Central American Revolutions*. Maryknoll, NY: Orbis Books, 1984.

Bloch, Ernst. *Avicenna und die Aristotelische Linke*. Frankfurt: Surkamp Verlag, 1963.

———. *Das Prinzip Hoffnung*. Frankfurt: Surkamp Verlag, 1959.

Block, Fred. *Revising State Theory: Essays in Politics and Postindustrialism*. Philadelphia: Temple University Press, 1987.

Bobbio, Norberto. *Which Socialism? Marxism, Socialism and Democracy*. Minneapolis: University of Minnesota Press, 1987.

Bodein, Vernon P. *The Social Gospel of Walter Rauschenbusch and Its Relation to Religious Education*. New Haven: Yale University Press, 1944.

Boff, Clodovis. *Theology and Praxis: Epistemological Foundations*. Maryknoll, NY: Orbis Books, 1987.

Boff, Leonardo. *Ecclesiogenesis: The Base Communities Reinvent the Church*. Maryknoll, NY: Orbis Books, 1986.

———. *Jesus Christ Liberator*. Maryknoll, NY: Orbis Books, 1978.

Bonhoeffer, Dietrich. *Letters and Papers from Prison*. Edited by Eberhard Bethge. New York: Macmillan, 1971.

Bonner, Raymond. "Peru's War." *New Yorker* (January 4, 1988).

Boulding, Kenneth E., and Tapan Mukerjee, eds. *Economic Imperialism*. Ann Arbor: University of Michigan Press, 1972.

Bricianer, Serge. *Pannekoek and the Workers' Councils*. St. Louis: Telos Press, 1978.

Brown, Robert McAfee. *Gustavo Gutiérrez: An Introduction to Liberation Theology*. Maryknoll, NY: Orbis Books, 1990.

———. "A Preface and a Conclusion." In *Theology in the Americas*, edited by Sergio Torres and John Eagleson. Maryknoll, NY: Orbis Books, 1976.

———. "Reinhold Niebuhr: His Theology in the 1980s." *The Christian Century* (January 22, 1986).

———. *Theology in a New Key: Responding to Liberation Themes*. Philadelphia: Westminster Press, 1978.

Brus, Wlodzimierz. *The Economics and Politics of Socialism*. London: Routledge & Kegan Paul, 1973.

———. *Socialist Ownership and Political Systems*. London: Routledge & Kegan Paul, 1975.

Buhlmann, Walbert. *The Coming of the Third Church*. Maryknoll, NY: Orbis Books, 1977.

Bultmann, Rudolf. *New Testament and Mythology and Other Basic Writings*. Edited by Schubert M. Ogden. Philadelphia: Fortress Press, 1984.

———. *Theology of the New Testament*. New York: Scribner's, 1951.

Bunzel, John H., ed. *Political Passages: Journeys of Change Through Two Decades, 1968-1988*. New York: Free Press, 1988.

Burbach, Roger and Patricia Flynn, eds. *The Politics of Intervention: The United States in Central America*. New York: Monthly Review Press, 1984.

Burnham, Frederick B., Charles S. McCoy, and M. Douglas Meeks, eds. *Love: The Foundation of Hope: The Theology of Jürgen Moltmann and Elisabeth Moltmann-Wendel*. San Francisco: Harper & Row, 1988.

Cabestrero, Teofilo, ed. *Faith: Conversations with Contemporary Theologians*. Maryknoll, NY: Orbis Books, 1980.

Cadorette, Curt. *From the Heart of the People: The Theology of Gustavo Gutiérrez*. Oak Park, IL: Meyer-Stone Books, 1988.

Cardoso, Fernando Henrique, and Enzo Falleto. *Dependencia y desarrollo en América Latina: ensayo de interpretacion sociologica*. Mexico City: Siglo Veintiuno, 1969.

Carnoy, Martin, and Derek Shearer. *Economic Democracy: The Challenge of the 1980s*. White Plains, NY: M.E. Sharpe, 1980.

Chopp, Rebecca. *The Praxis of Suffering: An Interpretation of Liberation and Political Theologies*. Maryknoll, NY: Orbis Books, 1986.

Cole, G. D. H. *Guild Socialism Restated*. New Brunswick, NJ: Transaction Books, 1980.

———. *Self Government in Industry*. London: Bell, 1929.

Comblin, José. *The Church and the National Security State*. Maryknoll, NY: Orbis Books, 1979.

Cone, James H. "The Black Church and Marxism: What Do They Have to Say to Each Other?" New York: Institute for Democratic Socialism, 1980.

———. *A Black Theology of Liberation*. Philadelphia: Lippincott, 1970.

————. *My Soul Looks Back.* Maryknoll, NY: Orbis Books, 1986.

————. *Speaking the Truth: Ecumenism, Liberation, and Black Theology.* Grand Rapids, MI: Eerdmans, 1986.

Cort, John C.. *Christian Socialism: An Informal History.* Maryknoll, NY: Orbis Books, 1988.

Cott, Nancy F. *The Grounding of Modern Feminism.* New Haven: Yale University Press, 1987.

Cox, Harvey. *Religion in the Secular City: Toward a Postmodern Theology.* New York: Simon & Schuster, 1984.

Crick, Bernard. *In Defence of Politics.* Chicago: University of Chicago Press, 1972.

Crosland, C.A.R. *The Future of Socialism.* New York: Macmillan, 1957.

Cunningham, Frank. *Democratic Theory and Socialism.* Cambridge: Cambridge University Press, 1987.

Dahl, Robert A. *Dilemmas of Pluralist Democracy: Autonomy vs. Control.* New Haven: Yale University Press, 1982.

————. *A Preface to Economic Democracy.* Berkeley: University of California Press, 1985.

Dallmayr, Fred. *Twilight of Subjectivity: Contributions to a Post-Individualist Theory of Politics.* Amherst: University of Massachusetts Press, 1981.

Daly, Mary. *Beyond God the Father: Toward a Philosophy of Women's Liberation.* Boston: Beacon Press, 1973.

Degler, Carl N. *Out of Our Past: The Forces That Shaped Modern America.* New York: Harper & Brothers, 1959.

Denitch, Bogdan. *Democratic Socialism: The Mass Left in Advanced Industrial Societies.* Montclair, NJ: Allanheld, Osmun, 1981.

Dickie, Robert B. and Leroy S. Rouner, eds. *Corporations and the Common Good.* Notre Dame: University of Notre Dame Press, 1986.

Dobb, Maurice. *Welfare Economics and the Economics of Socialism: Towards a Commonsense Critique.* Cambridge: Cambridge University Press, 1969.

Dorrien, Gary. *The Democratic Socialist Vision.* Totowa, NJ: Rowman and Littlefield, 1986.

Douglas, Ann. *The Feminization of American Culture.* New York: Anchor Press, 1988, c1977.

Duncan, Graeme, ed. *Democracy and the Capitalist State.* Cambridge: Cambridge University Press, 1989.

————. *Democratic Theory and Practice.* Cambridge: Cambridge University Press, 1983.

Dunn, John. *The Politics of Socialism: An Essay in Political Theory.* Cambridge: Cambridge University Press, 1984.

Dussel, Enrique. *Ethics and the Theology of Liberation.* Maryknoll, NY: Orbis Books, 1979.

Eagleson, John, ed. *Christians and Socialism: Documentation of the Christians for Socialism Movement in Latin America.* Maryknoll, NY: Orbis Books, 1975.

Eagleson, John, and Philip Sharper, eds. *Puebla and Beyond: Documentation and Commentary.* Maryknoll, NY: Orbis Books, 1979.

Einhorn, Eric C., and John Logue, eds. *Democracy on the Shop Floor?* Kent, OH: Kent Popular Press, 1982.

Eisenstein, Zillah R. *The Radical Future of Liberal Feminism.* New York: Longman, 1981.

Elden, J. Maxwell. "Political Efficacy at Work." *American Political Science Review* 75 (March 1981).

Elster, Jon. *Making Sense of Marx*. Cambridge: Cambridge University Press, 1985.

Epstein, Gerald. "The Triple Debt Crisis." *World Policy Journal* vol. 3, no. 4 (Fall 1985).

Erskine, Noel Leo. *Decolonizing Theology: A Caribbean Perspective*. Maryknoll, NY: Orbis Books, 1981.

Esping-Andersen, Gosta. *Politics Against Markets: The Social Democratic Road to Power*. Princeton: Princeton University Press, 1985.

Fabella, Virginia, and Sergio Torres, eds. *Irruption of the Third World: Challenge to Theology*. Maryknoll, NY: Orbis Books, 1983.

Fajnzylber, Fernando. *Estrategia Industrial y Empresas Internacionales: Posicion relativa de America y Brasil*. Rio de Janeiro: United Nations, CEPAL, 1970.

Ferber, Michael. "Religious Revival on the Left," *The Nation* (July 6/13, 1985).

Fierro, Alfredo. *The Militant Gospel: A Critical Introduction to Political Theologies*. Maryknoll, NY: Orbis Books, 1977.

Flexner, Eleanor. *Century of Struggle: The Woman's Rights Movement in the United States*. Cambridge: Harvard University Press, 1975.

Foner, Philip S. *American Socialism and Black Americans: From the Age of Jackson to World War II*. Westport, CT: Greenwood Press, 1977.

Fossedal, Gregory. "Corporate Welfare Out of Control." *The New Republic* (February 25, 1985).

Foucault, Michel. *Power/Knowledge: Selected Interviews and Other Writings*, edited by Colin Gordon. New York: Pantheon Books, 1980.

Frank, Andre Gunder. *Dependent Accumulation and Underdevelopment*. New York: Monthly Review Press, 1979.

Frei, Eduardo. *Latin America: The Hopeful Option*. Maryknoll, NY: Orbis Books, 1978.

Freire, Paulo. *Pedagogy of the Oppressed*. New York: Seabury Press, 1970.

Galbraith, John Kenneth, *Economics and the Public Purpose*. Boston: Houghton Mifflin, 1973.

Gallin, Alice. *Midwives to Nazism: University Professors in Weimar Germany, 1925-1933*. Macon, GA: Mercer University Press, 1986.

Gay, Peter. *The Dilemma of Democratic Socialism: Eduard Bernstein's Challenge to Marx*. New York: Columbia University Press, 1952.

Geertz, Clifford. *The Interpretation of Cultures*. New York: Basic Books, 1973.

George, Henry. *Progress and Poverty*. New York: Robert Schalkenbach Foundation, 1955, c1879.

Gibellini, Rosino, ed. *Frontiers of Theology in Latin America*. Maryknoll, NY: Orbis Books, 1979.

Gilder, George. *Sexual Suicide*. New York: Quadrangle/New York Times Book Company, 1973.

———. *Wealth and Poverty*. New York: Basic Books, 1981.

Gilkey, Langdon. *Naming the Whirlwind: The Renewal of God-Language*. New York: Bobbs-Merrill, 1969.

———. *Reaping the Whirlwind: A Christian Interpretation of History*. New York: Seabury Press, 1976.

Ginger, Ray. *The Bending Cross: A Biography of Eugene Victor Debs*. New Brunswick, NJ: Rutgers University Press, 1949.

Gorz, André. *Ecology as Politics*. Boston: South End Press, 1980.

Gunn, C. E. *Workers' Self-Management in the United States*. Ithaca, NY: Cornell University Press, 1984.

Gunnemann, Jon. *The Moral Meaning of Revolution*. New Haven: Yale University Press, 1979.

Gutiérrez, Gustavo. "Freedom and Salvation: A Political Problem." In *Liberation and Change*, edited by Ronald H. Stone. Atlanta: John Knox Press, 1977.

————. "Liberation Praxis and Christian Faith." In *Frontiers of Theology in Latin America*, edited by Rosino Gibellini. Maryknoll, NY: Orbis Books, 1979.

————. *On Job: God-Talk and the Suffering of the Innocent*. Maryknoll, NY: Orbis Books, 1973.

————. *The Power of the Poor in History*. Maryknoll, NY: Orbis Books, 1983.

————. "Terrorism, Liberation, and Sexuality." *Witness* (April 1977).

————. *A Theology of Liberation*. Maryknoll, NY: Orbis Books, 1973.

————. *A Theology of Liberation*, rev. ed.. Maryknoll, NY: Orbis Books, 1988.

————. "Two Theological Perspectives: Liberation Theology and Progressivist Theology." In *The Emergent Gospel: Theology from the Developing World*, edited by Sergio Torres and Virginia Fabella. Maryknoll, NY: Orbis Books, 1978.

————. *We Drink from Our Own Wells: The Spiritual Journey of a People*. Maryknoll, NY: Orbis Books, 1984.

Gutiérrez, Gustavo, and Richard Shaull. *Liberation and Change*. Atlanta: John Knox Press, 1977.

Gutmann, Amy. *Liberal Equality*. Cambridge: Cambridge University Press, 1980.

————, ed., *Democracy and the Welfare State*. Princeton: Princeton University Press, 1988.

Habermas, Jürgen. *Knowledge and Human Interests*. Boston: Beacon Press, 1971.

————. *Legitimation Crisis*. Boston: Beacon Press, 1975.

————. *The Theory of Communicative Action*. Vol. 1, *Reason and the Rationalization of Society*. Boston: Beacon Press, 1984.

Handy, Robert T., ed. *The Social Gospel in America*. New York: Oxford University Press, 1966.

Harnack, Adolf. *What Is Christianity?* New York: Putnam, 1901.

Harrington, Michael. "Corporate Collectivism: A System of Social Injustice." In *Contemporary Readings in Social and Political Ethics*, edited by Garry Brodsky, John Troyer, and David Vance. Buffalo: Prometheus Books, 1984.

————. *Decade of Decision: The Crisis of the American System*. New York: Simon & Schuster, 1980.

————. *Fragments of the Century*. New York: Saturday Review Press, 1973.

————. *The Long-Distance Runner: An Autobiography*. New York: Holt, 1988.

————. *The Next Left: The History of a Future*. New York: Holt, 1986.

————. *The Politics at God's Funeral: The Spiritual Crisis of Western Civilization*. New York: Penguin Books, 1983.

————. *Socialism*. New York: Saturday Review Press, 1972.

————. *The Twilight of Capitalism*. New York: Simon & Schuster, 1976.

————. *The Vast Majority: A Journey to the World's Poor*. New York: Simon & Schuster, 1977.

Harrison, Beverly Wildung. *Making the Connections: Essays in Feminist Social Ethics*. Boston: Beacon Press, 1985.

Heilbroner, Robert. *Marxism: For and Against*. New York: Norton, 1980.

————. *The Nature and Logic of Capitalism*. New York: Norton, 1985.

Heim, Karl. *Christian Faith and Natural Science*. New York: Harper & Brothers, 1953.

————. *The Transformation of the Scientific World View*. New York: Harper & Brothers, 1953.

Held, David. *Models of Democracy*. Stanford, CA: Stanford University Press, 1987.

Hennelly, Alfred. *Theologies in Conflict: The Challenge of Juan Luis Segundo*. Maryknoll, NY: Orbis Books, 1979.

Herzog, Frederick. "A New Spirituality: Shaping Doctrine at the Grass Roots." *The Christian Century* (July 30-August 6, 1986).

————, ed. *The Future of Hope: Theology as Eschatology*. New York: Herder & Herder, 1970.

Hinkelammert, Franz J. *The Ideological Weapons of Death: A Theological Critique of Capitalism*. Maryknoll, NY: Orbis Books, 1986.

Hobhouse, L. T. *Liberalism*. Oxford: Oxford University Press, 1964.

Hofstadter, Richard. *The Age of Reform: From Bryan to FDR*. New York: Knopf, 1955.

Hook, Sidney. *Revolution, Reform, and Social Justice: Studies in the Theory and Practice of Marxism*. New York: New York University Press, 1975.

Hooks, Bell. *Feminist Theory: From Margin to Center*. Boston: South End Press, 1984.

Hopkins, C. Howard. *The Rise of the Social Gospel in American Protestantism, 1865-1915*. New Haven: Yale University Press, 1940.

Horvat, Branko. *The Political Economy of Socialism: A Marxist Social Theory*. Armonk, NY: Sharpe, 1982.

Howe, Irving. *A Margin of Hope: An Intellectual Autobiography*. New York: Harcourt Brace Jovanovich, 1982.

————. *Socialism and America*. New York: Harcourt Brace Jovanovich, 1985.

————. *Steady Work: Essays in the Politics of Democratic Radicalism, 1953-1966*. New York: Harcourt, Brace & World, 1966.

Jagger, Alison M. *Feminist Politics and Human Nature*. Totowa, NJ: Rowman & Allenheld, 1983.

Johnson, Paul. *Modern Times: The World From the Twenties to the Eighties*. New York: Harper & Row, 1983.

Kegley, Charles W., and Robert W. Bretall, eds. *Reinhold Niebuhr: His Religious, Social, and Political Thought*. New York: Macmillan, 1956.

————, eds., *The Theology of Paul Tillich*. New York: Macmillan, 1952.

Kellerman, Bill. "Apologist of Power: The Long Shadow of Reinhold Niebuhr's Christian Realism." *Sojourners* (March 1987).

King, Martin Luther, Jr. "Pilgrimage to Nonviolence." *The Christian Century* 77 (April 13, 1960).

————. *Stride toward Freedom: The Montgomery Story*. New York: Harper, 1958.

Kliever, Lonnie D. *The Shattered Spectrum: A Survey of Contemporary Theology*. Atlanta: John Knox Press, 1981.

Kolakowski, Leszek. *Main Currents of Marxism: Its Origin, Growth, and Dissolution*. Vol. 3, *The Breakdown*. Oxford: Clarendon Press, 1976.

Kolakowski, Leszek, and Stuart Hampshire, eds. *The Socialist Idea: A Reappraisal*. New York: Basic Books, 1974.

Kuttner, Robert. *The Economic Illusion: False Choices Between Prosperity and Social Justice*. Boston: Houghton Mifflin, 1984.

Laclau, Ernesto, and Chantal Mouffe. *Hegemony and Socialist Strategy: Towards a Radical Democratic Politics*. London: Verso, 1984.

LaFeber, Walter. *Inevitable Revolutions: The United States in Central America*. New York: Norton, 1983.

Laidler, Harry. *A History of Socialist Thought*. New York: Crowell, 1933.

Lange, Oskar, and F. M. Taylor. *On the Economic Theory of Socialism*. New York: McGraw-Hill, 1964, c1931.

Leonhard, Wolfgang. *Three Faces of Marxism: The Political Concepts of Soviet Ideology, Maoism, and Humanist Marxism*. New York: Holt, Rinehart & Winston, 1974.

Levin, Michael. "Comparable Worth: The Feminist Road to Socialism." *Commentary*, vol. 78, 3 (September 1984).

———. *Feminism and Freedom*. New Brunswick, NJ: Transaction Books, 1987.

Lichtheim, George. *Marxism: An Historical and Critical Study*. New York: Columbia University Press, 1982, c1961.

Lindblom, Charles E. *Politics and Markets: The World's Political-Economic Systems*. New York: Basic Books, 1977.

Lindenfeld, Frank, and Joyce Rothschild-Whitt, eds. *Workplace Democracy and Social Change*. Boston: Porter Sargent, 1982.

Long, Edward L. *War and Conscience in America*. Philadelphia: Westminster Press, 1968.

Lovin, Robin W. *Christian Faith and Public Choices: The Social Ethics of Barth, Brunner, and Bonhoeffer*. Philadelphia: Fortress Press, 1984.

Lukes, Steven. *Marxism and Morality*. New York: Oxford University Press, 1987.

Luxemburg, Rosa. *Selected Political Writings of Rosa Luxemburg*. Edited by Dick Howard. New York: Monthly Review Press, 1971.

MacIntyre, Alasdair. *After Virtue: A Study in Moral Theology*. Notre Dame, IN: University of Notre Dame Press, 1981.

Mackintosh, Hugh Ross. *Types of Modern Theory: Schleiermacher to Barth*. New York: Scribner's, 1937.

Macpherson, C. B. *Democratic Theory: Essays in Retrieval*. Oxford: Oxford University Press, 1975.

———. *The Life and Times of Liberal Democracy*. Oxford: Oxford University Press, 1977.

———. *The Real World of Democracy*. Toronto: Canadian Broadcasting Corporation, 1965.

———. *The Rise and Fall of Economic Justice*. Oxford: Oxford University Press, 1985.

McCann, Dennis P. *Christian Realism and Liberation Theology: Practical Theologies in Creative Conflict*. Maryknoll, NY: Orbis Books, 1980.

McGovern, Authur F. "Latin America and Dependency Theory." *This World*, 14 (Spring/Summer 1986).

———. *Marxism: An American Christian Perspective*. Maryknoll, NY: Orbis Books, 1980.

Mahan, Brian, and L. Dale Richesin, eds. *The Challenge of Liberation Theology: A First World Response*. Maryknoll, NY: Orbis Books, 1981.

Marcuse, Herbert. *Eros and Civilization: A Philosophical Inquiry into Freud.* Boston: Beacon Press, 1955.

Marty, Martin E. *Modern American Religion.* Vol. l: *The Irony of It All, 1893-1919.* Chicago: University of Chicago Press, 1986.

———. *Righteous Empire: The Protestant Experience in America.* New York: Dial Press, 1970.

Marx, Karl. *Capital: A Critique of Political Economy.* Edited by Ernest Untermann. Vol. 1. Chicago: Kerr, 1906.

———. *Selected Writings.* Edited by David McLellan. Oxford: Oxford University Press, 1977.

Massanari, Ronald. "The Sacred Workshop of God: Reflections on the Historical Perspective of Walter Rauschenbusch." *Religion in Life,* 40, no. 2 (Summer 1971).

May, Henry F. *Protestant Churches and Industrial America.* New York: Harper & Row, 1949.

May, Rollo. *Paulus: Reminiscences of a Friendship.* New York: Harper & Row, 1973.

Mead, Sidney E. *The Lively Experiment: The Shaping of Christianity in America.* New York: Harper & Row, 1963.

Meidner, Rudolf. *Employee Investment Funds: An Approach to Collective Capital Formation.* London: Allen & Unwin, 1978.

———. "A Swedish Union Proposal for Collective Capital Sharing." In *Eurosocialism and America: Political Economy for the 1980s.* Edited by Nancy Lieber. Philadelphia: Temple University Press, 1982.

Metz, Johann Baptist. *The Emergent Church.* New York: Crossroad, 1981.

———. *Faith in History and Society.* New York: Seabury Press, 1969.

———. *Theology of the World.* New York: Seabury Press, 1969.

Míguez Bonino, José. *Christians and Marxists: The Mutual Challenge to Revolution.* Grand Rapids, MI: Eerdmans, 1976.

———. *Doing Theology in a Revolutionary Situation.* Philadelphia: Fortress Press, 1975.

———. "For Life and Against Death: A Theology That Takes Sides." In *Theologians in Transition,* edited by James M. Wall. New York: Crossroad, 1981.

———. "Historical Praxis and Christian Identity." In *Frontiers of Theology in Latin America,* edited by Rosino Gibellini. Maryknoll, NY: Orbis Books, 1979.

———. *Toward a Christian Political Ethics.* Philadelphia: Fortress Press, 1983.

———. "Violence: A Theological Reflection." In *Mission Trends No. 3: Third World Theologies,* edited by Gerald H. Anderson and Thomas F. Stransky, C.S.P. New York: Paulist Press, 1976.

Mill, John Stuart. *Principles of Political Economy.* Vol. 2. New York: Appleton, 1884.

Miller, William Robert, ed. *Contemporary American Protestant Thought, 1900-1970.* Indianapolis: Bobbs-Merrill, 1973.

Minus, Paul M. *Walter Rauschenbusch: American Reformer.* New York: Macmillan, 1988.

Miranda, José Porfirio. *Marx Against the Marxists.* Maryknoll, NY: Orbis Books, 1980.

———. *Marx and the Bible: A Critique of the Philosophy of Oppression.* Maryknoll, NY: Orbis Books, 1974.

Moltmann, Jürgen. *The Church in the Power of the Spirit: A Contribution to Messianic Ecclesiology.* New York: Harper & Row, 1977.

————. *Creating a Just Future: The Politics of Peace and the Ethics of Creation in a Threatened World*. Philadelphia: Trinity Press International, 1989.

————. *The Crucified God: The Cross of Christ as the Foundation and Criticism of Christian Theology*. New York: Harper & Row, 1974.

————. *Experiences of God*. Philadelphia: Fortress Press, 1980.

————. *The Experiment Hope*. Philadelphia: Fortress Press, 1975.

————. *The Future of Creation: Collected Essays*. Philadelphia: Fortress Press, 1979.

————. *God in Creation: A New Theology of Creation and the Spirit of God*. San Francisco: Harper & Row, 1985.

————. *On Human Dignity: Political Theology and Ethics*. Philadephia: Fortress Press, 1984.

————. "On Latin American Liberation Theology: An Open Letter to José Míguez Bonino." *Christianity & Crisis* (March 29, 1976). In *Liberation Theology: A Documentary History*. Edited by Alfred T. Hennelly. Maryknoll, NY: Orbis Books, 1990.

————. *Religion, Revolution, and the Future*. New York: Scribner's, 1969.

————. *Theology of Hope: On the Ground and the Implications of a Christian Eschatology*. London: SCM Press, 1967.

————. *The Trinity and the Kingdom of God: The Doctrine of God*. New York: Harper & Row, 1981.

Morse, Christopher. *The Logic of Promise in Moltmann's Theology*. Philadelphia: Fortress Press, 1975.

Mouffe, Chantal. "Towards a Radical Democratic Citizenship." *Democratic Left*, vol. 17, no. 2 (March/April 1989).

Murchland, Bernard. *The Dream of Christian Socialism: An Essay on Its European Origins*. Washington, DC: American Enterprise Institute, 1982.

Myrdal, Gunnar. *Against the Stream: Critical Essays on Economics*. New York: Pantheon Books, 1972.

————. *Beyond the Welfare State: Economic Planning and Its International Implications*. New Haven: Yale University Press, 1960.

Nash, Ronald, ed. *Liberation Theology*. Milford, MI: Mott Media, 1984.

Neal, Maria Augusta. *A Socio-Theology of Letting Go: The Role of a First World Church Facing Third World Peoples*. Paramus, NJ: Paulist Press, 1977.

Neuhaus, Richard John. "A Death Much Exaggerated." *National Review* (August 28, 1987).

————. "Liberation Theology and the Captivities of Jesus." In *Worldview* (June 1973), reprinted in *Mission Trends No. 3: Third World Theologies*, edited by Gerald H. Anderson and Thomas F. Stransky, C.S.P. New York: Paulist Press, 1976.

————. *The Naked Public Square: Religion and Democracy in America*. Grand Rapids, MI: Eerdmans, 1984.

————. "The Obligations and Limits of Political Commitment." *This World* 14 (Spring/Summer 1986).

————. "Theologian and Activist." *Commentary* (March 1986).

————. "The World Council of Churches and Radical Chic." Washington, DC: Georgetown University Ethics and Public Policy Center; Ethics and Public Policy Reprint 2 (December 1977).

Niebuhr, H. Richard. *Christ and Culture*. New York: Harper & Brothers, 1951.

Niebuhr, Reinhold. *The Children of Light and the Children of Darkness: A Vindication of Democracy and a Critique of its Traditional Defence*. New York: Scribner's, 1944.

———. *Christian Realism and Political Problems*. New York: Scribner's, 1953.

———. *An Interpretation of Christian Ethics*. New York: Harper & Brothers, 1935.

———. *Moral Man and Immoral Society: A Study in Ethics and Politics*. New York: Scribner's, 1947.

———. "Walter Rauschenbusch in Historical Perspective." *Religion in Life* 27 (1958).

Nietzsche, Friedrich. *The Antichrist*. In *The Portable Nietzsche*, edited and translated by Walter Kaufmann. New York: Viking Press, 1968.

Nisbet, Robert. *Twilight of Authority*. New York: Oxford University Press, 1975.

Norman, Edward. *Christianity and the World Order*. Oxford: Oxford University Press, 1979.

Novak, Michael. "The Case Against Liberation Theology." *New York Times Magazine* (October 21, 1984).

———. *Free Persons and the Common Good*. New York: Madison Books, 1989.

———. "Needing Niebuhr Again." *Commentary* (September 1972).

———. "Reinhold Niebuhr: Model for Neoconservatives." *The Christian Century* (January 22, 1986).

———. *The Spirit of Democratic Capitalism*. New York: American Enterprise Institute/Simon & Schuster, 1982.

———. *Will It Liberate? Questions about Liberation Theology*. New York: Paulist Press, 1986.

———, ed. *Liberation South, Liberation North*. Washington, DC: American Enterprise Institute, 1981.

———, ed. *Liberation Theology and the Liberal Society*. Washington, DC: American Enterprise Institute, 1987.

Nove, Alec. *The Economics of Feasible Socialism*. London: Allen & Unwin, 1983.

———. *Socialism, Economics, and Development*. London: Allen & Unwin, 1986.

O'Connor, James. *The Fiscal Crisis of the State*. New York: St. Martin's Press, 1973.

Offe, Claus. *Contradictions of the Welfare State*. Cambridge, MA: MIT Press, 1984.

———. *Disorganized Capitalism: Contemporary Transformations of Work and Politics*. Cambridge, MA: MIT Press, 1985.

Olmsted, Clifton E. *Religion in America: Past and Present*. Englewood Cliffs, NJ: Prentice-Hall, 1961.

Otto, Rudolf. *The Idea of the Holy*. London: Oxford University Press, 1977, c1923.

Pannenberg, Wolfhart. *Anthropology in Theological Perspective*. Philadelphia: Westminster Press, 1985.

———. *The Idea of God and Human Freedom*. Philadelphia: Westminster Press, 1985.

Pateman, Carole. *Participation and Democratic Theory*. Cambridge: Cambridge University Press, 1970.

Pauck, Wilhelm, and Marion Pauck. *Paul Tillich: His Life and Thought*. New York: Harper & Row, 1976.

Peruvian Bishops' Commission for Social Action. *Between Honesty and Hope: Documents from and about the Church in Latin America*. Maryknoll, NY: Maryknoll Publications, 1970.

Peruvian Bishops' Conference. "La Justicia en el Mundo" (1969). In *Development-*

Dependency: The Role of Multinational Corporations. Washington, DC: U.S. Catholic Conference, 1974.

Polsby, Nelson W. *Community Power and Political Theory*. New Haven: Yale University Press, 1963.

Prebisch, Raul. *The Economic Development of Latin America and Its Principal Problems*. New York: United Nations, 1950.

Preston, Ronald H. *The Future of Christian Ethics*. London: SCM, 1987.

Przeworski, Adam. *Capitalism and Social Democracy*. Cambridge: Cambridge University Press, 1986.

Ramsey, Paul. *The Just War: Force and Political Responsibility*. New York: Scribner's, 1968.

Rauschenbusch, Walter. *Christianity and the Social Crisis*. New York: Hodder & Stoughton/ Macmillan, 1907.

————. *Christianizing the Social Order*. New York: Macmillan, 1912.

————. *Das Leben Jesu: Ein Systematisher Studiengang für Jugendvereine und Bibelklassen*. Cleveland: P. Ritter, 1895.

————. *For God and the People: Prayers of the Social Awakening*. Boston: Pilgrim Press, 1910.

————. *The Righteousness of the Kingdom*. Edited by Max L. Stackhouse. Nashville, TN: Abingdon Press, 1968.

————. *Selected Writings*. Edited by Winthrop Hudson. New York: Paulist Press, 1984.

————. *The Social Principles of Jesus*. New York: Grosset & Dunlap, 1916.

————. *A Theology for the Social Gospel*. New York: Macmillan, 1917.

————. *Unto Me*. Boston: Pilgrim Press, 1912.

Rawls, John. *A Theory of Justice*. Cambridge: Harvard University Press, 1971.

Reynolds, Charles H., and Ralph V. Norman. *Community in America: The Challenge of "Habits of the Heart."* Berkeley: University of California Press, 1988.

Robinson, James M., ed. *The Beginnings of Dialectic Theology*. Richmond: John Knox Press, 1968.

Roemer, John, ed. *Analytical Marxism*. Cambridge: Cambridge University Press, 1986.

Rorty, Richard. "Post Modernist Bourgeois Liberalism." *Journal of Philosophy* 80 (1983).

————. "Thugs and Theorists: A Reply to Bernstein." *Political Theory* (November 1987).

Rothstein, Richard. "Give Them a Break: Third World Debtors and a Cure for Reaganomics." *The New Republic* (February 1, 1988).

Ruether, Rosemary Radford. "Feminist Theology and Spirituality." In *Christian Feminism: Visions of a New Humanity*, edited by Judith L. Weidman. New York: Harper & Row, 1984.

————. *Sexism and God-Talk: Toward a Feminist Theology*. Boston: Beacon Press, 1983.

Russell, Letty M. *Human Liberation in a Feminist Perspective—A Theology*. Philadelphia: Westminster Press, 1974.

Ryan, Alan. *Property and Political Theory*. New York: Basil Blackwell, 1984.

Salvatore, Nick. *Eugene V. Debs: Citizen and Socialist*. Urbana: University of Illinois Press, 1982.

Sandel, Michael. *Liberalism and the Limits of Justice*. Cambridge: Cambridge University Press, 1982.

Schall, James V., S.J., ed. *Liberation Theology in Latin America*. San Francisco: Ignatius Press, 1982.

Schleiermacher, Friedrich. *The Christian Faith*. Edited by H. R. Mackintosh and J. S. Stewart. Edinburgh: T. & T. Clark, 1968, c1928.

———. *On Religion: Addresses in Response to Its Cultured Critics*. Richmond: John Knox Press, 1969.

Schlesinger, Arthur M., Jr. *The Cycles of American History*. Boston: Houghton Mifflin, 1986.

Schweickart, David. *Capitalism or Worker Control? An Ethical and Economic Appraisal*. New York: Praeger, 1980.

Schweitzer Albert. *The Quest of the Historical Jesus*. New York: Macmillan, 1960, c1906.

Segundo, Juan Luis. "Capitalism versus Socialism: Crux Theologica." In *Frontiers of Theology in Latin America*, edited by Rosino Gibellini. Maryknoll, NY: Orbis Books, 1979.

———. *Faith and Ideologies*. Vol. 2, *Jesus of Nazareth Yesterday and Today*. Maryknoll, NY: Orbis Books, 1984.

———. *The Historical Jesus of the Synoptics*. Vol. 2, *Jesus of Nazareth*. Maryknoll, NY: Orbis Books, 1985.

———. *The Humanist Christology of Paul*. Vol. 3, *Jesus of Nazareth*. Maryknoll, NY: Orbis Books, 1986.

———. "Las 'elites' latinoamericanas: problematica humana y christian a ante el cambio social." In *Fe christiana y cambio social en America latina*. Salamanca: Sigueme, 1973.

———. *The Liberation of Theology*. Maryknoll, NY: Orbis Books, 1976.

———. *Masas y minorías en la dialéctica divina de la liberación*. Buenos Aires: La Aurora, 1973.

———. *Our Idea of God*. Vol. 3, *A Theology for Artisans of a New Humanity*. Maryknoll, NY: Orbis Books, 1974.

———. *The Sacraments Today*. Vol. 4, *Theology for Artisans*. Maryknoll, NY: Orbis Books, 1974.

———. *Theology and the Church: A Response to Cardinal Ratzinger and a Warning to the Whole Church*. Minneapolis: Winston Press, 1985.

Selucky, Radoslav. *Marxism, Socialism, and Freedom*. London: Macmillan, 1979.

Sharpe, Dores Robinson. *Walter Rauschenbusch*. New York: Macmillan, 1942.

Shaull, Richard. "Christian Faith as Scandal in a Technocratic World." In *New Theology*, no. 6, edited by Martin E. Marty and Dean G. Peerman. New York: Macmillan, 1969.

———. *Heralds of a New Reformation: The Poor of South and North America*. Maryknoll, NY: Orbis Books, 1984.

Sigmund, Paul E. *Multinationals in Latin America: The Politics of Nationalization*. Madison: University of Wisconsin Press, 1980.

Sobrino, Jon. *Christology at the Crossroads: A Latin American Approach*. Maryknoll, NY: Orbis Books, 1978.

———. *The True Church and the Poor*. Maryknoll, NY: Orbis Books, 1984.

Sölle, Dorothee. *Beyond Mere Dialogue: On Being Christian and Socialist*. Detroit: Christians for Socialism in the United States, 1978.

Sontag, Susan. "Communism and the Left." *The Nation* (February 27, 1982).

Steinberg, Ronnie. "The Debate on Comparable Worth." *New Politics* vol. 1, 1 (Summer 1986).

Steinberg, Ronnie, and Lois Haignere. "Separate but Equivalent: Equal Pay for Work of Comparable Worth." *Gender at Work: Perspectives on Occupational Segregation and Comparable Worth.* Washington, DC: Women's Research and Education Institute, 1984.

Stockman, David. *The Triumph of Politics: How the Reagan Revolution Failed.* New York: Harper & Row, 1986.

Stone, Ronald H. *Paul Tillich's Radical Social Thought.* Atlanta: John Knox Press, 1980.

Stout, Jeffrey. *Ethics After Babel: The Languages of Morals and Their Discontents.* Boston: Beacon Press, 1988.

Sullivan, William. *Reconstructing Public Philosophy.* Berkeley: University of California Press, 1982.

Tabb, William K., ed. *Churches in Struggle: Liberation Theologies and Social Change in North America.* New York: Monthly Review Press, 1986.

Tamez, Elsa. *Against Machismo.* Oak Park, IL: Meyer-Stone Books, 1987.

Tawney, R. H. *Religion and the Rise of Capitalism: A Historical Study.* New York: Harcourt, Brace, 1926.

Temple, William. *Christianity and the Social Order.* Middlesex, U.K.: Penguin Books, 1942.

———. *Christianity and the State.* London: Macmillan, 1928.

———. *Essays in Christian Politics and Kindred Subjects.* London: Longmans, Green, 1927.

Thistlethwaite, Susan, ed. *A Just-Peace Church.* New York: United Church Press, 1986.

Thomas, H., and C. Logan. *Mondragon: An Economic Analysis.* London: Allen & Unwin, 1982.

Thomas, Norman. *Socialism Reexamined.* New York: Norton, 1963.

———. *A Socialist's Faith.* New York: Norton, 1951.

Tillich, Hannah. *From Time to Time.* New York: Stein & Day, 1973.

Tillich, Paul, *Biblical Religion and the Search for Ultimate Reality.* Chicago: University of Chicago Press, 1955.

———. *Dynamics of Faith.* New York: Harper & Row, 1957.

———. *The Eternal Now.* New York: Scribner's, 1963.

———. *A History of Christian Thought: From its Judaic and Hellenistic Origins to Existentialism.* Edited by Carl E. Braaten. New York: Simon & Schuster, 1968.

———. *The Interpretation of History.* New York: Scribner's, 1936.

———. *Love, Power, and Justice: Ontological Analyses and Ethical Applications.* New York: Oxford University Press, 1954.

———. *My Search for Absolutes.* New York: Simon & Schuster, 1967.

———. *On the Boundary: An Autobiographical Sketch.* New York: Scribner's, 1966.

———. *Political Expectation.* Edited by James Luther Adams, Victor Nuovo, and Hannah Tillich. New York: Harper & Row, 1977.

———. *The Protestant Era.* Edited by James Luther Adams. London: Nisbet, 1951.

———. *The Religious Situation.* Cleveland: Meridian Books, 1956.

———. *The Socialist Decision.* New York: Harper & Row, 1977.

————. *Systematic Theology*. Three vols. Chicago: University of Chicago Press: 1951, 1957, 1963.

————. *Theology of Culture*. New York: Oxford University Press, 1959.

Torres, Camilo. *Revolutionary Priest: the Complete Writings and Messages of Camilo Torres*. Edited by John Gerassi. New York: Vintage Press, 1971.

Torres, Sergio, and John Eagleson, eds. *Theology in the Americas*. Maryknoll, NY: Orbis Books, 1976.

Torres, Sergio, and Virginia Fabella, eds. *The Emergent Gospel: Theology from the Developing World*. Maryknoll, NY: Orbis Books, 1978.

Tracy, David. *Blessed Rage for Order: The New Pluralism in Theology*. New York: Seabury Press, 1975.

Troeltsch, Ernst. *The Social Teaching of the Christian Churches*. Two vols. New York: Macmillan, 1931.

Tussie, Diana, ed. *Latin America in the World Economy*. New York: St. Martin's Press, 1983.

Unger, Roberto Mangabeira. *Knowledge and Politics*. New York: Free Press, 1975.

Vanek, Jaroslav, ed. *Self-Management*. Harmondsworth, U.K.: Penguin Books, 1975.

Wall, James M., ed. *Theologians in Transition*. New York: Crossroad, 1981.

Wallerstein, Immanuel. *The Capitalist World Economy*. Cambridge: Cambridge University Press, 1979.

Walzer, Michael. *Just and Unjust Wars: A Moral Argument with Historical Illustrations*. New York: Basic Books, 1977.

————. *Radical Principles: Reflections of an Unreconstructed Democrat*. New York: Basic Books, 1980.

————. *Spheres of Justice: A Defense of Pluralism and Equality*. New York: Basic Books, 1983.

Ward, Benjamin. *The Ideal Worlds of Economics: Liberal, Radical, and Conservative Economic World Views*. New York: Basic Books, 1979.

Welch, Claude. *Protestant Thought in the Nineteenth Century*. Two vols. New Haven: Yale University Press, 1972, 1985.

Welch, Sharon. *Communities of Resistance and Solidarity: A Feminist Theology of Liberation*. Maryknoll, NY: Orbis Books, 1985.

West, Cornel. "Afterword: The Politics of American Neo-Pragmatism." In *Post-Analytic Philosophy*, edited by John Rajchman and Cornel West. New York: Columbia University Press, 1985.

————. *Prophesy Deliverance! An Afro-American Revolutionary Christianity*. Philadelphia: Westminster Press, 1982.

————. *Prophetic Fragments*. Grand Rapids, MI: Eerdmans, 1988.

————. "Realign the Left," *Democratic Left* (January/February 1985).

Willams, Oliver F., and John W. Houck, eds. *The Common Good and U. S. Capitalism*. Lanham, MD: University Press of America, 1987.

Wilson, Donna, ed. *Democratic Socialism: The Challenge of the Eighties and Beyond*. Vancouver: New Star Books, 1985.

Winter, Gibson. *Elements for a Social Ethic: Scientific Perspectives on Social Process*. New York: Macmillan, 1968.

————. *Liberating Creation: Foundations of Religious Social Ethics*. New York: Crossroad, 1981.

Witte, John F. *Democracy, Authority, and Alienation in Work*. Chicago: University of Chicago Press, 1980.

Wittner, Lawrence. *Cold War America: From Hiroshima to Watergate.* New York: Holt, Rinehart & Winston, 1978.

Wolfe, Alan. *America's Impasse: The Rise and Fall of the Politics of Growth.* New York: Pantheon Books, 1981.

————. *The Limits of Legitimacy: Political Contradictions of Contemporary Capitalism.* New York: Free Press, 1977.

Wolterstorff, Nicholas. *Until Justice and Peace Embrace.* Grand Rapids, MI: Eerdmans, 1983.

Wood, Robert E. "Making Sense of the Debt Crisis." *Socialist Review.* No. 81. Vol. 15, no.3 (1985).

Wooton, Graham. *Workers, Unions, and the State.* London: Routledge & Kegan Paul, 1986.

Zea, Leopoldo. *The Latin American Mind.* Norman: OK: University of Oklahoma Press, 1963.

Index

Activism, political: Gutiérrez's involvement in, 103-4
Alves, Rubem, 119, 121
Ama y haz lo que quieras (Míguez Bonino), 130
American Baptist Home Mission, 41
American Popular Revolutionary Alliance (APRA), 123
Anabaptism: pacifism and, 92
Antichrist, The (Nietzsche), 7
Apocalypticism: Rauschenbusch's view of, 28-29
Arguedas, José María: friendship with Gutiérrez, 125
Assmann, Hugo, 167
Atheism: Marxism and, 113-14
Augsburg Confession, 92
Augustine, St., 95-96
Avicenna und die Aristotelische Linke (Bloch), 79
Background of the Social Gospel in America, The (Hooft), 16
Baptist Congress of 1892, 23
Barth, Karl, 60
"Basic Principles of Religious Socialism" (Tillich), 74
"Be Fair to Germany" (Rauschenbusch), 40
Bello, Andrés, 131
"Beneath the Glitter" (Rauschenbusch), 21
Bilbao, Francisco, 131-32
Bliss, W. D. P., 22
Bloch, Ernst, 79, 100; assessment of religion, 80; influence on Moltmann, 80; philosophy of, 79-80
Blumhardt, Christoph, 51
Boff, Leonardo, 172
Bonhoeffer, Dietrich, 90

Bowles, Samuel, 3
Brotherhood of the Kingdom, 24
Brown, Robert McAfee, 11
Brus, Wlodzimierz, 164
Bultmann, Rudolf, 77, 129, 147; critique by Moltmann, 83-84; doctrine of illumination, 86; Moltmann and, 82-83
Capitalism, 63: Catholic church and, 133; effects on Latin America, 131-38; Gutiérrez's views on, 109-10; politicization of, 14; Rauschenbusch's views of, 34-35; Segundo's view of, 112; socialism and, 4-5; Tillich's view of, 57-59
"Capitalism versus Socialism: Crux Theologica" (Segundo), 112
Cardoso, Fernando Henrique, 109, 137
Catholicism: Rauschenbusch's view of, 44
CELAM: See Second General Conference of the Latin American Episcopate
Children of Light and the Children of Darkness, The (Niebuhr), 13
Choice: personal vs. political, 93
Chopp, Rebecca, 99
Christianity and Social Crisis (Rauschenbusch), 20, 27, 28, 30, 31, 34
Christianity and the Social Order (Temple), 173
Christianity: Marxism and, 100; nonviolence and, 94; Socialism and, 26, 33
Christianizing the Social Order (Rauschenbusch), 32, 33, 34, 35
Christians and Marxists (Míguez Bonino), 129, 145, 146
Church, the: colonialism in Latin America and, 131; role of, 55-56,